Workshop on Creating, Enriching and Using Parliamentary Corpora (ParlaCLARIN III)

Held at LREC 2022

Marseille, France
20 – 25 June 2022

Editors:

Darja Fiser
Maria Eskevich
Jakob Lenardic
Franciska de Jong

ISBN: 978-1-7138-6132-4

Printed from e-media with permission by:

Curran Associates, Inc.
57 Morehouse Lane
Red Hook, NY 12571

Some format issues inherent in the e-media version may also appear in this print version.

Association for Computational Linguistics
209 N. Eighth Street
Stroudsburg, Pennsylvania 18360

Phone: 1-570-476-8006
Fax: 1-570-476-0860

acl@aclweb.org

Additional copies of this publication are available from:

Curran Associates, Inc.
57 Morehouse Lane
Red Hook, NY 12571 USA
Phone: 845-758-0400
Fax: 845-758-2633
Email: curran@proceedings.com
Web: www.proceedings.com

LREC 2022
Language Resources and Evaluation Conference
20-25 June 2022

ParlaCLARIN III
Workshop on Creating, Enriching and Using Parliamentary Corpora

PROCEEDINGS

Editors: Darja Fišer, Maria Eskevich, Jakob Lenardič,
Franciska de Jong

Proceedings of the LREC 2022 ParlaCLARIN III Workshop on Creating, Enriching and Using Parliamentary Corpora

Edited by:
Darja Fišer, Maria Eskevich, Jakob Lenardič, Franciska de Jong

Acknowledgements: Organisation of the workshop is supported by CLARIN ERIC.
https://www.clarin.eu/ParlaCLARIN-III

For more information:
European Language Resources Association (ELRA)
9 rue des Cordelières
75013, Paris
France
http://www.elra.info
Email: lrec@elda.org

Introduction

Parliamentary data is an important source of scholarly and socially relevant content, serving as a verified communication channel between the elected political representatives and members of the society. The development of accessible, comprehensive and well-annotated parliamentary corpora is therefore crucial for the information society, as such corpora help scientists and investigative journalists to ascertain the accuracy of socio-politically relevant information, and to inform the citizens about the trends and insights on the basis of such data explorations. Research-wise, parliamentary corpora are a quintessential resource for a number of disciplines in digital humanities and social sciences, such as political science, sociology, history, and (socio)linguistics.

The distinguishing characteristic of parliamentary data is that it is spoken language produced in controlled circumstances. Such data has traditionally been transcribed in a formal way but is now also increasingly released in the original audio and video formats, which encourages resource and software development and provides research opportunities related to structuring, synchronisation, visualisation, querying and analysis of parliamentary corpora. Therefore, a harmonised approach to data curation practises for this type of data can support the advancement of the field significantly. One of the ways in which the research community is supported in this line of work is through the conversion of existing corpora and further development of new cross-national parliamentary corpora into a highly comparable, harmonised set of multilingual resources. These allow researchers to share comparative perspectives and to perform multidisciplinary research on parliamentary data. We envision that the ParlaCLARIN III workshop, as a venue for knowledge and experience exchange on the topic, will contribute to the development and growth of the field of digital parliamentary science.

An inspiring and highly successful first edition of the ParlaCLARIN scientific workshop[1] was held at LREC 2018. A follow-up developmental workshop was organised by CLARIN ERIC in 2019 under the name ParlaFormat[2], while the second ParlaCLARIN workshop was held at LREC 2020.[3] These events led to a comprehensive overview[4] of a multitude of existing parliamentary resources worldwide as well as tangible first steps towards better harmonisation, interoperability and comparability of the resources and tools relevant for the study of parliamentary discussions and decisions.

This third ParlaCLARIN workshop is a continuation of the 2018 and 2020 editions. On the one hand, it continues to bring together developers, curators and researchers of regional, national and international parliamentary debates from across diverse disciplines in the Humanities and Social Sciences. On the other hand, we envisage the appearance of new discussion threads, tasks, and challenges that are partially inspired by or related to the new data releases such as ParlaMint [5] and data formats such as Parla-CLARIN.[6]

The Call for Papers has invited original, overview and position papers with the focus on one of the following topics:

- Compilation, annotation, visualisation and utilisation of parliamentary records;
- Harmonisation of existing multilingual parliamentary resources, containing either synchronic or diachronic data or both;
- Linking or comparing of parliamentary records with other sources of structured knowledge, such as formal ontologies and LOD datasets (in particular for the description of speakers, political parties, etc.).

[1]https://www.clarin.eu/ParlaCLARIN
[2]https://www.clarin.eu/event/2019/parlaformat-workshop
[3]https://www.clarin.eu/ParlaCLARIN-II
[4]https://www.clarin.eu/resource-families/parliamentary-corpora
[5]https://www.clarin.eu/parlamint
[6]https://github.com/clarin-eric/parla-clarin

In 2022 the following special themes were also brought for discussion at the workshop:

- Machine translation of parliamentary proceedings and research using machine translated parliamentary data;
- Semantic tagging of parliamentary proceedings and research using semantically tagged parliamentary data;
- Digital Humanities and Social Sciences research into parliamentary proceedings.

The workshop programme is composed of a keynote talk by Luke Blaxill from the University of Oxford and 18 peer-reviewed papers by 66 authors from 15 countries (the 5 most represented: Germany (10), Italy (10), Slovenia (8), Austria (6) Spain (6)). Two papers report on the work that was carried out by the co-authors representing the institutions in more than one country, and one group of authors represent Canadian studies.

We would like to thank the reviewers for their careful and constructive reviews which have contributed to the quality of the event.

The ParlaCLARIN III workshop was held in person with the a possibility of hybrid attendance in Marseille (France), as part of the 13th edition of the Language Resources and Evaluation Conference (LREC2022).

D. Fišer, M. Eskevich, J. Lenardič , F. de Jong June 2022

Organizers

Darja Fišer, University of Ljubljana and Jožef Stefan Institute, Slovenia
Maria Eskevich, CLARIN ERIC, The Netherlands
Jakob Lenardič, University of Ljubljana and Jožef Stefan Institute, Slovenia
Franciska de Jong, CLARIN ERIC, The Netherlands

Program Committee:

Ahlame Bedgouri, Faculty of Sciences and Technology of Fez, University of Sidi Mohamed Ben Abdellah, Morocco
Çağrı Çöltekin, University of Tübingen, Germany
Jesse de Does, Dutch Language Institute, The Netherlands
Tomaž Erjavec, Jožef Stefan Institute, Slovenia
Francesca Frontini, Istituto di Linguistica Computazionale "A. Zampolli", CNR Pisa, Italy
Maria Gavriilidou, ILSP/Athena RC, Greece
Barbora Hladká, Charles University, Czechia
Haidee Kotze, Utrecht University, The Netherlands
Nikola Ljubešić, Jožef Stefan Institute, Slovenia
Bente Maegaard, CST, Department of Nordic Languages and Linguistics, University of Copenhagen, Denmark
Maarten Marx, University of Amsterdam, The Netherlands
Stefano Menini, Fondazione Bruno Kessler, Trento, Italy
Robert Muthuri, Anjarwalla & Khanna LLP, Kenya
Maciej Ogrodniczuk, Institute of Computer Science, Polish Academy of Sciences, Poland
Petya Osenova, IICT-BAS and Sofia University 'St. Kl. Ohridski', Bulgaria
Stelios Piperidis, ILSP/Athena RC, Greece
Simone Paolo Ponzetto, Mannheim University, Germany
Paul Rayson, Lancaster University, United Kingdom
Sara Tonelli, Fondazione Bruno Kessler, Italy
Daniela Trotta, University of Salerno, Italy

Invited Speaker:

Luke Blaxill, University of Oxford, United Kingdom

Table of Contents

Conference Program

20 June 2022

9:15–9:30 **Welcome and Introduction**

9:30–10:30 **Session 1: Corpus Creation 1**

ParlaMint II: The Show Must Go On
Maciej Ogrodniczuk, Petya Osenova, Tomaž Erjavec, Darja Fišer, Nikola Ljubešić, Çağrı Çöltekin, Matyáš Kopp and Meden Katja

How GermaParl Evolves: Improving Data Quality by Reproducible Corpus Preparation and User Involvement
Andreas Blaette, Julia Rakers and Christoph Leonhardt

Between History and Natural Language Processing: Study, Enrichment and Online Publication of French Parliamentary Debates of the Early Third Republic (1881-1899)
Marie Puren, Aurélien Pellet, Nicolas Bourgeois, Pierre Vernus and Fanny Lebreton

A French Corpus of Québec's Parliamentary Debates
Pierre André Ménard and Desislava Aleksandrova

11:00–12:00 **Keynote**

Parliamentary Corpora and Research in Political Science and Political History
Luke Blaxill

12:00–13:00 **Session 2: Corpus Enhancement**

Error Correction Environment for the Polish Parliamentary Corpus
Maciej Ogrodniczuk, Michał Rudolf, Beata Wójtowicz and Sonia Janicka

Clustering Similar Amendments at the Italian Senate
Tommaso Agnoloni, Carlo Marchetti, Roberto Battistoni and Giuseppe Briotti

Entity Linking in the ParlaMint Corpus
Ruben van Heusden, Maarten Marx and Jaap Kamps

Visualizing Parliamentary Speeches as Networks: the DYLEN Tool
Seung-bin Yim, Katharina Wünsche, Asil Cetin, Julia Neidhardt, Andreas Baumann and Tanja Wissik

20 June 2022 (continued)

14:00–15:15 Session 3: Corpus Analysis

Emotions Running High? A Synopsis of the state of Turkish Politics through the ParlaMint Corpus
Gül M. Kurtoğlu Eskişar and Çağrı Çöltekin

Immigration in the Manifestos and Parliament Speeches of Danish Left and Right Wing Parties between 2009 and 2020
Costanza Navarretta, Dorte Haltrup Hansen and Bart Jongejan

Parliamentary Discourse Research in Sociology: Literature Review
Jure Skubic and Darja Fišer

FrameASt: A Framework for Second-level Agenda Setting in Parliamentary Debates through the Lense of Comparative Agenda Topics
Christopher Klamm, Ines Rehbein and Simone Paolo Ponzetto

Comparing Formulaic Language in Human and Machine Translation: Insight from a Parliamentary Corpus
Yves Bestgen

15:15–16:00 Panel

16:30–17:45 Session 4: Corpus Creation 2

Adding the Basque Parliament Corpus to ParlaMint Project
Jon Alkorta and Mikel Iruskieta Quintian

ParlaSpeech-HR - a Freely Available ASR Dataset for Croatian Bootstrapped from the ParlaMint Corpus
Nikola Ljubešić, Danijel Koržinek, Peter Rupnik and Ivo-Pavao Jazbec

Making Italian Parliamentary Records Machine-Actionable: the Construction of the ParlaMint-IT corpus
Tommaso Agnoloni, Roberto Bartolini, Francesca Frontini, Simonetta Montemagni, Carlo Marchetti, Valeria Quochi, Manuela Ruisi and Giulia Venturi

ParlamentParla: A Speech Corpus of Catalan Parliamentary Sessions
Baybars Kulebi, Carme Armentano-Oller, Carlos Rodriguez-Penagos and Marta Villegas

ParlaMint-RO: Chamber of the Eternal Future
Petru Rebeja, Mădălina Chitez, Roxana Rogobete, Andreea Dincă and Loredana Bercuci

17:45–18:00 Pitches of relevant initiatives in the field

Proceedings of ParlaCLARIN III @ LREC2022 pages 1–6
Marseille, 20 June 2022

ParlaMint II: The Show Must Go On

Maciej Ogrodniczuk, Petya Osenova, Tomaž Erjavec, Darja Fišer, Nikola Ljubešić, Çagrı Çöltekin, Matyáš Kopp, Katja Meden

maciej.ogrodniczuk@ipipan.waw.pl,
petya@bultreebank.org, tomaz.erjavec@ijs.si, darja.fiser@ff.uni-lj.si,
nikola.ljubesic@ijs.si, ccoltekin@sfs.uni-tuebingen.de,
kopp@ufal.mff.cuni.cz, katja.meden@ijs.si

Abstract

In ParlaMint I, a CLARIN-ERIC supported project, a set of comparable and uniformly annotated multilingual corpora for 17 national parliaments was developed and released. Currently on-going is the ParlaMint II project, where the main goals are to upgrade the annotation guidelines, XML schema and Git-related workflow; enhance the existing corpora with new metadata and newer data; add corpora for 10 new parliaments; add machine-translated and semantically annotated English texts to the corpora; for a few corpora add speech data; and provide more use cases. The paper reports on these planned steps, including some that have already been taken, and outlines future plans.

Keywords: parliamentary debates, parliamentary records, parliamentary corpora, ParlaMint, linguistic annotation, metadata

1. Introduction

The ParlaMint project produced uniformly sampled, annotated and encoded comparable parliamentary corpora for 17 European countries with almost half a billion words in total (Erjavec et al., 2022). The corpora, which comprise reference and COVID-19 sections, contain rich metadata about the mandates, sessions, and speakers and their political party affiliations etc., are linguistically annotated for named entities and Universal Dependencies morphological features and syntax, and encoded to a common and very strict schema, so their format is not merely interchangeable but also interoperable. This has been validated in practice, as the corpora have been mounted on the CLARIN.SI concordancers, i.e. they can be explored and analyzed in a common and very powerful environment. The corpus development and a part of the communication took place on GitHub, the corpora have been released under the CC BY licence in the scope of a CLARIN repository (Erjavec et al., 2021a; Erjavec et al., 2021b)[1], not only in their source XML TEI format, but also in a number of derived and immediately useful formats.

The ParlaMint corpora have also been used in the Helsinki Digital Humanities Hackathon (Calabretta et al., 2021)[2], giving them increased visibility as well as providing useful feedback for the structure of the final version 2.1 corpora of the project. The project has thus produced a novel and highly valuable resource for a broad range of comparative trans-national SSH studies that is openly available and has already proved itself in practice.

However, during the compilation and especially DHH use of the ParlaMint corpora, a number of relatively straightforward as well as some more complex upgrades were identified, which would make the corpora even more useful. In particular, the structure, accessibility and metadata of the corpora need to be improved in order to maximize interoperability and comparative research. These issues are discussed in Section 2.

Due to the prolonged pandemics, the COVID-19 section of the existing corpora also needs to be extended with new data. To make the resource as valuable for SSH scholars as possible, parliamentary corpora of additional countries and languages need to be provided as well. The data extension is the focus of Section 3.

The ParlaMint corpus family will be enriched by adding machine translations into English, thus allowing for comparative analyses across parliaments. Also, integration of speech data will be piloted for selected parliaments. These topics are presented in Section 4.

Last but not least, the corpora will be utilised in new and more varied user scenarios. The engagement activities like the hackathon with the ParlaMint data, as well as the shared task and other related showcases, are outlined in Section 5.

Section 6 concludes and lists some directions to follow beyond the time and resource limits of the project.

2. Schema and Metadata Improvements

The encoding of ParlaMint I corpora followed the previously developed TEI-based Parla-CLARIN recommendations for encoding parliamentary corpora (Erjavec and Pančur, 2019)[3], which provide extensive textual guidelines but are very permissive in their formal

[1] `http://hdl.handle.net/11356/1432` and `http://hdl.handle.net/11356/1431`

[2] `https://dhhackathon.wordpress.com/2021/05/28/parliamentary-debates-in-the-covid-times/`

[3] `https://github.com/clarin-eric/parla-clarin`

XML schema. To enable interoperability of the produced corpora, ParlaMint required much stricter encoding, so we started the project by defining a RelaxNG schema for corpus validation, which was then refined during most of the lifetime of the ParlaMint I project.

However, the Parla-CLARIN textual recommendations were not updated during this time, so Parla-CLARIN was lagging behind ParlaMint. On the other hand, there were no ParlaMint-specific encoding guidelines, and the project partners – those with sufficient digital skills – had to rely on inspecting the formal schema or the already submitted and validated samples of their corpora and try to adapt them to their circumstances. Towards the end of the project, when all corpora were already available, some of the encoding decisions were also discovered to be questionable, however, it was too late to re-encode the corpora by then. Finally, the ParlaMint project had to absorb many corpora in a relatively short time, so many aspects of the encoding were not unified nor harmonised, in particular the status and roles of speakers, the encoding of sessions, meetings, and agendas, the distinction between political parties vs. parliamentary groups etc.

For interoperability of ParlaMint corpora, as well as a step towards standardisation of information (taxonomies/ontologies) associated with parliamentary debates in ParlaMint II, it is was deemed highly beneficial if the encoding and metadata of the current ParlaMint corpora were harmonised and unified, and the Parla-CLARIN recommendations updated to reflect the experience gained in ParlaMint I. This is also strategically important as several corpora being developed independently of the ParlaMint project have already started using the Parla-CLARIN schema, which was the ultimate goal for future sustainability and interoperability of the Parliamentary Resource Family.

ParlaMint II involves more than 30 partners that are all required to submit large and heavily annotated corpora with rich metadata. Yet the corpora will come from completely different sources and embodying different parliamentary procedures and traditions, while the partners will be using different tools for their annotation, and have very different backgrounds and familiarity with TEI, XML, its schema languages, and XSLT. It is, therefore, crucial to establish validation procedures that will result in useful, i.e. correctly and consistently encoded ParlaMint II corpora. Parla-CLARIN, as well as ParlaMint I, have already shown that git is a highly versatile environment for keeping track not only of program code but also documentation. Hosting platforms, in particular GitHub, also provide the means of recorded and structured communication via issues; however, this communication and data exchange policy was not really enforced in ParlaMint I.

Finally, a large part of the value of the ParlaMint corpora comes from their extensive metadata on speakers, which, however, can be very labour intensive to find and add to the corpora for some parliaments, which is why some corpora are missing some metadata that others have. Already in the first use cases, it also turned out that even more metadata would be highly beneficial to enable increasingly wider analyses, as this is unavailable in most related resources.

2.1. Harmonisation of Encoding

In the first phase of the ParlaMint II project, the Parla-CLARIN recommendations were updated adopting the solutions and examples from the ParlaMint corpora, yet still allowing for project-specific extensions.
On the basis of the updated Parla-CLARIN recommendations, but highly specific to ParlaMint, we made a new set of recommendations, including the schema (i.e. a XML TEI ODD document), and made the text guidelines available via GitHub pages[4]. These guidelines are meant to serve as the basis for adding new corpora and extending the existing ones. It should be noted that while the ParlaMint RelaxNG schemas derived from the ParlaMint ODD can be used for validation, more precise validation is still achieved with the native ParlaMint RelaxNG schemas and even more with developed validating XSLT scripts.
The encoding of ParlaMint corpora was further unified as regards the use of attributes and their values, including legislative taxonomies and vocabularies (mostly in both source language and English), speaker roles and affiliations etc. The existing ParlaMint schema and corpora were modified to reflect the ParlaMint best practice. In the course of these modifications, all observed open problems were documented via project GitHub issues.

2.2. Git Management

Both Parla-CLARIN and ParlaMint are completely or largely hosted on GitHub, and both need to be updated in a harmonised and controlled fashion, also providing support for the existing and new corpora developers, as well as to the use cases working with the data. In ParlaMint II, we have already improved the usage of GitHub, e.g. we implemented much stricter validation of commits, encoding and statistical documentation of the corpora in HTML, regular milestones and releases, and are responsive to communication via issues. While in ParlaMint I, quite a lot of support was done via individual emails, this is, given the even larger number of partners in ParlaMint II, now unmanageable, so all communication is to be via GitHub issues, and the validation of corpora the direct responsibility of the partners.

2.3. Adding Metadata to Existing Corpora

Additional metadata, in particular the information about whether the speakers are members of the government (ministers), and the positioning of political parties on the left-right spectrum, are planned to be added

[4] `https://clarin-eric.github.io/ParlaMint/`

to the corpora in ParlaMint II. The partners who will encode this information in their corpora can take advantage of a pipeline that transforms the data entered in spreadsheets into the required XML encoding. In addition to this, a taxonomy of common ministry types is planned to be added to enable cross-corpus comparisons.
After the initial discussion, it became clear that these tasks might present us with some difficulties, stemming mainly from the fact that the structure of political systems differs severely from one country to another. Primary tasks for this section are therefore finding common ground to facilitate encoding of the additional information about members of the government (and the taxonomy) as well as finding the appropriate scale for encoding political orientation (left-right scale, political compass scale or other).

3. Corpus Expansion

New corpora will be added to ParlaMint, and existing corpora will be updated with newer materials. All new resources will contain material from the same minimum periods, the same metadata as existing ParlaMint corpora and linguistic annotations. This will extend the ParlaMint scope in countries, languages and time to make it even more interesting for researchers.
As with previous versions of ParlaMint, both new and updated corpora will be validated, converted to derived formats (plain text, metadata files, CoNLL-U, vertical files), mounted on the CLARIN.SI concordancers, and deposited in the CLARIN.SI repository. We envision three releases: 3.0 at the half-way mark, 3.1 shortly before the end, and 3.2 at the conclusion of the project.

3.1. Adding New Corpora

New parliamentary corpora will be prepared by 10 new project partners (from Austria, Basque Country, Catalonia, Estonia, Finland, Greece, Norway, Portugal, Romania and Sweden) according to ParlaMint specifications and guidelines. The parliamentary transcripts will cover the period at least between January 1, 2015, and February 1, 2022. The texts in the corpora will be split into reference (until October 31, 2019) and COVID parts (later data).
Following the ParlaMint I model, each corpus will have to be delivered in two variants, the TEI encoded plain text one with the metadata and transcripts of the speeches, and the linguistically annotated one (so-called TEI.ana) with added linguistic annotations.
Corpus metadata should contain at least type of parliament (unicameral, bicameral), which speeches are included (lower/upper house, mandates) and the structure of the proceedings (taxonomy with types of meetings, types of speakers, legislative periods). Corpus element structure should encompass date-stamped mandates, sessions and speeches. Each speech can, minimally, contain only the pure transcripts of the speeches divided into paragraphs. However, many transcripts also contain commentary by the transcribers, which are then also retained and encoded.
Metadata on speakers should contain speaker role (regular, chair, guest), their analysed name (forename, surname), gender, MP status and political affiliation(s). If their MP status and political affiliation changed in the time frame of the corpus, it needs to be time-stamped. Political parties and/or political groups should be marked with name, short name (initials) and possibly start/end of existence. Coalitions/oppositions of parties should also be marked in the time frame of the corpus.
A linguistic annotation should encompass tokenisation and sentence segmentation, lemmatisation and UD morphological features, UD syntactic annotations and NE marking (PER, LOC, ORG, MISC).

3.2. Extending Existing Corpora

Recent data (up to June 2022) will also be added to the existing ParlaMint dataset, and the corpora will be further fixed for the found errors and missing metadata. Concerning COVID, it is difficult at this point to consider what period would be viewed as in-pandemic and post-pandemic but we can update our categorization accordingly later.

4. Corpus Enrichment

In this task, we will enhance the ParlaMint corpora with a translation of all non-English transcriptions into English. Having all the corpora in English will enable treating them as one corpus, and using identical queries to view and analyse the data from various parliaments. This opens the way for simple translingual comparative analyses among more than 20 national and regional parliaments, importantly increasing the usability of the ParlaMint corpora, making them an even more globally relevant research dataset. Furthermore, we will semantically tag the translated corpus, which will significantly increase the value of the ParlaMint corpora for SSH scholars.
As a proof of concept, we will also add a subset of recordings of parliamentary debates for selected parliaments, and align them with the available transcriptions. This will have a multiplier effect on improving interoperability of speech / multimodal data and tools in CLARIN well beyond parliamentary records, and will enable novel dimensions of SSH research on ParlaMint corpora that is currently not possible with most related resources, such as comparisons of official transcriptions with actual parliamentary discussions within and across parliaments.

4.1. Machine Translation

As part of the preparation of the DHH 2021 hackathon, we already machine translated 10 of the ParlaMint I corpora to English using the OpenNMT system (Klein et al., 2017)[5]. Now we plan to machine translate all

[5] https://opennmt.net/

the ParlaMint II corpora to English, with the best-performing model at the time of the translation task. We also plan to explore automatic post-editing to fix the most frequent translation errors, in particular the frequently incorrect "translation" of names. The translations will be performed on the sentence level, so that the sentence-level alignment between the originals and translations to English are available.

4.2. Semantic Tagging

The resulting texts will then be encoded and linguistically annotated in the same way as the other corpora. We will also add semantic annotations to the translated corpora using the UCREL Semantic Analysis System, USAS (Rayson et al., 2004)[6], which has been developed by the U.K. ParlaMint partner. The USAS tagger will assign semantic fields from a taxonomy of 232 tags to words and multi-word expressions in the corpus, representing coarse-grained word senses. The system for English has been developed and applied over the last 30 years, and assigning semantic tags to the English translations (as well as the original UK subcorpus) will facilitate future work on bootstrapping prototype semantic taggers in other languages via sentence and word alignment. USAS tagging accuracy for English is 91% and the tagger is already freely available via the UCREL website and REST API. In parallel, the Lancaster UCREL centre will develop a Python open-source version of the USAS tagger.

4.3. Multimodality

We will also gather, process and align audio recordings with the transcriptions for a selected list of languages. The alignments will be performed on the level of segments lasting 5 to 30 seconds. The possibility of making the aligned audio available through the KonText concordancer (Machálek, 2020) will be investigated as well.

Due to the high technical complexity of this task, it will be run as a proof-of-concept on three selected languages (Czech, Polish and Croatian), where audio alignment activities have already been applied to some level. Each of the selected languages will deliver at least 50 hours of high-quality audio alignment as well as the code base and a report of the used alignment procedure. The aim of this task is not only to obtain aligned audio data for the selected the ParlaMint corpora, but to identify best practices in the currently highly vibrant area of speech processing, to be used on the remaining ParlaMint languages in a possible follow-up project.

Although the project has started only recently, we can already report on the first freely-available dataset for training automatic-speech-recognition systems for Croatian, ParlaSpeech-HR (Ljubešić et al., 2022). It is based on the ParlaMint I corpus and the available video recordings of the Croatian parliament, resulting in a dataset of 1,816 hours. A similar availability of the speech and transcript data will be ensured for the remaining languages as well. The bootstrapping approach to building the dataset, consisting of using Google speech-to-text for constructing an initial dataset, and then training a transformer-based ASR system from this initial dataset, and using it to to build the final dataset, is described in (Ljubešić et al., 2022).

In implementing the alignment of Czech audio and transcription, we plan to utilize tools used to create the ParCzech 3.0 corpus (Kopp et al., 2021). This corpus covers the same period as the ParlaMint I Czech corpus and contains more than 3,000 hours of aligned audio. The audio recordings provided on the Czech Chamber of Deputies web pages are about 14 minutes long with only the approximately middle 10 minutes corresponding to the transcript on one web page, making it difficult to determine the alignment of the audio with the transcript. The alignment algorithm currently used in ParCzech 3.0 does try to determine the beginning of transcription in the audio file but because the transcription is redacted (i.e. does not fully correspond to the audio), the algorithm does not always work correctly. We believe that there is room for improvement by modifying the algorithm to also take into account the alignments made on the previous web page, and we will investigate this upgrade in ParlaMint II.

5. Engagement Activities

5.1. Tutorial

After performing a literature review and interacting with the relevant national and European projects and networks is being documented and made available (Skubic and Fišer, 2022), a tutorial and showcases will be developed for SSH scholars and students which demonstrates the use of ParlaMint data, metadata and linguistic annotations.

The tutorial will be developed around relevant SSH research questions on the theme of "opposition in times of crisis" using topic modelling, one of the most popular methods in the DH community. The tutorial will be complementary to the previous one, *Voices of the Parliament* [7], developed by the same team outside the ParlaMint project, which demonstrates the potential of parliamentary corpora research via concordancers. The new tutorial will be aimed at students and scholars of digital humanities and social sciences who are interested in the study of socio-cultural phenomena through language and to engage with the user-friendly text-mining tool *Orange* [8].

The theoretical part of the tutorial will introduce the characteristics of parliamentary records, the construction of the ParlaMint corpora and topic modelling. The practical part will demonstrate how topic modelling

[6] https://ucrel.lancs.ac.uk/usas/

[7] https://sidih.github.io/voices/index.html

[8] https://orangedatamining.com

and the Orange text mining tool can be utilized to answer three concrete research questions. In Task 1, we will analyze the basic characteristics of parliamentary speeches before and during the pandemic using interactive visualizations. In Task 2, we will identify the central topics of discussions in the two periods. In Task 3, we will explore topic distributions using heatmaps.

5.2. Showcases

Informed by the literature review and interactions with the relevant national and European projects and networks, a collection of showcases will be developed that will demonstrate the value of the ParlaMint corpora for SSH researchers and will serve as an instrument for cross-disciplinary method and knowledge transfer.

5.3. Hackathon

After the successful participation of the ParlaMint community in the Helsinki Digital Humanities Hackathon 2021, ParlaMint corpora will also be used at the DHH Hackathon 2022[9]. This time the participants will focus on the comparison of parliamentary debates from a sociological, politological, and computational perspective. Political decision-making is organised in party groups, committees, and informal networks among members of parliament and civil servants. In the plenary session, we see these networks manifest themselves as speakers represent their respective groups and refer to one another. The degree to which these networks display exceptional polarisation, centralization of parliamentary voices, or an imbalance in the dynamic between government and opposition, is telling of how the principle of parliamentarism is concretely playing out in the different countries. The networks can also be studied from the perspective of gender, party affiliation, and party stability. By comparing the data synchronically and diachronically in a cross-lingual context, we can obtain important insights into transnational characteristics.

This is why the objective of the hackathon will be to learn how to use comparable parliamentary corpora from various European countries that are annotated with rich metadata and linguistic annotations, enabling various analytical directions. The group will take a network analysis perspective on parliament debates to answer questions on the influence of members, the polarisation of groups, and information spreading in parliament. The group will make use of the linguistic annotations, Named Entities, and metadata coded in the ParlaMint data. Additionally, the group will learn to utilise *Google Colab* [10] and network analysis tools such as *Gephi* [11] and *NetworkX* [12] to bring together the disciplines of computer science and humanities in gaining knowledge on the Networks of Power. The results from the hackathon will be published on the CLARIN website.

5.4. Shared Task

To address a very different but important community of users and expose the created resources to novel approaches, a shared task will be organized in which the ParlaMint corpora will be used to predict whether a speech belongs to a governing or opposition party member (and possibly additional tasks for party affiliation and political ideologies). The corpora released in ParlaMint I will be used as training data, and the newly developed but withheld ParlaMint II corpora will be used as test data. The results from the shared task will be published in open-access proceedings. The details about the shared task will be communicated when this information is ready.

6. Beyond ParlaMint II

Even though ParlaMint II will run until 2023, we are already planning how it could be extended in the future and become a sustainable initiative. Apart from such obvious directions as including more data (from the European Parliament, regional parliaments or national parliaments beyond Europe) or historical data, we are also planning to link our datasets with additional data sources, e.g. by adding voting results, referencing social media content or introducing newspaper and TV news mentions.

ParlaMint data could also be extended to include multimodal aligned corpora (with speech and video), gesture annotated corpora or live corpora produced and used as streamed and on the fly.

Acknowledgements

The ParlaMint project is supported by: CLARIN ERIC – 'ParlaMint: Towards Comparable Parliamentary Corpora' • H2020-INFRAEOSC-04-2018 #823782 'SSHOC: Social Sciences and Humanities Open Cloud' • ARRS (Slovenian Research Agency) P2-103 'Knowledge Technologies' • ARRS (Slovenian Research Agency) P6-0411 'Language Resources and Technologies for Slovene' • ARRS (Slovenian Research Agency) P6-0436 'Digital Humanities: resources, tools and methods' • Ministry of Education and Science Republic of Bulgaria DO01-272/16.12.2019 'Bulgarian National Interdisciplinary Research e-Infrastructure for Resources and Technologies CLaDA-BG' • LINDAT/CLARIAH-CZ LM2018101 'Digital Research Infrastructure for Language Technologies, Arts and Humanities' • Spanish Ministry of Science and Innovation PID2019-108866RB-I0 / AEI / 10.13039/501100011033 'Original, Translated and Interpreted Representations of the Refugee Cris(e)s: Methodological Triangulation

[9] `https://www2.helsinki.fi/en/helsinki-centre-for-digital-humanities/helsinki-digital-humanities-hackathon-2022-dhh22`

[10] `https://colab.research.google.com`

[11] `https://gephi.org`

[12] `https://networkx.org`

within Corpus-Based Discourse Studies' • The Research Council of Lithuania P-MIP-20-373 "Policy Agenda of the Lithuanian Seimas and its Framing: The Analysis of the Seimas Debates in 1990 2020" • CLARIN-LV, European Regional Development Fund project 1.1.1.5/18/I/016 'University of Latvia and Institutes in the European Research Area – Excellency, Activity, Mobility, Capacity' • CLARIN-PL-Biz, financed by the European Regional Development Fund as a part of the 2014-2020 Smart Growth Operational Programme, CLARIN – Common Language Resources and Technology Infrastructure, project no. POIR.04.02.00-00C002/19

Bibliographical References

Calabretta, I., Dalton, C., Griscom, R., Kołczyńska, M., Pahor de Maiti, K., and Ros, R. (2021). Parliamentary debates in the COVID times. https://dhhackathon.wordpress.com/2021/05/28/parliamentary-debates-in-the-covid.

Erjavec, T. and Pančur, A. (2019). Parla-CLARIN: TEI guidelines for corpora of parliamentary proceedings, September. https://doi.org/10.5281/zenodo.3446164.

Erjavec, T., Ogrodniczuk, M., Osenova, P., Ljubešić, N., Simov, K., Grigorova, V., Rudolf, M., Pančur, A., Kopp, M., Barkarson, S., Steingrímsson, S., van der Pol, H., Depoorter, G., de Does, J., Jongejan, B., Haltrup Hansen, D., Navarretta, C., Calzada Pérez, M., de Macedo, L. D., van Heusden, R., Marx, M., Çöltekin, Ç., Coole, M., Agnoloni, T., Frontini, F., Montemagni, S., Quochi, V., Venturi, G., Ruisi, M., Marchetti, C., Battistoni, R., Sebők, M., Ring, O., Darģis, R., Utka, A., Petkevičius, M., Briedienė, M., Krilavičius, T., Morkevičius, V., Bartolini, R., Cimino, A., Diwersy, S., Luxardo, G., and Rayson, P. (2021a). Linguistically annotated multilingual comparable corpora of parliamentary debates ParlaMint.ana 2.1. Slovenian language resource repository CLARIN.SI. http://hdl.handle.net/11356/1431.

Erjavec, T., Ogrodniczuk, M., Osenova, P., Ljubešić, N., Simov, K., Grigorova, V., Rudolf, M., Pančur, A., Kopp, M., Barkarson, S., Steingrímsson, S., van der Pol, H., Depoorter, G., de Does, J., Jongejan, B., Haltrup Hansen, D., Navarretta, C., Calzada Pérez, M., de Macedo, L. D., van Heusden, R., Marx, M., Çöltekin, Ç., Coole, M., Agnoloni, T., Frontini, F., Montemagni, S., Quochi, V., Venturi, G., Ruisi, M., Marchetti, C., Battistoni, R., Sebők, M., Ring, O., Darģis, R., Utka, A., Petkevičius, M., Briedienė, M., Krilavičius, T., Morkevičius, V., Diwersy, S., Luxardo, G., and Rayson, P. (2021b). Multilingual comparable corpora of parliamentary debates ParlaMint 2.1. Slovenian language resource repository CLARIN.SI, http://hdl.handle.net/11356/1432.

Erjavec, T., Ogrodniczuk, M., Osenova, P., Ljubešić, N., Simov, K., Pančur, A., Rudolf, M., Kopp, M., Barkarson, S., Steingrímsson, S., Çöltekin, Ç., de Does, J., Depuydt, K., Agnoloni, T., Venturi, G., Pérez, M. C., de Macedo, L. D., Navarretta, C., Luxardo, G., Coole, M., Rayson, P., Morkevičius, V., Krilavičius, T., Darģis, R., Ring, O., van Heusden, R., Marx, M., and Fišer, D. (2022). The ParlaMint Corpora of Parliamentary Proceedings. *Language Resources and Evaluation*. https://doi.org/10.1007/s10579-021-09574-0.

Klein, G., Kim, Y., Deng, Y., Senellart, J., and Rush, A. (2017). OpenNMT: Open-source toolkit for neural machine translation. In *Proceedings of ACL 2017, System Demonstrations*, pages 67–72, Vancouver, Canada, July. Association for Computational Linguistics. https://www.aclweb.org/anthology/P17-4012.

Kopp, M., Stankov, V., Krůza, J. O., Straňák, P., and Bojar, O. (2021). ParCzech 3.0: A Large Czech Speech Corpus with Rich Metadata. In *24th International Conference on Text, Speech and Dialogue*, pages 293–304, Cham, Switzerland. Springer. https://link.springer.com/chapter/10.1007/978-3-030-83527-9_25.

Ljubešić, N., Korzinek, D., Rupnik, P., and Jazbec, I.-P. (2022). ParlaSpeech-HR – a freely available ASR dataset for Croatian bootstrapped from the ParlaMint corpus. In *Proceedings of the Third ParlaCLARIN Workshop*, Marseille, France.

Ljubešić, N., Koržinek, D., Rupnik, P., Jazbec, I.-P., Batanović, V., Bajčetić, L., and Evkoski, B. (2022). ASR training dataset for Croatian ParlaSpeech-HR v1.0. Slovenian language resource repository CLARIN.SI, http://hdl.handle.net/11356/1494.

Machálek, T. (2020). KonText: Advanced and Flexible Corpus Query Interface. In *Proceedings of the 12th Language Resources and Evaluation Conference*, pages 7003–7008, Marseille, France, May. European Language Resources Association. https://www.aclweb.org/anthology/2020.lrec-1.865.

Rayson, P., Dawn Archer, S. P., and McEnery, T. (2004). The UCREL semantic analysis system. In *Proceedings of the Workshop "Beyond Named Entity Recognition – Semantic labelling for NLP tasks*, pages 7–12. https://eprints.lancs.ac.uk/id/eprint/1783/.

Skubic, J. and Fišer, D. (2022). Parliamentary discourse research in sociology: Literature review. In *Proceedings of the Third ParlaCLARIN Workshop*, Marseille, France.

Proceedings of ParlaCLARIN III @ LREC2022 pages 7–15
Marseille, 20 June 2022

How GermaParl Evolves: Improving Data Quality by Reproducible Corpus Preparation and User Involvement

Andreas Blätte, Julia Rakers, Christoph Leonhardt
University of Duisburg-Essen
{andreas.blaette, julia.rakers, christoph.leonhardt}@uni-due.de

Abstract

The development and curation of large-scale corpora of plenary debates requires not only care and attention to detail when the data is created but also effective means of sustainable quality control. This paper makes two contributions: Firstly, it presents an updated version of the GermaParl corpus of parliamentary debates in the German *Bundestag*. Secondly, it shows how the corpus preparation pipeline is designed to serve the quality of the resource by facilitating effective community involvement. Centered around a workflow which combines reproducibility, transparency and version control, the pipeline allows for continuous improvements to the corpus.

Keywords: corpus creation, reproducibility, FAIR, community involvement, parliamentary debates, German Bundestag

1. Introduction[1]

Parliaments are at the heart of democracy and institutions with rich traditions. Nonetheless, the datafication of parliamentary resources is a relatively recent trend for research on parliaments and representative democracy. Plenary protocols prepared as corpora serve many research objectives – such as assessing party positions between elections, the (substantial) representativeness of parliamentarians, and much more (Fernandes et al., 2021).

One reason for the increasing use of parliamentary debates as research data – apart from their substantial meaning for democracy – is that tools and techniques to process large amounts of plenary data have become widely accessible and affordable. If data quality does not matter too much, the technically savvy will soon attain large-scale data, yet with a hacky prototyping approach. But the challenges to develop corpora of plenary data as a sustainable, multifunctional research resource are not to be underestimated.

Making data "FAIR" (Findable, Accessible, Interoperable, Reusable) (Wilkinson et al., 2016) has emerged as a new gold standard. In the case of parliamentary data, being FAIR means that corpora need to be findable in common repositories, data and workflows should be publicly available for download - in our case as open access resources -, should function across different technical environments, and should be applicable to different research objectives.

For good research data, just being "FAIR" is not enough. Data quality is as important as it has always been. We posit that in the case of large-scale corpora, data quality is hard to reach without explicit community involvement and a reproducible data preparation workflow. Moreover, without usability, there will not be users for the data. To be widely usable (and used), community efforts are needed to spot errors and flaws in a large quantity of data and to improve data quality. Furthermore, community efforts can improve the usability of tools. Even the best data and tools will not be used widely if their use is not intuitive. Scholars focused on a particular research question favor data and tools which are intuitive, easy to use, reliable, and with good performance.

Against this background, we suggest a process for evolving data quality with a reproducible data preparation workflow and community feedback as central building blocks. Issue tracking, transparent workflows, reproducibility, and versioning play important roles in this process. The use case for presenting this model is the GermaParl corpus of parliamentary debates in the German *Bundestag* that covers Germany's entire postwar history (1949 to 2021) in terms of parliamentary proceedings. We introduce this resource in the context of other corpora of debates in the *Bundestag*, and then discuss how reproducible data preparation and user involvement contribute to an evolving data quality.

In this contribution, a broad understanding of reproducibility is applied. We assume that data is created in a reproducible manner when a specific workflow reliably results in the same output given the same raw data. This definition is less granular than those of oth-

[1]The development of this version of the GermaParl corpus was supported by the team of the SOLDISK project at the University of Hildesheim (https://www.uni-hildesheim.de/soldisk/en/soldisk/). GermaParl has benefitted significantly from SOLDISK's comprehensive manual quality control of the data. Our special thanks goes to Hannes Schammann, Max Kisselew, Franziska Ziegler, Carina Böker, Jennifer Elsner and Carolin McCrea. Funding from KonsortSWD has advanced the data preparation tool set (namely the bignlp R package) to facilitate annotation layers relevant for data linkage. Funding from the Text+ consortium warrants updates of the corpus, quality control and keeping data formats up with current and future developments.The authors also want to thank Isabelle Borucki and the three anonymous reviewers for their valuable feedback on the first draft of this paper.

ers which differentiate, for example, between replicability, reproducibility and repeatability (Pawlik et al., 2019, p. 107). In practical terms, this means that the GermaParl corpus can be rebuilt from scratch in an automated and transparent fashion.

2. Existing Resources

The making and evolution of new the version of the GermaParl corpus of parliamentary debates shall illustrate how a reproducible data preparation pipeline is the essential counterpart to community involvement to improve data quality and usability. In line with the relevance of this conceptual and technical approach and the increasing popularity of plenary debates in research, multiple corpora of the German *Bundestag* exist nowadays. Before turning to GermaParl, the benefits and limitations of the siblings of GermaParl shall be considered.[2]

Three of those are summarized in table 1: The DeuParl corpus (Kirschner et al., 2021) covers the most extensive period of all corpora and covers the period from 1867 to 2020. However, the corpus lacks structural annotations that might be needed for more fine-grained analyses. In contrast to that, the ParlSpeech corpus (Rauh and Schwalbach, 2020) encompasses extensive metadata – for example the name of agenda items and speakers as well as their party affiliations, including Party Facts IDs (Döring and Regel, 2019) – and covers nine parliamentary chambers including the German *Bundestag* (from 1991 until 2018). While the ParlSpeech corpus is a significant resource for comparative parliamentary research, the authors' intention to continuously update the corpus and improve its quality is not clear and thus future availability and sustained improvements are not guaranteed. Another non-profit resource for parliamentary data is the Open Discourse Project (Richter et al., 2020). It includes plenary protocols and metadata from the so-called *Stammdaten* of the German *Bundestag* (Deutscher Bundestag, 2021) and Wikipedia. The authors offer a graphical user interface, the code how to build the corpus, the data itself, and a GitHub page to encourage user pull requests. Furthermore, the authors aim to continuously update the corpus. However, the Open Discourse Project has one important drawback for scientific use: While it is thoroughly documented from a technical perspective and comprehensively presented on their website, the data paper is not available as of the time of writing. As a result, substantial documentation about design decisions is still missing.

Apart from scientific projects, commercial newspapers leaping into data journalism provide corpora. The German weekly newspaper *Die Zeit* covers 70 years of German parliamentary activity in its corpus (Biermann et al., 2019). However, this is not an open research resource and only accessible through a graphical user interface with limited functionality. It is a great information tool for interested newspaper readers but not for researchers with specific questions in mind. Apart from *Die Zeit*, the *Süddeutsche Zeitung* offers different corpora covering German parliamentary debates. Under #sprachemachtpolitik, the newspaper offers different analyses about discursive changes and topics in the *Bundestag* (Schories, without year), covering 70 years of parliamentary activity. However, this larger corpus is not publicly accessible. In addition, the *Süddeutsche Zeitung* compiled an earlier corpus of the German *Bundestag* and published their code on GitHub (Brunner and Schories, 2018). Of all corpora mentioned, the smaller *Süddeutsche* corpus is the smallest one covering six months of plenary activity to assess changes of parliamentary habits after the advent of the right-wing populist AfD in Germany's national parliament in 2017/2018. The analysis was updated in 2020 to cover 2019 as well. Despite this transparency, the limited coverage is a limitation of this corpus for many research questions.

Besides these general-purpose corpora for the German *Bundestag*, there are specialized corpora covering German politics. A corpus prepared by Barbaresi (2018) includes political speeches of the four highest ranked political functionaries in Germany. The MigParl corpus (Blätte and Leonhardt, 2020) focuses on migration and integration related speeches in the German *Länder*. Corpora like these may be a suitable option for research projects closely related to the authors' initial projects. Nonetheless, many projects will require a general-purpose, multi-functional resource.

A final flavor of *Bundestag* debates to be addressed are XML documents of parliamentary protocols directly issued by the German *Bundestag*. Of course, it would be a great relief for researchers if standardized XML was prepared right at the origin. The XML offered by the German *Bundestag* is a disappointment in this respect. Documents for older legislative periods are just plain text wrapped into a very slim header. New documents need considerable transformation and consolidation to serve as a research resource.

Preparing corpora or parliamentary debates for scientific purposes costs time and demands technical knowledge. Distinguishing it from the resources that have been introduced, the GermaParl is comprehensively ambitious to serve as a sustainable research resource. Firstly, by providing extensive coverage and metadata, we aim to provide a resource that is suitable for many different research projects on parliamentary debates in Germany. Secondly, we aim to actively engage the scientific community to enhance data quality. Thirdly, we offer our data as an open access resource for research.

As a follow-up to the previous release of GermaParl covering twenty years of parliamentary debates in Germany (1996-2016), the first comprehensive version of GermaParl is published in 2022. The release of the cor-

[2]While the following overview is our own, the OPTED project, for example, currently works on a systematic inventory of available parliamentary corpora (Sebők et al., 2021).

	DeuParl (Kirschner et al., 2021)	ParlSpeech (Rauh and Schwalbach, 2020)	Open Discourse (Richter et al., 2020)
Size	5,446 protocols from the Reichstag; 4,260 from the Bundestag	more than 6.3 million speeches	more than 4,000 protocols; 907,644 speeches
Scope	German Reichstag and German Bundestag	9 parliamentary chambers: Austrian Nationalrat, the Czech Poslanecká sněmovna Parlamentu, the Danish Folketing, the Dutch Tweede Kammer, the German Bundestag, the New Zealand House of Representatives, the Spanish Congreso de los Disputados, the Swedish Riksdag, the UK House of Commons	German Bundestag
Time periods	1867 - 2020	Differs per parliament: 1987-2019	1949 – 2021 (19 legislatures)
Meta data	year/date	Date, speech number, speaker, party, Party Facts ID, speaker's position as chair, speech length, name of the agenda item	among others: id; session; electoral term; first name; last name; politician id; speech_content; faction id; document url; position short; position_long; date; search_speech_content; multiple variables on politicians, electoral terms and factions
Raw text available	yes	yes	yes
Publicly available	Via university's repository	Via Harvard Dataverse	Via Harvard Dataverse
Context of origin	Data is part of a research paper	Along authors' research goals	Non-profit project

Table 1: Other Resources concerned with German Parliamentary Data

pus follows a two-stage scheme that is laid out in detail in section 5 of this paper.

3. The GermaParl Corpus 1949 - 2021

Covering the years from 1996 to 2016, the initial release of GermaParl corpus is an established resource for the analysis of parliamentary debates in the German *Bundestag*. It is available in two editions. The first is an interoperable XML format inspired by the standards of the Text Encoding Initiative (TEI).[3] In addition, the data has been imported into the IMS Open Corpus Workbench (CWB) (Evert and Hardie, 2011) which facilitates the management of large corpora and provides a powerful query language (the Corpus Query Processor / CQP) to make use of additional linguistic annotation layers which come with this version of the corpus.[4] The corpus has been introduced by Blätte and Blessing (2018) and has been used, inter alia, to investigate discourses on economic inequality and taxation (Smith Ochoa, 2020; Hilmar and Sachweh, 2022) and the politics of parliamentary speech-making (Müller et al., 2021).

Users of the R programming language will just need the following snippet to install GermaParl locally.

```
install.packages("polmineR")
install.packages("cwbtools")
doi <- "10.5281/zenodo.3742113"
cwbtools::corpus_install(doi = doi)
```

After the installation, users are ready to load polmineR as a toolset for corpus analysis and run some initial queries.

```
library(polmineR)
kwic(
  "GERMAPARL",
  query = "Integration"
)
```

[3]See https://github.com/PolMine/GermaParlTEI.

[4]The CWB corpus can be downloaded from Zenodo: https://zenodo.org/record/3742113.

The Comprehensive R Archive Network (CRAN) takes extraordinary care that all published R packages are interoperable. So this code is proven to work on Windows, macOS and several flavors of Linux.

In the following section, we present the corpus which extends the coverage of the previous one, describe the workflow used to create it and discuss how this addresses the need for reproducible workflows to facilitate community involvement. This workflow might provide some inspiration for the creation of other corpora with comparable goals.

3.1. Data Report

The 2022 release of GermaParl covers all debates of the first 19 legislative periods of the German *Bundestag*. In its current state, the corpus comprises about 271 million tokens in total. Figure 1 shows the size of the corpus per legislative period.[5] In both the TEI and the CWB version, the corpus is enriched with a number of metadata which makes it possible to create meaningful subcorpora. In the terminology of the CWB, these are called structural attributes. These are presented in the subsequent section. The CWB version also contains additional linguistic annotation layers which are mostly added at the level of individual tokens. These are called positional attributes in the CWB terminology and are presented thereafter.

3.2. Structural Attributes

To create useful subcorpora, a number of structural attributes is available. An overview is provided in table 2. Firstly, there is document level metadata such as the legislative period and session number, the date and, derived from that, the year. Figure 1 already showed the corpus size by legislative period. Figure 2 adds granularity by providing the same information by year and

[5]All reported numbers and visualizations in this contribution are based on the CWB version of the corpus.

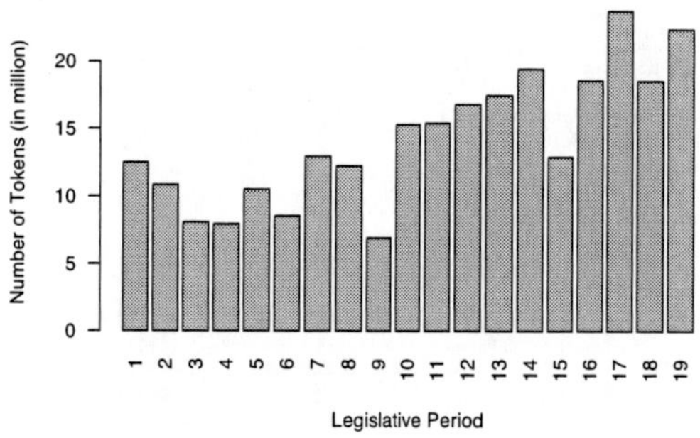

Figure 1: Number of Tokens by Legislative Period

reveals that election years usually contain less tokens than regular years. In addition, it also shows that the first and the last legislative period covered by the corpus include a smaller number of tokens because legislative periods do not align with calendar years. Finally, the long-term trend towards more words in parliament indicates a general increase in the number of delivered speeches per year.

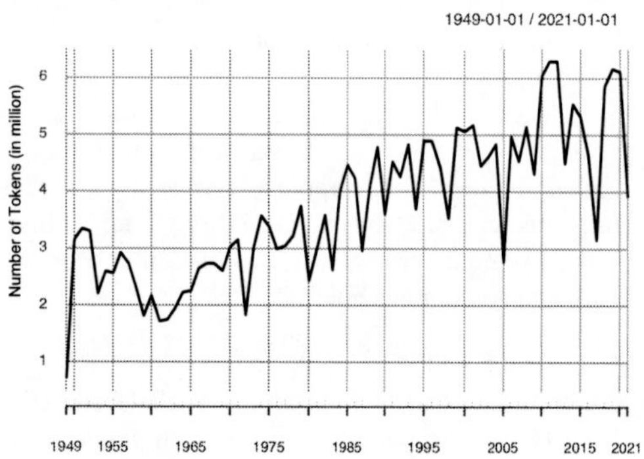

Figure 2: Number of Tokens by Year

Secondly, there is information on speaker level. This means that subsets of the corpus can be created for individual speakers, parliamentary groups and other attributes. Some of these attributes are part of the initial plenary protocols while others were added using additional external resources. Prominent examples for these attributes are full speaker names as well as party affiliations. The assignment of these attributes is discussed in detail later, but to provide a glimpse into the data, there are 4303 unique speaker names and 22 unique parliamentary groups included in the current version of the corpus. Thirdly, some linguistic features (named entities with types for persons, organizations, locations and miscellaneous named entities as well as paragraphs and sentences) are encoded as structural attributes. Finally, there are some technical structural attributes like the URL or the type of the source material.

3.3. Positional Attributes

The corpus contains linguistic features beyond the word form of a token. Two different Part-of-Speech tag sets (the Universal Dependencies tag set and the Stuttgart-Tübingen tag set) and lemmata have been added to the corpus at the token level. Table 3 represents a token stream extracted from the corpus to illustrate the available positional attributes.

4. A Reproducible Corpus Preparation Pipeline

While the corpus has been prepared with great care, remaining flaws in the data cannot be ruled out. Unknown variations or simply typos in the original data can cause speakers to be missed, for example. Despite systematic checks, some of these flaws will be encountered only after release by researchers who actually work with the corpus. The data is simply too big to be aware of all potential shortcomings.

We see it as a precondition for a culture of suggesting improvements, reporting bugs and an approximation to fundamental Open Science principles, that the corpus is prepared in a transparent and reproducible fashion.[6] This is the technical basis for a feedback loop for quality control (see also Blätte and Blessing (2018, p. 813)). Reproducibility facilitates that community involvement and feedback can improve resources and tools.

The following workflow is based on the preparation pipeline initially presented by Blätte and Blessing (2018). The initial steps are thus similar to the workflow presented there. Due to changes in data coverage and availability, some stages differ. In general, the corpus preparation workflow still comprises the three steps described by Blätte and Blessing (2018, p. 812):

- Preprocessing
- XMLification
- Consolidating

4.1. Preprocessing

The corpus preparation starts with the download of the raw data from the website of the German *Bundestag*.[7] The first 13 legislative periods as well as the 18th legislative period are downloaded as XML files. The existing GermaParl data is incorporated into the new version of the corpus. The existing corpus can be retrieved from GitHub and covers the years between 1996 and 2016 (about the second half of the 13th legislative period until about the first half of the 18th legislative period).[8] For reasons explained below, protocols of the 18th legislative period are extracted from PDF files.[9]

[6] See `https://openscience.org/what-exactly-is-open-science/`.

[7] See `https://www.bundestag.de/services/opendata`.

[8] See `https://github.com/PolMine/GermaParlTEI`.

[9] The XML files for the 18th legislative period are used to retrieve the metadata of the documents while the PDF files are used to retrieve the text of the protocols.

Structural Attribute	Level	In initial protocols	Description
lp	document level	yes	Legislative period
protocol_no	document level	yes	Session number
date	document level	yes	Date of the protocol
year	document level	yes	Year derived from date
speaker	text level	partially	Full name of the speaker, including regional specification when necessary
parliamentary_group	speaker level	yes	Parliamentary group of a speaker, corrected errors when necessary
party	speaker level	no	Party affiliation of a speaker, retrieved from Wikipedia
role	speaker level	yes	Parliamentary role of a speaker, derived from speaker call
stage_type	text level	yes	Type of stage comment, if segment is not speech but some form of comment or interjection
ner_type	text level	no	Type of named entity, if a sequence is a named entity
p	text level	partially	paragraph
s	text level	yes	sentence

Table 2: Structural Attributes in the GermaParl Corpus

cpos	word	upos	xpos	lemma
0	Meine	PRON	PPOSAT	mein
1	Damen	NOUN	NN	Dame
2	und	CCONJ	KON	und
3	Herren	NOUN	NN	Herr
4	!	PUNCT	$.	!
5	Abgeordnete	NOUN	NN	Abgeordnete
6	des	DET	ART	die
7	Deutschen	PROPN	ADJA	deutsch
8	Bundestags	PROPN	NN	Bundestag
9	!	PUNCT	$.	!

Speech by Paul Löbe on 1949-09-07

Table 3: Beginning of GermaParl as a Token Stream

During preprocessing, the protocols of the first 13 legislative periods are extracted from the downloaded XML files. Aside from some document-level metadata, these files only contain a single text node in which the entire text of the protocol is found. Compared to the PDF versions of the document, this has the advantage that the initial two column layout is already resolved. However, header lines as well as the table of contents and appendices are still part of the text and have to be removed. This is also a reason why we still use the PDF files for the 18th legislative period because they are sufficiently formatted to be extracted via the trickypdf R package, removing margin columns as well as header and footer lines.[10]

4.2. XMLification

After extracting the raw text from the XML and PDF files and removing header lines, table of contents and appendices where necessary, the data for legislative periods 1 to 13 and 18 is processed in the same workflow. Using the Framework for Parsing Plenary Protocols (frappp) which provides a generic workflow to parse unstructured protocols into structured XML (implemented as an R package), the raw text is XMLified. This follows the process described in Blätte and Blessing (2018): Based on the notion that regular expressions can be used to identify metadata as well as speaker calls, interjections or agenda items, an iterative process is used to formulate a battery of specific regular expressions for different speaker types and other structural elements such as interjections. The result is an XML format which resembles the standards of the Text Encoding Initiative (TEI) for performance text.[11] It is envisioned to extend the output format to also include a format compatible with the ParlaMint project (Erjavec et al., 2022). This would further increase the interoperability of the data.

4.3. The 19th Legislative Period as a Special Case

The 19th legislative period is a special case: Compared to earlier legislative periods, the format of the XML files issued by the German *Bundestag* changes completely, from an essentially unstructured plain text format with XML headers to a comprehensively annotated, structured XML format. Thus, the preprocessing for this legislative period follows a separate pro-

[10]See `https://github.com/PolMine/trickypdf`.

[11]See `https://www.tei-c.org/release/doc/tei-p5-doc/en/html/DR.html`.

cess. Providing an already comprehensively annotated XML, the central task is to convert this XML to the same TEI-inspired output format used for the other legislative periods. The most significant hurdle is the decision in the original XML specification to include presidential speakers of the *Bundestag* as child nodes of the current speaker. Resolving this robustly can be challenging. In addition, specific conditions apply for specific types of debates, in particular question time, in which not all utterances are actually speech nodes in their own right. In consequence, we flatten this structure by assigning speech nodes to each individual utterance.

4.4. Consolidating

When consolidating the data, apart from the volume and the resulting variations in the data, there is one difference: While the previous version of GermaParl used Wikipedia for all parliamentary actors, in this new iteration, members of parliament are consolidated using the so-called "*Stammdaten*" of the German *Bundestag* (Deutscher Bundestag, 2021) to provide canonical names. The comprehensive *Stammdaten* file contains information for each member of parliament in the history of the *Bundestag*, including biographical as well as political data. In contrast, the plenary protocols issued by the *Bundestag* itself contain the speaker name in various formats. From the first to the 11th legislative period, the protocols contain only family names (sometimes with a speaker's constituency for disambiguation) when speakers are called. At the beginning of the 12th legislative period, this changed and full names are used thereafter in the speaker call. To harmonize the names of speakers in the corpus, the names found in the initial protocols were matched against the data in the *Stammdaten* file, using an approach to match the name, parliamentary group and legislative period of a speaker found in the speaker call with the *Stammdaten*. Like in the previous version of GermaParl, it was necessary to account for alternative names in some cases as well as to deploy fuzzy matching and make manual interventions in case of typos, missing information in either the protocols or the *Stammdaten* and other errors or divergences. To keep the results of these interventions reproducible, they are done programmatically during the corpus preparation. Similarly, the party affiliation is not part of the initial protocols. We use the data provided on the Wikipedia pages for each legislative period to add this information to the corpus. This has been done for the previous version of GermaParl as well (Blätte and Blessing, 2018, p. 813). This enables us to add a party affiliation specific to the legislative period to a speaker. In contrast, the *Stammdaten* file only reports a single party assignment for each member of parliament for the entire time, not documenting switches between parties. This still does not equate to date-specific party assignments, though: It must be noted that the information extracted from these tables on Wikipedia does not account for changes during legislative periods in a structured fashion. In addition, they are not entirely homogeneous when it comes to the point in time (beginning or end of the legislative period) which is used to determine the current party affiliation of a speaker. A remaining challenge is the annotation of agenda items. While these will be of great interest for a number of analyses, their identification is challenging as they are called in a great variety of forms. Using sentence similarities to find agenda item calls which are similar to those found in the 19th legislative period, a first implementation of an agenda item annotation is included in the TEI version of the corpus. The CWB version does not contain agenda items yet.

4.5. Linguistic Annotation and Import into the Corpus Workbench

As a result, we end up with 4340 structurally annotated plenary protocols in the TEI format described earlier. For the linguistic annotation which is part of the CWB corpus we first use Stanford CoreNLP (version 4.2) (Manning et al., 2014) to segment the textual data into tokens, sentences and paragraphs, add Part-of-Speech Tags (in the Universal Dependencies tag set) and perform named entity recognition. To use Stanford CoreNLP from within R, a wrapper called bignlp was developed that exposes the Java implementation of Stanford CoreNLP in a way that allows the processing of large amounts of text in parallel.[12] This both should speed up the process and increase robustness, at least vis-a-vis problems concerned with limited memory. The intermediate result is a vertical XML format which contains segmented tokens as well as named entities and part-of-speech annotation. This vertical XML format can then be imported into the Corpus Workbench. Finally, based on the CWB corpus, we use the TreeTagger (Schmid, 1995) to add Part-of-Speech tags in the Stuttgart-Tübingen tag set as well as lemmata to the corpus. More recent developments like the RNNTagger (Schmid, 2019) may be used in the future.

4.6. Reproducibility

To ensure that feedback can be incorporated into the data preparation and maintenance workflow, the process needs to be designed in a reproducible fashion and should be centered around open source tools. To this end, the entire workflow is set up in R (R Core Team, 2021) (as explained earlier, also accessing resources implemented in other programming languages via wrappers) and can theoretically be executed in a single R script. While this might not be advisable for each phase of corpus creation - especially when a large amount of quality control including iterative and manual optimization is involved at the beginning of the process - this facilitates a reproducible workflow in later stages. For example, it is possible to adjust a regular expression to improve the matching of specific speak-

[12]See `https://github.com/PolMine/bignlp`.

ers and re-run the script to create an updated version of the corpus. Combined with dissemination methods like GitHub and Zenodo (providing digital object identifiers), the process is transparent and both workflow and output are subject to version control. With most steps being realized via documented R packages which are under version control, this workflow was developed with a long-term perspective in mind.

5. The Role of Community Involvement

As argued above, aside from a workflow that allows for reproducibility, involving an active community is a crucial precondition for high quality data on a large scale. This involvement includes both the creation of the data as well as later stages. During the development, the community takes part in a two-stage release process. Firstly, researchers are offered access to the corpus during a beta phase starting in May 2022. Researchers can get access after expressing their interest.[13] During this stage, we encourage feedback from beta users to improve data quality and workflows. Apart from established feedback mechanisms such as GitHub issues, a community workshop provides an opportunity to gain more detailed insights about the user experience when working with the corpus. These insights go beyond dealing with outright flaws and errors in the data. Participants discuss aspects like the (non)intuitive conventions and workflows as well as potential difficulties when using the corpus and tools for analysis. Secondly, after this initial stage of testing and improving the corpus, a general release is planned in October 2022. Subsequently, GermaParl is available as an open research resource with a proportionately open license. The corpus will be available from GitHub (in the specific XML format described above) and Zenodo (as a CWB corpus). More information and documentation will be provided on the GermaParl website. Workflows used when the corpus was built will be documented on GitHub to increase transparency.

This two-stage release process aims at improving both the quality of the data and its usability before the general release of the data. After the initial open release, feedback mechanisms such as issues via GitHub are available to report remaining flaws, improve the documentation of the data or to suggest additional features which should be considered and incorporated on a regular basis in subsequent releases. Closely related to community involvement is community outreach: While GermaParl is an established resource, its active community should be engaged, maintained and grown. Amongst others, we use GermaParl and related R-packages in university courses. Furthermore, we present GermaParl-based research at national and international political science conferences. Talks and forums of the National Research Data Infrastructure Germany (NFDI) are an important dissemination mechanism. These events are only the most visible among a number of different exchange formats for the PolMine Project to reach out.

[13] See `https://zenodo.org/record/6539967` for further information.

6. Discussion and Outlook

Reproducibility is the core idea of the workflow behind GermaParl. Being based around a set of generic tools, especially the Framework for Parsing Plenary Protocols (frappp), it should facilitate an iterative process of data creation and quality control. Given the size of the corpus and the number of protocols, even the most thorough checks during the creation of the corpus cannot guarantee the identification of all possible flaws. The names of speakers might contain typos which prevent regular expressions to match them, for example. These are scenarios which benefit from an active community in which researchers and other interested persons use the data and report errors when they encounter them. However, reporting errors is not enough when these errors cannot be fixed. And here, a reproducible workflow is a central requirement.

We conceive GermaParl as a comprehensively annotated and thoroughly checked high-quality research resource. Going beyond other existing resources for parliamentary debates in Germany, the focus is on reproducibility and community involvement, transparency and long-term perspectives as well as multifunctionality - the usability in different research projects. Unlike other resources on the *Bundestag*, GermaParl is available in two editions: 1) a TEI-inspired XML edition which makes it interoperable, 2) a linguistically annotated Corpus Workbench (CWB) corpus. This opens up the potentials of the CWB as a powerful corpus management tool and query engine. Moreover, it makes the analysis of large amounts of textual data accessible when analyzed with the polmineR (Blätte, 2020) analysis environment shown earlier.

The development does not stop here. For instance, Wikidata-IDs for persons will be added to the corpus to facilitate the linkage of parliamentary data to other resources such as, for example, roll call vote data. This would allow even more comprehensive analyses, for example concerning the relationship between parliamentary speech and other public arenas or how specific characteristics on the individual level contribute to parliamentary discourse.

7. References

Barbaresi, A. (2018). A corpus of German political speeches from the 21st century. In *Proceedings of the Eleventh International Conference on Language Resources and Evaluation (LREC 2018)*, pages 792–797, Miyazaki, Japan, May. European Language Resources Association (ELRA).

Biermann, K., Blickle, P., Drongowski, R., Ehmann, A., Erdmann, E., Gortana, F., Lindhoff, A., Möller, C., Rauscher, C., Scheying, S., Schlieben, M., Stahnke, J., Tröger, J., and Venohr, S.

(2019). Darüber spricht der Bundestag. Zeit Online. https://www.zeit.de/politik/deutschland/2019-09/bundestag-jubilaeum-70-jahre-parlament-reden-woerter-sprache-wandel. Accessed: 2022-05-20.

Blätte, A. and Blessing, A. (2018). The GermaParl Corpus of Parliamentary Protocols. In *Proceedings of the Eleventh International Conference on Language Resources and Evaluation (LREC 2018)*, pages 810–816, Miyazaki, Japan, May. European Language Resources Association (ELRA).

Blätte, A. and Leonhardt, C. (2020). MigParl. A Corpus of Speeches on Migration and Integration in Germany's Regional Parliaments. https://doi.org/10.5281/zenodo.3872263.

Blätte, A. (2020). polmineR: Verbs and Nouns for Corpus Analysis. https://doi.org/10.5281/zenodo.4042093.

Brunner, K. and Schories, M. (2018). Das steckt in den Bundestagsprotokollen. Süddeutsche Zeitung Online. https://www.sueddeutsche.de/politik/bundestag-analyse-plenarprotokolle-1.3944784. Accessed: 2022-05-20.

Deutscher Bundestag. (2021). Stammdaten aller Abgeordneten seit 1949 im XML-Format. https://www.bundestag.de/resource/blob/472878/d5743e6ffabe14af60d0c9ddd9a3a516/MdB-Stammdaten-data.zip.

Döring, H. and Regel, S. (2019). Party Facts: A database of political parties worldwide. *Party Politics*, 25(2):97–109.

Erjavec, T., Ogrodniczuk, M., Osenova, P., Ljubešić, N., Simov, K., Pančur, A., Rudolf, M., Kopp, M., Barkarson, S., Steingrímsson, S., Çöltekin, Ç., de Does, J., Depuydt, K., Agnoloni, T., Venturi, G., Pérez, M. C., de Macedo, L. D., Navarretta, C., Luxardo, G., Coole, M., Rayson, P., Morkevičius, V., Krilavičius, T., Darģis, R., Ring, O., van Heusden, R., Marx, M., and Fišer, D. (2022). The ParlaMint corpora of parliamentary proceedings. *Language Resources and Evaluation*.

Evert, S. and Hardie, A. (2011). Twenty-first century Corpus Workbench: Updating a query architecture for the new millennium. In *Proceedings of the Corpus Linguistics 2011 conference*, University of Birmingham, UK.

Fernandes, J. M., Debus, M., and Bäck, H. (2021). Unpacking the politics of legislative debates. *European Journal of Political Research*, 60(4):1032–1045.

Hilmar, T. and Sachweh, P. (2022). "Poison to the Economy": (Un-)Taxing the Wealthy in the German Federal Parliament from 1996 to 2016. *Social Justice Research*.

Kirschner, C., Walter, T., Eger, S., Glavas, G., Lauscher, A., and Ponzetto, S. P. (2021). DeuParl. https://tudatalib.ulb.tu-darmstadt.de/handle/tudatalib/2889.

Manning, C., Surdeanu, M., Bauer, J., Finkel, J., Bethard, S., and McClosky, D. (2014). The Stanford CoreNLP Natural Language Processing Toolkit. In *Proceedings of 52nd Annual Meeting of the Association for Computational Linguistics: System Demonstrations*, pages 55–60, Baltimore, Maryland, June. Association for Computational Linguistics.

Müller, J., Stecker, C., and Blätte, A. (2021). Germany: Strong Party Groups and Debates among Policy Specialists. In Hanna Bäck, et al., editors, *The Politics of Legislative Debates*, pages 376–398. Oxford University Press, Oxford.

Pawlik, M., Hütter, T., Kocher, D., Mann, W., and Augsten, N. (2019). A Link is not Enough – Reproducibility of Data. *Datenbank Spektrum*, 19:107–115.

R Core Team. (2021). R: A Language and Environment for Statistical Computing. https://www.R-project.org/.

Rauh, C. and Schwalbach, J. (2020). The ParlSpeech V2 data set: Full-text corpora of 6.3 million parliamentary speeches in the key legislative chambers of nine representative democracies. Harvard Dataverse, V1. https://doi.org/10.7910/DVN/L4OAKN.

Richter, F., Koch, P., Franke, O., Kraus, J., Kuruc, F., Thiem, A., Högerl, J., Heine, S., and Schöps, K. (2020). Open Discourse. Harvard Dataverse, V3. https://doi.org/10.7910/DVN/FIKIBO.

Schmid, H. (1995). Improvements in Part-of-Speech Tagging With an Application To German. Revised version of a paper originally presented at the EACL SIGDAT workshop in Dublin in 1995. https://www.cis.uni-muenchen.de/~schmid/tools/TreeTagger/data/tree-tagger2.pdf.

Schmid, H. (2019). Deep Learning-Based Morphological Taggers and Lemmatizers for Annotating Historical Texts. In *Proceedings of the 3rd International Conference on Digital Access to Textual Cultural Heritage*, DATeCH2019, New York, NY, USA. Association for Computing Machinery. https://www.cis.uni-muenchen.de/~schmid/papers/Datech2019.pdf.

Schories, M. (without year). So haben wir den Bundestag ausgerechnet. Süddeutsche Zeitung Online. https://www.sueddeutsche.de/projekte/artikel/politik/so-haben-wir-den-bundestag-ausgerechnet-e893391/. Accessed: 2022-05-20.

Sebők, M., Proksch, S.-O., and Rauh, C. (2021). OPTED. Review of available parliamentary corpora. Deliverable D5.1. https://opted.eu/fileadmin/user_upload/k_opted/OPTED_Deliverable_D5.1.pdf.

Smith Ochoa, C. (2020). Trivializing inequality by

narrating facts: a discourse analysis of contending storylines in Germany. *Critical Policy Studies*, 14(3):319–338.

Wilkinson, M. D., Dumontier, M., Aalbersberg, I. J., Appleton, G., Axton, M., Baak, A., Blomberg, N., Boiten, J.-W., da Silva Santos, L. B., Bourne, P. E., Bouwman, J., Brookes, A. J., Clark, T., Crosas, M., Dillo, I., Dumon, O., Edmunds, S., Evelo, C. T., Finkers, R., Gonzalez-Beltran, A., Gray, A. J. G., Groth, P., Goble, C., Grethe, J. S., Heringa, J., 't Hoen, P. A. C., Hooft, R., Kuhn, T., Kok, R., Kok, J., Lusher, S. J., Martone, M. E., Mons, A., Packer, A. L., Persson, B., Rocca-Serra, P., Roos, M., van Schaik, R., Sansone, S.-A., Schultes, E., Sengstag, T., Slater, T., Strawn, G., Swertz, M. A., Thompson, M., van der Lei, J., van Mulligen, E., Velterop, J., Waagmeester, A., Wittenburg, P., Wolstencroft, K., Zhao, J., and Mons, B. (2016). The FAIR Guiding Principles for scientific data management and stewardship. *Scientific Data*, 3:160018.

Proceedings of ParlaCLARIN III @ LREC2022 pages 16–24
Marseille, 20 June 2022

Between History and Natural Language Processing: Study, Enrichment and Online Publication of French Parliamentary Debates of the Early Third Republic (1881–1899)

Marie Puren[1 2], Aurélien Pellet[1], Nicolas Bourgeois[1], Pierre Vernus[3 4], Fanny Lebreton[5]
[1]MNSHS-Epitech, [2]Centre Jean Mabillon, [3]LARHRA, [4]Université Lumière Lyon 2,
[5] École nationale des chartes
[1]Le Kremlin-Bicêtre (France), [2 5]Paris (France), [3 4]Lyon (France)
{marie.puren, aurelien.pellet, nicolas.bourgeois}@epitech.eu, pierre.vernus@msh-lse.fr,
fanny.lebreton@chartes.psl.eu

Abstract

We present the AGODA (*Analyse sémantique et Graphes relationnels pour l'Ouverture des Débats à l'Assemblée nationale*) project, which aims to create a platform for consulting and exploring digitised French parliamentary debates (1881-1940) available in the digital library of the National Library of France. This project brings together historians and NLP specialists: parliamentary debates are indeed an essential source for French history of the contemporary period, but also for linguistics. This project therefore aims to produce a corpus of texts that can be easily exploited with computational methods, and that respect the TEI standard. Ancient parliamentary debates are also an excellent case study for the development and application of tools for publishing and exploring large historical corpora. In this paper, we present the steps necessary to produce such a corpus. We detail the processing and publication chain of these documents, in particular by mentioning the problems linked to the extraction of texts from digitised images. We also introduce the first analyses that we have carried out on this corpus with "bag-of-words" techniques not too sensitive to OCR quality (namely topic modelling and word embedding).

Keywords: parliamentary debates, France, Third Republic, OCR, XML-TEI, topic modelling, word embedding

1. Introduction

In this paper, we present the objectives of AGODA[1] (2021-2022) (Puren and Vernus, 2021), one of the five pilot projects supported by the DataLab of the National Library of France[2]. It aims to create an online platform for consulting and exploring parliamentary debates in the Chamber of Deputies (1881-1940), transcribed in the *Journal officiel de la République française. Débats parlementaires. Chambre des députés : compte rendu in-extenso*, available online on *Gallica* (the digital library of the National Library of France[3]), in the form of structured and semantically enriched textual data.

This project has the particularity of bringing together computer scientists (in particular NLP specialists) and historians: the aim is not only to produce annotated data from digitised documents, but also to offer historians functionalities that allow them to explore these sources according to their research interests. The editorialization and enrichment of these data require the design of a workflow adapted to the production and analysis of such large corpora of historical documents. During this project, we try to develop such a workflow, while demonstrating its feasibility and reusability. This is why we have adopted a "proof of concept" approach: we are working on a test sub-corpus, namely the parliamentary debates of the early Third Republic, in order to test our hypotheses on a smaller data set. In the (limited) framework of the AGODA project, we are mainly interested in the parliamentary cycle from 1889 to 1893[4] which is of major interest for historians; but we apply topic modelling and word embedding on a larger corpus (1881-1899) because both methods (and especially word embedding) require a large amount of text.

From January 1881 and throughout the Third Republic[5], the debates in the lower house of the French Parliament were published in the *Journal Officiel* (this is still the case today). Since its establishment in the nineteenth century, the Chamber of Deputies has played a central role in French politics, especially during the Third Republic (1870-1940). Proclaimed on 4 September 1870, constitutionally founded in 1875 as a temporary solution, the Third Republic only became fully republican between 1876 and 1879 with the conquest of the Chamber of Deputies and the Senate by the Republicans. From then on, the Republicans established a parliamentary system of government that placed the Chamber of Deputies at the heart of the system. This is why the government paid particular attention to the reactions of this assembly throughout the Third Republic (Coniez, 2010). We are fortunate to have access to detailed transcripts of the debates held in the Cham-

[1]Analyse sémantique et Graphes relationnels pour l'Ouverture et l'étude des Débats à l'Assemblée nationale.

[2]https://www.bnf.fr/fr/les-projets-de-recherche

[3]Available on Gallica

[4]This parliamentary cycle or "5th *législature*" took place between 12 November 1889 and 14 October 1893.

[5]The Third Republic was the republican system of government in effect in France from September 1870 to July 1940.

ber: in the context of the increasing publicisation of parliamentary debates (Lavoinne, 1999), a body of specialised civil servants was set up in 1847 to transcribe the debates in detail, while trying to render the naturalness of the discussions (Gardey, 2010).
In this article, we will introduce the rationale of the project, showing what it can bring to history but also to other different disciplines. We will then present the corpus, and the processing and publication chain that we are developing. Finally, we will discuss two examples of exploration - topic modelling and word embedding - that have been tested on the corpus.

2. Background and Aims

These sources were digitised and put online between 2008 and 2016, as part of the French digitisation program for legal science[6] (Alix, 2008). For the past sixty years, parliamentary debates have been a source used by the humanities, as shown for example by the work carried out on the British Parliament (Chester and Bowring, 1962; Franklin and Norton, 1993). They are indeed very valuable for historians, particularly those interested in political history (Ouellet and Roussel-Beaulieu, 2003) and comparative history (Ihalainen et al., 2016) but also in social, economic or religious history (Lemercier, 2021; Marnot, 2000). We are also aware of the importance that this corpus may have for other disciplines such as the history of law (Fournier and Pépratx, 1991), political science(Van Dijk, 2010), sociology (Cheng, 2015) or linguistics (de Galembert et al., 2013; Hirst et al., 2014; Rheault et al., 2016).
This historical source is not unknown to historians, and its digitisation can be expected to give rise to new projects[7]. But it turns out that the French parliamentary debates in the Chamber of Deputies are still little known to the general public, and are still under-used by specialists (Coniez, 2010). Despite the fact that the entire historical French parliamentary debates are available online, it is still difficult to manipulate these digitised documents, which constitute a particularly large corpus of texts[8]. The apprehension of such material requires a good prior knowledge of the source, and very often, to know precisely what one is looking for. On the other hand, the online availability of Hansard[9], the Anglo-Saxon equivalent of the *Journal Officiel* for parliamentary debates, has led to the emergence of new works in history and political science (Bonin, 2020). More generally, access to digitised and ocerised debates seems to have a positive effect on the number of historical works using these documents (Mela et al., 2022). The same effect can be observed for other disciplines using textual data from contemporary debates (Fišer et al., 2018; Fišer et al., 2020).
The Hansard also allows its users to explore the debates in a very intuitive way and makes the textual data easily exploitable. We believe that building a similar platform for French parliamentary debates, especially historical ones, would increase the number of users and thus the exploitation of these documents. The AGODA project therefore aims to facilitate access to these documents for Internet users, whether they are researchers or the general public. AGODA is therefore not only about doing research, but also about promoting a little-known heritage collection.

3. Related Works

The AGODA project is part of a wider movement to improve knowledge and exploitation of parliamentary data. Two trends, which are not exclusive, can be distinguished: on the one hand, the production of corpora exploitable by researchers and, on the other, the desire to facilitate the exploration of these debates by the general public.
The ParlaClarin (Fišer and Lenardič, 2018) and ParlaMint (Erjavec et al., 2022b) projects propose to produce comparable and multilingual Parliamentary Proceedings Corpora (PPCs). These two projects have produced corpora according to the XML-TEI standard (TEI, 2017), accompanied by adapted XML schemas (Erjavec et al., 2022a; Erjavec et al., 2022c). As part of her dissertation, Naomi Truan also produced a corpus of parliamentary debates encoded in XML-TEI (Truan, 2019; Truan and Romary, 2021; Tóth-Czifra and Truan, 2021). The production of this type of resource facilitates the publication of works exploiting these textual data to better understand the French political discourse (Diwersy et al., 2018; Diwersy and Luxardo, 2020; Blaette et al., 2020). The online publication of Hansard is part of this line of work, but it also offers an interface for the visualisation of the debates, facilitating their exploration by various users (researchers and the general public). The *Fabrique de la loi* project[10] aims to propose a new way of exploring parliamentary debates by making it possible to follow the evolution of a law - from its proposal to its publication. AGODA is at the crossroads of these different projects, producing both new PPCs respecting the XML-TEI standard and giving access to these corpora via an online platform.
From a methodological point of view, parliamentary debates also constitute an excellent case study for the development of tools for publishing and exploring large historical corpora. While digitisation provides access to an increasingly large mass of textual data, especially

[6]Cf. La Mission de recherche Droit et Justice et le programme national de numérisation concertée en sciences juridiques

[7]Such as Political Representation - Tensions between Parliament and the People from the Age of Revolutions to the 21st Century

[8]There were 14 parliamentary cycles or *législatures* between 1881 and 1940 ; and the debates for a parliamentary cycle consist of about 10-12,000 pages.

[9]For example, the British Hansard : https://hansard.parliament.uk/

[10]https://www.lafabriquedelaloi.fr

for history, it requires the implementation of "new modes of reading sources" (Clavert, 2014). Building on the work carried out during the ANR project TIME-US (2018-2021)[11], we propose to make it easier to access to, to search into and to visualize parliamentary debates. TIME-US has indeed led to the publishing of a corpus of contemporary historical documents respecting TEI standards stored in an eXist-db database and queryable through TEI Publisher (Chagué et al., 2019; Le Fourner, 2019; Génèro, 2020; Génèro et al., 2021).

4. Data Set

The issues of the *Journal Officiel* available on *Gallica* have been digitised by the National Library of France and the archives of the National Assembly. Between 1881 and 1899, 2596 issues were published, or 50791 images[12]. For the parliamentary cycle 1889-1893, 10418 images are available. The digital images of the documents available in JPG format can be downloaded via the *Gallica* API. The debates are also downloadable in TXT format. *ABBY FineReader* automatic transcription (OCR) software was used to extract the text of the debates on the fly, as they were being digitised. The generated text was made available online, but without extensive post-correction.

We roughly measured the quality of the OCR by estimating the number of words present in the ocerised texts, from the French dictionnary (which consists of a word frequency list) provided with the Python library *pyspellchecker*[13]. In practice, we selected 20 documents at random between 1889 and 1892. We counted the number of unique words present in the text automatically extracted from these digitised documents. We then calculated the number of unique words present in both the OCR results and the dictionary. We then divided this result by the total number of unique words in the digitised texts. We used unique words so that our results would not be biased, for example, by the name of a speaker that would not be present in the dictionary. Figure 1 shows that the quality of the OCR varies greatly. Various factors explain the high variability of the quality of the ocerised texts. The curvature of the page, due to the binding, results in "curving" the text, sometimes even cutting off part of it or casting shadows on the pages. Besides the quality of the documents themselves (stains, overprinted text) is also at issue.

5. Processing and Publishing Chain

AGODA aims to offer users easier access to these debates (full-text search, navigation, selection of homogeneous sub-corpuses, etc.) and to allow them to explore and analyse this corpus with "distant reading" methods (Moretti, 2013).

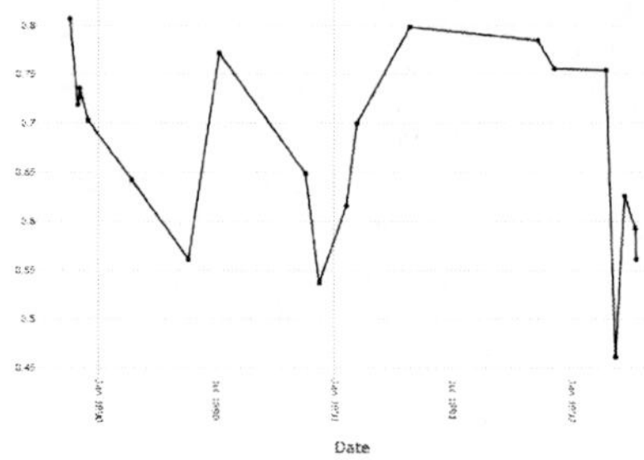

Figure 1: OCR quality evaluation (OCR retrieved from *Gallica*).

5.1. Ocerisation and Postprocessing

Large-scale analysis of digitised historical sources requires the ability to extract data (in our case, textual data) from these documents. As we have seen, the quality of OCR is not sufficient to provide a satisfactory online browsing experience; it could also have a negative impact on the analyses conducted on these texts (van Strien et al., 2020). We chose to ocerise the text again, in order to obtain a better quality result. We first used Tesseract, an open source OCR engine [14], but the results obtained were somewhat mitigated on our corpus as shown in Figure 2. We used both default Tesseract method and Tesseract pre-trained on a French corpus. To estimate the quality of the OCR, we use the same method as described in section 4. Although the Tesseract French model greatly increases the quality of the OCR, the results are sometimes inferior to those obtained with *ABBY FineReader*.

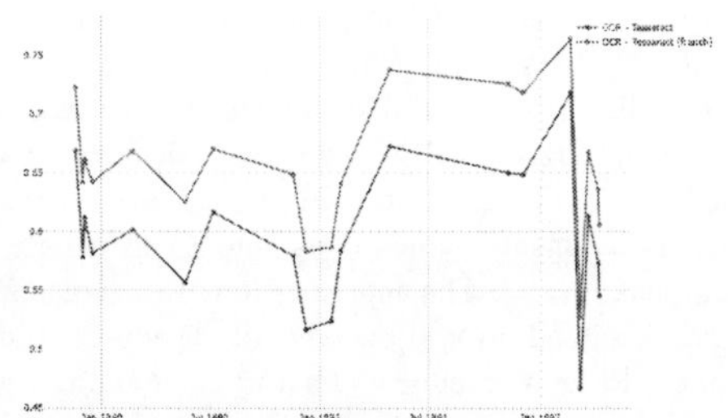

Figure 2: OCR quality evaluation (Tesseract).

As a result, we decided to use the OCR tool developed in the framework of the ANR SODUCO project[15]. Figure 3 shows a view of the tool. It should be noted

[11] https://timeus.hypotheses.org/

[12] One image corresponding to one page.

[13] https://pyspellchecker.readthedocs.io/en/latest/index.html

[14] https://tesseract-ocr.github.io/

[15] https://soduco.github.io/, https://anr.fr/Projet-ANR-18-CE38-0013

that this tool not only ocerises texts but also recognises named entities (such as speakers' names). OCR is performed using the PERO OCR engine (Kišš et al., 2021; Kodym and Hradiš, 2021; Kohút and Hradiš, 2021), which performs particularly well on historical printed texts. Currently in private alpha version, this tool was used, for example, to prepare the data used in (Abadie et al., 2022). This dataset, which will be freely available on Zenodo [16], consists of texts ocerised from a corpus of printed trade directories of Paris from the XIXth century.

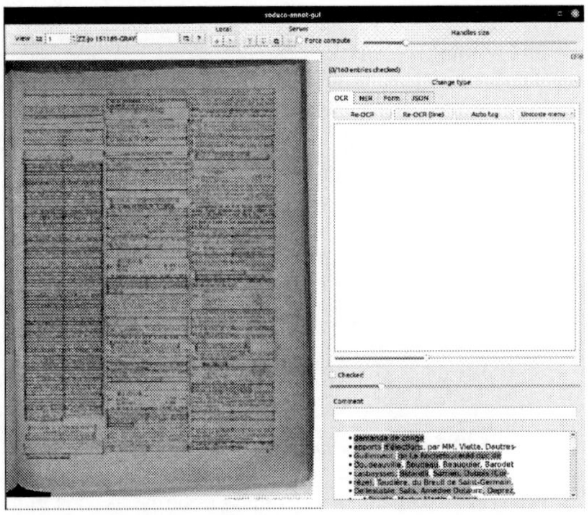

Figure 3: Interface of the OCR tool developed by SODUCO.

With this tool, we obtain the ocerised texts in JSON format. But we are aware that the use of an OCR engine will not allow us to obtain error-free texts, and that it will be necessary to go through a post-correction phase. We used the Python library *pyspellchecker*, setting up a simple spell checking algorithm. *pyspellchecker* uses a dictionary based on a word frequency list extracted from film and TV subtitles (*OpenSubtitles*). To correct misspelled words, *pyspellchecker* uses the Levenshtein distance. This metric measures the distance between two words based on the characters that compose them. The distance is the shortest number of operations required to move from one word to another using three operations: insertions, deletions or substitutions. We used a distance of 1 as a post-correction rule, i.e. we allowed only one transformation to correct erroneous words. The results were disappointing, as it turns out that the French dictionary is not suitable for our corpus. It contains too much contemporary vocabulary, especially by integrating English words ("PC" for "*ordinateur*", "deal" instead of "*accord*", etc.). Some faulty words were thus corrected with words from the dictionary that had no relation to their original meaning: we can speak of "over-interpretation" of the correction. We are thus creating a dictionary based on French novels published between 1870 and 1920, texts from French press documents from the same period[17], and the list of names of MPs elected to the Chamber between 1889 and 1893[18].

5.2. Annotation in XML-TEI

These corrected texts will then be annotated in XML-TEI. The modelling in TEI will be formalised by using an adapted XML schema, created by means of a documented ODD (Rahtz and Burnard, 2013).

To create this ODD, we drew on the ODD produced by ParlaClarin (Erjavec and Pančur, 2021), and the work carried out by ParlaMint (Erjavec et al., 2022a; Erjavec et al., 2022c) on contemporary parliamentary debates. In the case of France, the rules governing the transcription of debates were set in the 19th century (cf. Section 1); the records of today's debates are therefore very similar to those produced under the Third Republic. A first version of the ODD as well as examples of encoding the parliamentary debates in TEI can be found on Github[19]

However, the annotation rules need to be adapted to the historical sources we are working on. For example, we have removed the <recordingStmt> element (and the elements contained in this element), as it will be useless in the context of AGODA. In addition, the presentation of the votes and their results is quite different: they are referred to in an appendix, and one finds there both numerical results and the names of the voters. This presentation of the results requires a modification of the proposed model for contemporary debates. There is also the question of layout: the TEI does not allow the use of <pb/>, <cb/> or <lb/> elements in the <incident> element that we use to encode all events disrupting the debates (usually interventions by other députies). We have adopted a middle ground: we do not retain the page layout (columns and line breaks), but we do retain the page number with a <pb/> element contained within a <floatingText>. .

We will focus on two types of annotations specific to our project. Firstly, we wish to keep track of the corrections made to the ocerised text. For this purpose, we propose to use the <corr> tag which allows us to mark the corrected text string and the nature of the correction:

```
[...]
<p>dans le scrutin sur
    <corr>
        <orig>lçi</orig>
        <reg>la</reg>
    </corr>
motion de M. Millerand</p>
[...]
```

[16]https://zenodo.org/record/6394464

[17]*OCR corrigé de documents de presse de Gallica*

[18]Extracted from the *Base de données des députés français depuis 1789*

[19]https://github.com/mpuren/agoda/tree/ODD

We also wish to add semantic annotations resulting from analyses performed on our corpus with topic modelling. Topic modelling is an unsupervised learning method that discovers the latent semantic structures of a text corpus, without using semantic and lexical resources (Blei et al., 2003)[20]. Basically, the result of topic modelling consists of weighted lists of words (each list corresponding to one topic). The topic name is not generated automatically, but chosen by hand according to the distribution of the vocabulary in the list of words considered. To attach this semantic annotation to the corresponding list of words, we chose to use the mechanism offered by the <span> element which allows to attach an analytical note to passages in the text. Each word in the text is encoded with a <w> element accompanied by a unique identifier composed of the document identifier[21] and a number corresponding to the place of the word in the text. A *ref* attribute then associates the topic with the corresponding words. We have also chosen to group the semantic annotations in the <standOff> element to facilitate their management. These <span> tags are also grouped in a <spanGrp> element associated with a *type* attribute with the value "topic":

```
[...]
<standOff>
    <spanGrp type="topic">
        <span target="#ps1895022_119">
        army</span>
        <span target="_#ps1895022_123">
         colonisation</span>
</spanGrp>
</standOff>
<text>
    <body>
        <p> <w xml:id="ps1895022_116">
        une</w>
            <w xml:id="ps1895022_117">
            partie</w>
            <w xml:id="ps1895022_118">
            du</w>
            <w xml:id="ps1895022_119">
            matériel</w>
            <w xml:id="ps1895022_120">
            de</w>
            <w xml:id="ps1895022_121">
            guerre</w>
            <w xml:id="ps1895022_122">
            à</w>
            <w xml:id="ps1895022_123">
            Madagascar</w>.</p>
    </body>
</text>
[...]
```

[20]The method is described in detail in section 6.1

[21]Formed by the prefix "ps" for parliamentary sitting, followed by the date of the sitting

Given the size of the corpus, we intend to use a method of automatic annotation of these documents. We are currently developing rule-based Python scripts to transform the files into JSON obtained with the OCR tool[22].

5.3. Online Publication with eXist-db and TEI Publisher

The TEI-encoded corpus will be stored in an eXist-db database[23]. TEI Publisher application is able transform the source data, stored in the XML database, into HTML web pages for publication[24]. The parliamentary debates will thus be available to users online as a digital edition, and integrated into an application context with the addition of navigation, full-text search and facsimile display. In addition, new functionality can be added as required using Web Components technology. The AGODA project will use components natively offered by TEI Publisher, implement components developed in the framework of TIME-US[25], and create new ones.

6. Topic Modelling and Word Embedding Applied to Parliamentary Debates

We also wish to facilitate the exploration of these debates by offering new ways to "reading" these documents, in particular by allowing users to use the results of the analyses carried out on the corpus. To gain an in-depth understanding of these documents, it is indeed necessary to adopt computational methods to analyse such a large corpus of sources (Pančur and Šorn, 2016; Bonin, 2020). As seen in section 5.2, we also plan to use the possibilities offered by the XML-TEI to add and make accessible the semantic annotations resulting from downstream NLP tasks such as Latent Dirichlet Allocation and Latent Semantic Analysis. In this section, we will present some examples of lexical analysis that have been performed on the parliamentary corpus (Bourgeois et al., 2022), using the original ocerised text provided by the Bibliothèque nationale de France.

6.1. LDA

Latent Dirichlet Allocation is a Bayesian model based on a strong hypothesis (Blei et al., 2003), that fits extremely well our corpus. The underlying model is that there exist hidden variables, namely the topics, which consist of weighted lists of words (the more significant, the higher their probability). Then, every text from the corpus is generated by (1) picking at random a limited number of topics and (2) selecting words from these

[22]Following the example of the scripts developed for XML in the TIME US project, such as the LSE-OD2M script (https://github.com/TimeUs-ANR/LSE-OD2M), or those written by Victoria Le Fourner (https://gitlab.inria.fr/almanach/time-us/schema-tei).

[23]http://exist-db.org/exist/apps/homepage/index.html

[24]https://teipublisher.com/index.html

[25]The corpora produced by the project are accessible online via a TEI Publisher instance.

topics, according to their probability distribution. The role of LDA is to revert this generation process in order to retrieve the original topics, with the hope that their statistical coherence reflects some semantic homogeneity.

Topic 8	Topic 11	Topic 15
salaire	général	pari
question	commission	télégraphe
gouvernement	régiment	faire
jour	troupe	ingénieur
patron	monsieur	train
chambre	année	ligne
droit	jeune	chambre
syndicat	temps	personnel
délégué	faire	etat
monsieur	corps	administration
travail	soldat	employé
travaux	ministre	poste
ministre	homme	public
grève	loi	travaux
faire	an	service
mineur	guerre	agent
mine	service	ministre
loi	militaire	fer
compagnie	officier	chemin
ouvrier	armée	compagnie

Table 1: Three topics among 40: the working class (8), the army (11) and the state infrastructures (15).

The difficulties of LDA include determining the number of topics, ensuring their coherence, naming them and aggregating those who are highly correlated (Newman et al., 2010). We can for instance produce a large number of topics (Table 1 shows only 3 of the 40 topics identified), then use an agglomerative clustering to build coherent classes and proof-check them with a qualitative survey. Hence we obtain 15 classes with each a strong identity and limited correlation (Figure 4).

The main drawback of this analysis is that a single parliamentary sitting is in fact a rather long text, in which a possibly large sequence of topics are addressed one after the other. It is therefore preferable to divide it into several smaller chunks of texts that better fit the hypothesis of the model. Theoretically, the structure of the document provides a perfect tool for this division, since the different parts of a parliamentary session are easily recognisable by their titles in capital letters. However, the recognition of these titles is very imperfect in the original OCR, so we resorted to fixed-length divisions. We hope that as the quality of the text improves, we will be able to use a semantic-based division instead of this arbitrary division.

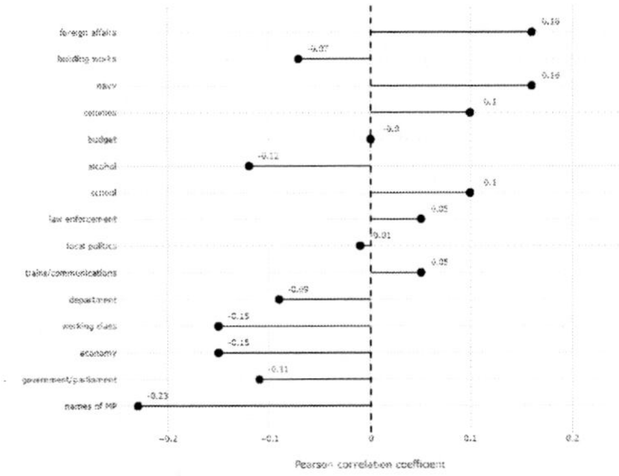

Figure 4: Correlation between the topic "army" and the other identified topics (by month).

6.2. Word Embedding

By definition, Latent Dirichlet Allocation builds a limited number of large semantic units and allow little control over the process. Alternatively, we may use word embedding to reduce the dimension of the original space from tenth of thousands of forms to a hundred of axes, and then apply classical data science tools such a clustering or correlation analysis on the reduced space (Mikolov et al., 2013). Word embedding has also shown its value in the study of parliamentary debates (Rheault and Cochrane, 2020).

We used a CBOW (Continuous Bag of Words) model for dimension reduction and an unsupervised classification algorithm - in this case DBSCAN (density-based spatial clustering of applications with noise) - to group words into clusters. This method worked well, mainly because the sample size is huge in terms of vocabulary and because similar patterns tend to occur regularly throughout the corpus (discussions on military service, taxes, colonies, etc.).

With word embedding, we obtain a large number (113) of highly coherent clusters (Table 2 shows three of the 113 clusters identified), which we can study in relation to each other, or in relation to other parameters such as time. We can recombine them, for example through agglomerative clustering (Figure 5): with some choices of linkage, we can find superclasses that are very similar to the topic models ; while with others, we get more detailed information about some aspects of the corpus.

However, word embedding is probably more sensitive than LDA to the quality of the OCR, since a clustering of documents requires that each text belongs to a single class, whereas several topics can be combined. Therefore, a good segmentation of the debate reports (according to the different parts of a parliamentary sitting) should have a significant impact on the results.

Cluster 55	Cluster 68	Cluster 70
victimes	divorce	enveloppes
inondations	epoux	timbres
secourir	mariage	poste
eprouvees	conjugal	postale
orages	divorces	timbre
sinistres	adultere	recepisses
grele	conjugale	postes
secours	remarier	postaux
venir	separation	telegraphes
infortunes	indissolubilite	colis
ravages	conjoints	fixe
miseres	mutuel	recouvrements
catastrophe	separations	graphes
evenements	mari	postales
repartition	mariages	taxe
incendies	femme	decide
soulager	conjoint	soit

Table 2: Three clusters among 113: storms (55), divorce (68) and the post office (70).

Figure 5: t-SNE projection of the centroïds of the clusters.

7. Conclusions

The AGODA project aims to produce a corpus of parliamentary debates, based on digitised old documents. The aim is to produce a resource that can be used both by historians and by researchers from other disciplines (in particular, linguists, science-politicians, sociologists). To this end, AGODA has three objectives: (1) to produce a new linguistic resource for French, respecting the TEI standard; (2) to create a processing chain that will be reusable in other contexts; (3) to make this corpus better known, by setting up an online consultation interface.

As in any project working with digitised ancient documents, one of the main obstacles is to extract (as clean as possible) text from images. We hope to achieve a very low error text at the end of the project, by combining both re-ocerisation of the documents and post-correction of the texts. We also hope to improve the results we obtain with topic modeling and word embedding. Although these "bag-of-words" techniques are not as sensitive to OCR quality as specific tasks such as name entity recognition, there is a strong incentive to use corrected text to perform natural language processing (van Strien et al., 2020; Mutuvi et al., 2018).

8. Acknowledgements

We would like to thank the National Library of France and Huma-Num for their support in the framework of the BnF DataLab.

9. Bibliographical References

Abadie, N., Carlinet, E., Chazalon, J., and Dumenieu, B. (2022). A Benchmark of Named Entity Recognition Approaches in Historical Documents. Application to 19th Century French Directories. DAS 2022 15th IAPR International Workshop on Document Analysis Systems `https://das2022.univ-lr.fr/`, La Rochelle.

Alix, Y. (2008). La numérisation concertée en sciences juridiques. *Bulletin des bibliothèques de France (BBF)*, 5:93–94.

Blaette, A., Gehlhar, S., and Leonhardt, C. (2020). The Europeanization of Parliamentary Debates on Migration in Austria, France, Germany, and the Netherlands. In *Proceedings of the Second ParlaCLARIN Workshop*, pages 66–74, Marseille, France, May. European Language Resources Association.

Blei, D., Ng, A., and Jordan, M. (2003). Latent Dirichlet Allocation. *Journal of Machine Learning Research*, 3:993–1022.

Bonin, H. (2020). From antagonist to protagonist: 'Democracy' and 'people' in British parliamentary debates, 1775–1885. *Digital Scholarship in the Humanities*, 35(4):759–775.

Bourgeois, N., Pellet, A., and Puren, M. (2022). Using Topic Generation Model to explore the French Parliamentary Debates during the early Third Republic (1881-1899). In *DHNB 2022 – Digital Humanities in Action - Workshop "Digital Parliamentary Data in Action*.

Chagué, A., Le Fourner, V., Martini, M., and Villemonte De La Clergerie, E. (2019). Deux siècles de sources disparates sur l'industrie textile en France : comment automatiser les traitements d'un corpus non-uniforme ?

Cheng, J. E. (2015). Islamophobia, Muslimophobia or racism? Parliamentary discourses on Islam and Muslims in debates on the minaret ban in Switzerland. *Discourse Society*, 26(5):562–586.

Chester, D. N. and Bowring, N. (1962). *Questions in parliament*. Clarendon Press, London.

Clavert, F. (2014). Vers de nouveaux modes de lecture des sources. In *Le temps des humanités digitales*. FYP EDITIONS.

Coniez, H. (2010). L'Invention du compte rendu intégral des débats en France (1789-1848). *Parlement[s], Revue d'histoire politique*, 2(14):146–159.

de Galembert, C., Rozenberg, O., and Vigour, C. (2013). *Faire parler le parlement: méthodes et enjeux de l'analyse des débats parlementaires pour les sciences sociales*. LGDJ-Lextenso éditions, Issy-les-Moulineaux.

Diwersy, S. and Luxardo, G. (2020). Querying a large annotated corpus of parliamentary debates. In *Proceedings of the Second ParlaCLARIN Workshop*, pages 75–79, Marseille, France, May. European Language Resources Association.

Diwersy, S., Frontini, F., and Luxardo, G. (2018). The Parliamentary Debates as a Resource for the Textometric Study of the French Political Discourse. In *Proceedings of the ParlaCLARIN@LREC2018 workshop*, Miyazaki, Japan.

Erjavec, T. and Pančur, A. (2021). Parla-CLARIN: a TEI schema for corpora of parliamentary proceedings. `https://clarin-eric.github.io/parla-clarin/`.

Erjavec, T., Kopp, M., Rebeja, P., de Joes, J., and Longejan, B. (2022a). Parla-CLARIN. `https://github.com/clarin-eric/parla-clarin`.

Erjavec, T., Ogrodniczuk, M., Osenova, P., Ljubešić, N., Simov, K., Pančur, A., Rudolf, M., Kopp, M., Steingrímsso, S. B. Çağrı Çölteki, de Doeso and-Katrien Depuydto, J., Agnolonio, T., Venturio, G., Pérezo, M. C., de Macedoo, L. D., Navarrettao, C., Luxardoo, G., Cooleo, M., Raysono, P., Morkevičiuso, V., Krilavičiuso, T., Dargiso, R., Ringo, O., van Heusdeno, R., Marx, M., and Fišer, D. (2022b). The ParlaMint corpora of parliamentary proceedings. In *Language Resources and Evaluation*.

Erjavec, T., Pančur, A., and Kopp, M. (2022c). Parlamint: Comparable parliamentary corpora. `https://github.com/clarin-eric/ParlaMint`.

Fišer, D. and Lenardič, J. (2018). CLARIN resources for parliamentary discourse research. In *Proceedings of the Eleventh International Conference on Language Resources and Evaluation (LREC 2018)*, pages 2–7. European Language Resources Association (ELRA).

Darja Fišer, et al., editors. (2018). *Proceedings of the Eleventh International Conference on Language Resources and Evaluation (LREC 2018)*, Paris, France, may. European Language Resources Association (ELRA).

Darja Fišer, et al., editors. (2020). *Proceedings of the Second ParlaCLARIN Workshop*, Marseille, France, May. European Language Resources Association.

Fournier, B. and Pépratx, F. (1991). La majorité politique : Étude des débats parlementaires sur la fixation d'un seuil. In Annick Percheron et al., editors, *Age et politique*, La vie politique, pages 85–110. Economica, Paris.

Franklin, M. and Norton, P. (1993). *Parliamentary questions*. Oxford University Press, Oxford.

Gardey, D. (2010). Scriptes de la démocratie : les sténographes et rédacteurs des débats (1848–2005). *Sociologie du travail*, 52(2).

Génèro, J.-D., Chagué, A., Le Fourner, V., and Puren, M. (2021). Transcribing and editing digitized sources on work in the textile industry. In *Rémunérations et usages du temps des hommes et des femmes dans le textile en France de la fin du XVIIe au début du XXe siècle*, Lyon, France. Manuela Martini.

Génèro, J.-D. (2020). Le corpus des Ouvriers des deux mondes : des images et des URLs. Billet du carnet de recherche de l'ANR Time Us relatif aux fichiers XML-TEI de transcription des volumes des Ouvriers des deux mondes et au lien entre ceux-ci et les images numérisées d'origine.

Hirst, G., Feng, V. W., C. C., , and Naderi, N. (2014). Argumentation, ideology, and issue framing in parliamentary discourse. In A.Z. Wyner E. Cabrio, S. Villata, editor, *Proceedings of the Workshop on Frontiers and Connections between Argumentation Theory and Natural Language Processing*.

Ihalainen, P., Ilie, C., and Palonen, K. (2016). *Parliament and Parliamentarism: A Comparative History of a European Concept*. Berghahn Books, Oxford, NY.

Kišš, M., Beneš, K., and Hradiš, M. (2021). At-st: Self-training adaptation strategy for ocr in domains with limited transcriptions. In J. Lladós, et al., editors, *Document Analysis and Recognition – ICDAR 2021. ICDAR 2021. Lecture Notes in Computer Science*, pages 130–146. Cham: Springer.

Kodym, O. and Hradiš, M. (2021). Page layout analysis system for unconstrained historic documents. In J. Lladós, et al., editors, *Document Analysis and Recognition – ICDAR 2021: 16th International Conference*, page 492–506, Lausanne, Switzerland, september. Heidelberg: Springer-Verlag.

Kohút, J. and Hradiš, M. (2021). Ts-net: Ocr trained to switch between text transcription styless. In J. Lladós, et al., editors, *Document Analysis and Recognition – ICDAR 2021. ICDAR 2021. Lecture Notes in Computer Science*, pages 130–146. Cham: Springer.

Lavoinne, Y. (1999). Publicité des débats et espace public. *Études de communication*, 22:115–132.

Le Fourner, V. (2019). Étude de la structuration automatique et de l'éditorialisation d'un corpus hétérogène.

Lemercier, C. (2021). Un catholique libéral dans le débat parlementaire sur le travail des enfants dans l'industrie (1840). *Parlement[s], Revue d'histoire politique*, pages 197–208.

Marnot, B. (2000). *Les ingénieurs au Parlement sous la IIIe République*. CNRS histoire. CNRS Editions, Paris.

Mela, M. L., Norén, F., and Hyvönen, E. (2022). Digital parliamentary data in action (dipada 2022). workshop co-located with the 6th digital humanities in the nordic and baltic countries conference (dhnb 2022). `https://dhnb.eu/conferences/dhnb2022/workshops/dipada/`.

Mikolov, T., Chen, K., Corrado, G. S., and Dean, J. (2013). Efficient Estimation of Word Representations in Vector Space. In *ICLR*.

Moretti, F. (2013). *Distant reading*. Verso, London.

Mutuvi, S., Doucet, A., Odeo, M., and Jatowt, A. (2018). Evaluating the Impact of OCR Errors on Topic Modeling. In *Maturity and Innovation in Digital Libraries. 20th International Conference on Asia-Pacific Digital Libraries, ICADL 2018, Hamilton, New Zealand, November 19-22, 2018, Proceedings*, pages 3 – 14.

Newman, D., Lau, J. H., Grieser, K., and Baldwin, T. (2010). Automatic Evaluation of Topic Coherence. In *Human Language Technologies: The 2010 Annual Conference of the North American Chapter of the Association for Computational Linguistics*, pages 100–108.

Ouellet, J. and Roussel-Beaulieu, F. (2003). Les débats parlementaires au service de l'histoire politique. *Bulletin d'histoire politique*, 11(3):23–40.

Pančur, A. and Šorn, M. (2016). Smart big data : Use of slovenian parliamentary papers in digital history. *Contributions to Contemporary History*, 56(3):130–146.

Puren, M. and Vernus, P. (2021). AGODA : Analyse sémantique et Graphes relationnels pour l'Ouverture et l'étude des Débats à l'Assemblée nationale. Inauguration du BnF DataLab.

Rahtz, S. and Burnard, L. (2013). Reviewing the TEI ODD system. In *Proceedings of the 2013 ACM Symposium on Document Engineering*, DocEng '13, page 193–196, New York, NY, USA. Association for Computing Machinery.

Rheault, L. and Cochrane, C. (2020). Word embeddings for the analysis of ideological placement in parliamentary corpora. *Political Analysis*, 28(1):112–133.

Rheault, L., Beelen, K., Cochrane, C., and Hirst., G. (2016). Measuring Emotion in Parliamentary Debates with Automated Textual Analysis. *PLoS ONE*, 11(12).

TEI Consortium, (2017). *TEI P5: Guidelines for electronic text encoding and interchange*.

Tóth-Czifra, E. and Truan, N. (2021). Creating and analyzing multilingual parliamentary corpora.

Truan, N. and Romary, L. (2021). Building, Encoding, and Annotating a Corpus of Parliamentary Debates in XML-TEI: A Cross-Linguistic Account. *Journal of the Text Encoding Initiative*.

Truan, N. (2019). Débats parlementaires sur l'Europe à l'Assemblée nationale (2002-2012). `https://hdl.handle.net/11403/fr-parl/v1.1`. ORTOLANG (Open Resources and TOols for LANGuage).

Van Dijk, T. A. (2010). Political identities in parliamentary debates. european parliaments under scrutiny. In Cornelia Ilie, editor, *European Parliaments under Scrutiny: Discourse strategies and interaction practices*, pages 29–56. John Benjamins Publishing Company.

van Strien, D., Beelen, K., Ardanuy, M., Hosseini, K., McGillivray, B., and Colavizza, G. (2020). Assessing the Impact of OCR Quality on Downstream NLP Tasks. *Proceedings of the 12th International Conference on Agents and Artificial Intelligence*, 21:484–496.

Proceedings of ParlaCLARIN III @ LREC2022 pages 25–32
Marseille, 20 June 2022

A French Corpus of Québec's Parliamentary Debates

Pierre André Ménard, Desislava Aleksandrova
Centre de Recherche Informatique de Montréal, Université de Montréal
menardpa@crim.ca, desislava.aleksandrova@umontreal.ca

Abstract

Parliamentary debates offer a window on political stances as well as a repository of linguistic and semantic knowledge. They provide insights and reasons for laws and regulations that impact electors in their everyday life. One such resource is the transcribed debates available online from the *Assemblée Nationale du Québec* (ANQ). This paper describes the effort to convert the online ANQ debates from various HTML formats into a standardized ParlaMint TEI annotated corpus and to enrich it with annotations extracted from related unstructured members and political parties list. The resulting resource includes 88 years of debates over a span of 114 years with more than 33.3 billion words. The addition of linguistic annotations is detailed as well as a quantitative analysis of part-of-speech tags and distribution of utterances across the corpus.

Keywords: French, Québec, ParlaMint, Provincial Parliament

1. Introduction

A critical mass of parliamentary corpora (Erjavec et al., 2021) has been published in recent years in many countries (Andrej Pančur and Erjavec, 2018; Onur Gungor and Çağıl Sönmez, 2018; Steingrímsson et al., 2018; Eide, 2020), helping digital humanities research in fields such as political science (Abercrombie and Batista-Navarro, 2020), sociology (Naderi and Hirst, 2018; Dorte Haltrup Hansen and Offersgaard, 2018), etc. Every one of these corpora also informs linguists and natural language processing experts on multiple phenomenon such as named entities, multi-word expressions, sentiment and emotion expressions, regionalisms, foreign words, to name a few. For some languages, national or provincial parliament corpora are the only large, publicly available textual resource serving as a witness to cultural and linguistic change.

This is the case for the *Assemblée Nationale du Québec* (ANQ), or National Assembly of Quebec in English, the legislative body of the only province with French as the official language in a country with both French and English as official languages. One other province is officially bilingual and the others have English as their official language. The main contribution of this paper is the transformation of ANQ's parliamentary proceedings into a TEI formatted resource which is currently only available for collaborative research, together with the annotations, either extracted from the source data or compiled from other sources.

This article begins with a presentation of the main content source (Section 2) and a detailed account of the acquisition process including processing and XML structure (Section 3). Details on both derived and linguistic annotations (Section 4) are followed by a selection of descriptive statistics (Section 5) to better illustrate the content and potential usage of the corpus.

2. Source Content

The transcriptions of parliamentary debates of the National Assembly of Québec are available as HTML on their website[1]. They are organized in *legislatures*, where a legislature designates the collective mandate of the members of a legislative assembly between two general elections.

Each legislature consists of one or more separate *sessions*, at the discretion of the government. A session designates the period that the Assembly sits, including periods of adjournment. It corresponds to the period of time, within a legislature, that elapses between the convocation of the Assembly and its prorogation or dissolution. The government convenes a new session when it intends to breathe new life into a legislature or to specify the objectives of its mandate. To this day, a legislature has had no more than six sessions and some have lasted a single day.

While the current structure is unicameral, it had a second non-elected high chamber from 1867 to 1963 called the *Conseil Législatif* (Legislative Council). Since then, this second chamber has never been reactivated. The other nine provinces and three territories that make up Canada are also unicameral, while the federal structure is bicameral.

The first provincial legislature of Quebec (not available in the online corpus) was formed in 1867 and had 71 elected members of the National Assembly (MNAs), one for each provincial electoral division. Some electoral divisions may span over a whole administrative region of the province while others, in large cities, are restricted to a single neighbourhood.

The current National Assembly is composed of 125 women and men elected in an electoral division under the first-past-the-post system. The leader of the political party that wins the most seats in the general election normally becomes prime minister. Each elected member, past or present, has an online information

[1] http://www.assnat.qc.ca/en/.

page describing aspects of their political and professional life, as well as their involvement in different organisations.
The earlier debates available online, from 1908 to 1963, were reconstituted from members' notes, assembly summaries, newspaper reports and other sources by a team of historians at the Library of the National Assembly of Quebec (Gallichan, 1988; Gallichan, 2004; Saint-Pierre, 2003). The resulting text is mostly in narrative form with the speaker's name and function in the speech turn followed by their words or actions. Between 1964 and 1989, the transcribed debates were curated in order to remove syntactical and style errors. Word order was modified to better follow syntactic logic. Anglicisms were systematically removed and synonyms were used to avoid repetitions.
Since 1989, the respect of the verbatim of statements requires that only minor spelling or grammatical changes may be made to adapt spoken language to written language (e.g. gender and number agreements). No corrections that modify the style or vocabulary are authorized, even slips of the tongue are transcribed verbatim. As a result, the proceedings of the last three decades contain more examples of spontaneous, unscripted speech. Such speech can be seen in Example 1.

"Ça, c'est la réalité concrète, M. le Président. Et, quant à la députée, peut-être, quand elle va se relever... Elle a eu le temps de réfléchir. Les discussions qu'elle a eues avec M. Arsenault pour qu'elle continue à voter contre la tenue d'une commission d'enquête, là, à quel endroit... C'était quoi, le deal avec lui, là? C'était quoi, l'entente que vous avez eue pour refuser aux Québécois d'avoir une commission d'enquête..."

(Free translation)
"That is the concrete reality, M. President. And, about the member, maybe, when she gets up... She had time to think. The discussions she had with M. Arsenault for her to continue to vote against the holding of a commission of inquiry there, where... What was the deal with him there? What was it, the agreement you had to refuse to Quebecers to have a commission of inquiry..."

Example 1: Excerpt of an unscripted utterance on February 20th, 2014.

Currently, the transcribers at the ANQ publish a preliminary draft of the proceedings at the end of each day of debates. This temporary version is available in a formatted HTML page. A few days later, a revised and approved version (still in HTML) is made available, along with additional documents such as recordings of the debates (audio and video), order paper and notices (pdf), documents tabled, bills introduced, votes and proceedings detailing each vote (pdf). While the accompanying documents are available in both French and English, the debates in both videos and transcribed versions are only in French. As such, this resource this gives a rare historical view of French spoken in Québec since the start of the previous century, as it can differs from other international or regional variances.
The elements distinguishable on a proceeding's page are as follows (Figure 1):
speech turn: A string of text announcing the author of the utterance that follows. It may or may not be contained in the same HTML tag as that utterance and usually ends with a colon. It identifies the speaker by their name (1), their function (2) or both, or it describes the source of the unidentifiable speech (e.g., voices, one voice, ministers, a speaker, cries, a journalist, etc.) (3, 4).
utterance: A string of text consisting of one or more sentences in one or more paragraphs which follows a speech turn (5).
non-verbal block content: Any non-verbal content formatted in a separate HTML tag (most often, centered and in bold). These elements are written testimonials of either document depositions or announcements of actions and speakers.
non-verbal inline content: Inline strings enclosed in parentheses or <b> tags are occurrences of non-verbal content of one of several types: applause, adjournment, indentation, editor note, reference resolution, written clarification, textual reference.
time: emphasized text in parentheses (6).
pre-formatted content: The contents of HTML tags used consistently across periods <table>, <i>, <acronym>, <a>.
Table 1 provides an overview of the available online content. Some years, especially around the first and second World Wars, are unavailable, which explains the difference between total and spanning period.

Legislature	28
Sessions	78
Total period	88 years
Spanning period	114 years
Debates periods	5,948 days
Members	1,310

Table 1: Overview of available content data from the ANQ source website.

3. Corpus Creation

Converting the online ANQ corpus from HTML to a fully TEI-encoded corpus involved many steps and required a series of design decisions. Since the ANQ corpus is being served online for consultation purposes, there was no available API or any convenient download functionality to rely upon. As such, this section details some particular aspects of the source data and design decisions made during the process.

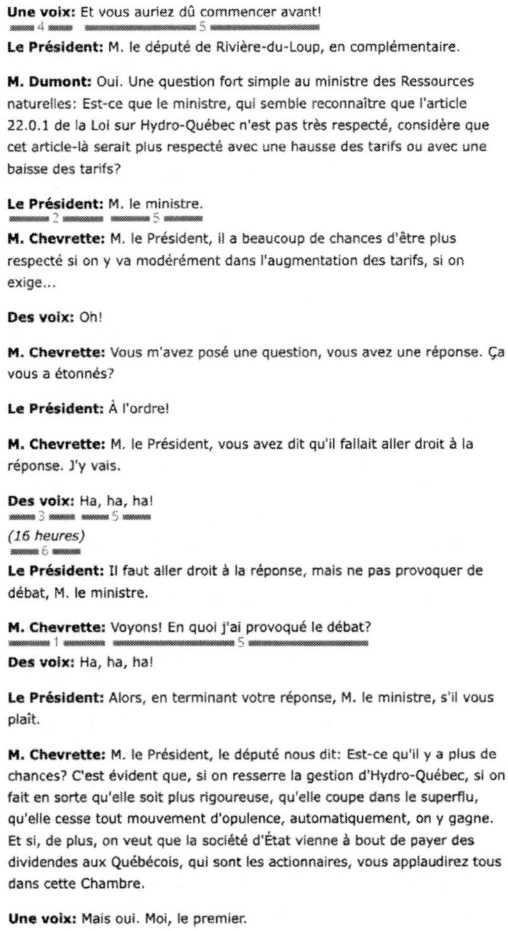
Une voix: Et vous auriez dû commencer avant!
4 5

Le Président: M. le député de Rivière-du-Loup, en complémentaire.

M. Dumont: Oui. Une question fort simple au ministre des Ressources naturelles: Est-ce que le ministre, qui semble reconnaître que l'article 22.0.1 de la Loi sur Hydro-Québec n'est pas très respecté, considère que cet article-là serait plus respecté avec une hausse des tarifs ou avec une baisse des tarifs?

Le Président: M. le ministre.
2 5

M. Chevrette: M. le Président, il a beaucoup de chances d'être plus respecté si on y va modérément dans l'augmentation des tarifs, si on exige...

Des voix: Oh!

M. Chevrette: Vous m'avez posé une question, vous avez une réponse. Ça vous a étonnés?

Le Président: À l'ordre!

M. Chevrette: M. le Président, vous avez dit qu'il fallait aller droit à la réponse. J'y vais.

Des voix: Ha, ha, ha!
3 5

(16 heures)
6

Le Président: Il faut aller droit à la réponse, mais ne pas provoquer de débat, M. le ministre.

M. Chevrette: Voyons! En quoi j'ai provoqué le débat?
1 5

Des voix: Ha, ha, ha!

Le Président: Alors, en terminant votre réponse, M. le ministre, s'il vous plaît.

M. Chevrette: M. le Président, le député nous dit: Est-ce qu'il y a plus de chances? C'est évident que, si on resserre la gestion d'Hydro-Québec, si on fait en sorte qu'elle soit plus rigoureuse, qu'elle coupe dans le superflu, qu'elle cesse tout mouvement d'opulence, automatiquement, on y gagne. Et si, de plus, on veut que la société d'État vienne à bout de payer des dividendes aux Québécois, qui sont les actionnaires, vous applaudirez tous dans cette Chambre.

Une voix: Mais oui. Moi, le premier.

Figure 1: Excerpt of a proceeding's web page from March 12, 1996 with annotated elements.

3.1. Acquisition

Two main sections were targeted on the ANQ website: the proceedings of each sitting and the individual pages of MNAs who took part in them.

The proceedings were crawled semi-automatically, starting from a list of sittings for a given month. These lists are accessed by selecting a session from a legislature (ex: 42th legislature, 1st session) followed by the desired month. The lists were parsed using the Beautiful Soup HTML parser (Richardson, 2007) to obtain the debates' URLs. The links were then followed to retrieve the complete HTML source of the web page. The page was then cached locally for further processing (i.e. text extraction, normalisation, annotations, etc.) and to avoid retrieving it multiple times. Politeness constraints were applied to the crawler to limit the public server load.

Starting from an online list of all MNAs since 1764, the information page of each member was crawled automatically. Current members have HTML-tabbed information page listing their function, biography, indexed interventions in the proceedings, press review, submitted bills, expense reports and contact information. The page's header also details the member's electoral division, the political party they are affiliated with (if not independent) and the role they occupy as a MNA (e.g., opposition's speaker on matters of justice, economy, etc.) The information pages of some members (from earlier legislatures) contain an unstructured summary on a single page which makes it more difficult to parse the information reliably.

To complete the information on MNAs and associate each member with an electoral division, we crawled another section of the ANQ website providing an index of MNAs for each legislature. This was essential to disambiguate the family names used to specify the speaker of an utterance, as they were normalized with fully upper-cased surnames followed by capitalized first name and the electoral division separated with a dash (e.g. SURNAME Forename - Division).

Finally, a list of political parties was parsed semi-automatically from Wikipedia [2] to obtain the official names of the current and historical political organisations with elected members. The acquisitions of members' information pages followed the same overall processing steps (HTML parsing, caching, etc.) as the proceedings.

3.2. Processing

To extract the text from the HTML code and to automatically annotate it, we developed a script using Python, BeautifulSoup, and regular expressions. In the process, we discovered five distinct HTML structures used over various periods of the corpus. The first period spans from 1908 to 1963 and contains the reconstructed proceedings. The second (until 1975) is defined by a lack of formatting around the speech turn segments, making them more difficult to identify and extract. The third period (1975 - 2000) contains some noise as a result of it being automatically digitized (by OCR). The final two periods hold the most recent debates (from October 2000 to the end of 2021) and are relatively clean and well-structured. The text in each of the five periods required a slightly different processing approach.

For each sitting, we parsed its HTML and performed an initial cleanup and correction of erroneous HTML tags (e.g. `<ahref>` instead of `<a href>`). We then attempted to identify and annotate each element of the proceeding (section title, non-verbal element, speech turn, speech, table, etc.) according to its related period. Some elements we could reliably identify based on their HTML encoding alone. Others would have different encoding across periods while remaining visually the same. For example, a section title is always displayed centered and in bold letters, but the 1st period uses a `<b>` tag contained

[2] Wikipedia's list of Quebec's political parties.

in a <p align="center">, while the 5th period employs an <a> tag contained in a <p style="font-weight:bold; text-align: center;">. Finally, to distinguish the speech turn (e.g. Mme Kirkland-Casgrain:) from the actual speech segment in one of the periods, we had to rely on positional clues and punctuation. This is because a single paragraph contained both elements. We made a distinction between indirect (from 1908 to 1960) and direct (from 1963 to present) utterances and speech turn annotations because the indirect ones have the speech turn included in the utterance (Figure 2).

L'honorable M. Gouin (Portneuf) propose, selon l'ordre du jour, que la Chambre se forme en comité général pour prendre en considération un projet de résolution relative au bill 192 concernant le Code municipal de la province de Québec.

Figure 2: Excerpt of a proceeding's web page from March 5, 1915.

Prior to saving the text, the following transformations were applied: corrected common typing errors; standardized spaces, hyphens and line breaks; stripped decorative symbols; reconstructed hyphenated words and concatenated sentences spanning across consecutive paragraphs. The spelling mistakes in the text or in the names of the speakers were not corrected.

In addition to annotating the core elements of a proceeding, we further analysed each speech turn and extracted the available structured data on the speaker. Our custom parser relies on regular expressions and string manipulations to detect and extract, as accurately as possible, the various combinations of surname, forename, division and function contained in a speech turn. Figure 3 illustrates a fraction of the variability of the source, while Listing 1 presents an example of input and output.

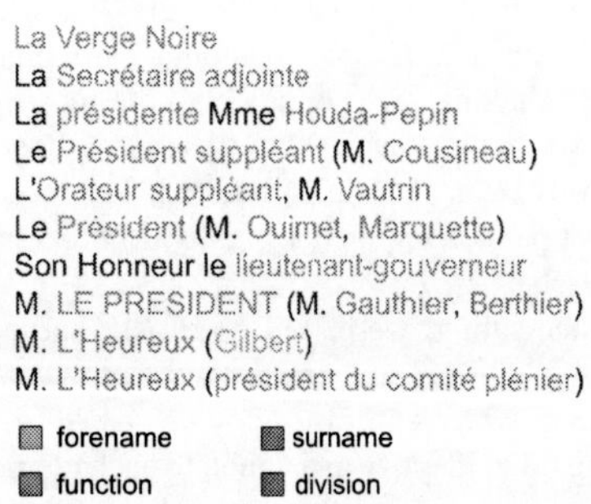

Figure 3: Examples of speech turns and their components

3.3. Corpus Structure

For the TEI version of the ANQ corpus, the schema of ParlaMint CLARIN was followed and each daily proceeding was encoded in a separate XML file.

```
M. LE PRESIDENT (M. Gauthier, Berthier)
{
    "surname": "Gauthier",
    "forename": "",
    "position": "président",
    "sex": "M",
    "division": "Berthier",
    "type": "person" }
}
```

Listing 1: Speech turn from the corpus followed by the corresponding structured data on the speaker.

The root XML element <teiCorpus> contains the <teiHeader> of the corpus, which in turn contains the metadata for the corpus as a whole. It also includes a list of all identified MNAs with their metadata (forename, surname, division, party, URL) and references to their speeches. The <teiHeader> of the corpus is followed by a series of included <TEI> elements where each of them contains one corpus component (one daily proceeding).

The <teiHeader> of a single TEI file contains document-level metadata: legislative period, session number, date, language, place, as well as a list of identified MNAs whose speeches the file contains, followed by text and tag occurrence statistics.

The body of the document lists in order of appearance all elements of a sitting's proceeding, both verbal and non-verbal. The non-verbal elements were annotated using the tag <note> and the @type attribute was used to categorize them based on their form or function (vote, narrative, summary, comment, time). The speech turn segment, which precedes an utterance and contains the name and/or function of the speaker was annotated as a note of @type "speaker". This choice of annotation allows the inclusion of speech turns (as they appear in the source) but also to signal their non-verbal character. A special case of this rule, where the speech turn is also part of the utterance annotation, is applied to all (reconstructed) proceedings between 1908 and 1963.

Utterances were annotated as <u> and were attributed to speakers with the help of the @who attribute. In a standard TEI file, an utterance contains segments <seg> of text corresponding to paragraphs in the source transcription. In the linguistically annotated TEI file, an utterance contains sentences <s> which contain words <w> and punctuation <pc>. Each word is accompanied by its @lemma and @msd attributes. The components of contracted determiners (e.g. du = de + le) were also included. The @msd attributes details features like the UD part-of-speech tag, gender and number, verb tense and form, pronoun type, depending on the syntactic role of each word.

4. Corpus Annotations

In order to produce a fully annotated TEI corpus, some specialized processing of data sources had to be done to combine extracted and automatically annotated information. This section details these steps, their implications and their limits.

4.1. Speaker Annotation

Linking rich speaker information to each utterance in the ANQ transcriptions required transformation and coupling of multiple sources. The main issue is that MNAs are not referred in a uniform and standardized way in the source content, causing misalignment when combining information. A fuzzy matching algorithm was used when no direct fit was found between the MNAs by division list and the MNAs by legislature and session list. This produced a combined list of each MNA for each session with their associated division.

The association links between MNAs and political parties were then extracted from the historical information pages on MNAs described in Section 3.1. Except for recent members who had their political affiliation described in the header of the page, there are no other standardized expressions of this link. The political party was often mentioned with a contextual template in the form of "...elected member of <party> in <division> in <date>..." with some variations. Some other pages indicated the party as an adjective like "...elected in <year> as a <party>" when the name of the party allowed such adaptation. Then some cases were referred by a short name like the "Bleu" (*blue*) instead of their full name like "Parti Bleu" (*Blue Party*), sometimes even as a single word sentence to denote the affiliation. These texts also contain failed election mentions, which were sometimes written in a similar way as winning elections.

A list of official political party names with corresponding short or adjectival forms was compiled. Every form of this list was used to find exact matches in a description with a known contextual template as shown above. For the description without a match, a fuzzy matching algorithm was applied, falling back to a fuzzy search of standalone party names if no matching context was found. A majority vote was then applied to select the most probable associated party of each MNA, with identified ties to be validated manually. Some of the rare cases of defection where members changed party affiliation after being elected might be missed by this approach.

The combination of these two lists resulted in a speaker reference dataset. It was used jointly with the structured data obtained from parsing the speech turn to identify and attribute utterances to their speakers. When generating the TEI file of a proceeding, a speech turn of multiple people (e.g. M. Galipeault (Bellechasse) et l'honorable M. Gouin (Portneuf)) indicated a summary instead of an utterance. A speech turn of a single person referenced by their function (e.g. L'Orateur, Le Président, etc.) was annotated with an ID combining the name of the function and the numbers of the legislature and session (to allow for further disambiguation in a later version of the corpus). A speech turn of a single person containing their division was unambiguously identified using the speaker reference dataset, since there is a single representative per division per session[3]. A speech turn of a single person containing their name(s) was identified (via the @who attribute) using a fuzzy match against the speaker reference dataset and the list of MNAs for the respective session and legislature. Each utterance tag includes information on the role of the speaker (président, vice-président, lieutenant-gouverneur, greffier, etc.) in the @ana attribute. If no role is indicated in the speech turn segment, the role of "député" is attributed. This current method overgeneralizes and fails to distinguish names of guest speakers from names of MNAs. We consider improving it in future work.

4.2. Linguistic Annotations

In order to produce the linguistically annotated version of the TEI corpus, all the debates were annotated using Trankit 1.0.0 (Nguyen et al., 2021). This tool is a multilingual model based on the Transformer architecture (Vaswani et al., 2017) using the large XLM-roberta model (Conneau et al., 2019) with fine-tuned adapters inserted between the language model's layers, instead of a fully fine-tuned language model. While the model is multilingual and some very rare sentences in the ANQ corpus might be in other languages (like English), only the French annotation pipeline was used.

Each utterance is annotated in a separate CONLL-U formatted file with each single daily debate file generating numerous annotated utterance files. For example, the first session of the 37 legislatures has 200 days of debates and 44,375 utterances. Applying the model on the content of this legislature with a single Titan X 12G GPU took approximately 14 hours, averaging at 52,5 utterances annotated per minute, depending on the length of each utterance. While the process was parallelized, the sum of all annotation times amounted to 28 days for the current version of the corpus. Each parallel process ran a single instance of Trankit over all sittings of a legislature, creating a single CONLL-U file for each day of proceedings.

The model produces universal dependencies (Nivre et al., 2016) part-of-speech labels, morphological features and lemmas used in the annotated TEI. While not included in the current TEI format, it also performed syntactic parsing for future use. Morphosyntactic features (number for nouns and adjectives, person, form and tense for verbs, pronoun gender, etc.) are added in the @msd attribute of the <w> TEI element. The lemma of each word is assigned as the value of the @lemma attribute. Table 2 lists the approximate quantity of each part-of-speech tag in the ANQ corpus,

[3]Barring a few exceptions handled separately.

with nouns (NOUN), determiner (DET) and adposition (ADP) as the top three categories. The "other" (X), particle (PART) and symbol (SYM) categories trail the list with the lowest number of occurrences.

Category	Occurrences (by 1M)
ADJ	1,441
ADP	3,467
ADV	1,987
AUX	1,109
CCONJ	0,677
DET	4,672
INTJ	0,081
NOUN	5,801
NUM	0,400
PART	0,014
PRON	3,253
PROPN	0,705
PUNCT	3,902
SCONJ	0,748
SYM	0,085
VERB	3,381
X	0,025
Total	33,312

Table 2: Part-of-speech categories distribution in the ANQ corpus.

While this tool was trained using mostly international French, like the French version of Wikipedia and other online resources, performance on Québec's French was not an issue as the goal was to give a first overview of the distribution of parts-of-speech in the corpus. A more in-depth inspection of resulting annotations might reveal issues with specific regionalisms or specific idiomatic expressions which sometimes differs from one country to another.

4.3. Non-parliamentary expressions

The ANQ has an official procedure where members can denounce words or expressions which they deem inappropriate in the daily working of the chamber. These expressions can include personal attacks (i.e. idiot, bigot, stupid, liar), unfounded claims or accusations (i.e. racket, collusion, criminal action, stealing surplus, nepotism), associations (i.e. friend of a criminal, friends of the party), unflattering comparisons (i.e. Pontius Pilate, Tartuffe, barking like a wild dog, clown, shylock, eunuch, door mat), among many other types.
The ANQ keeps a record of each time such expressions have been denounced by a member of the national assembly by recording the day, who denounced it, the expression and how many times it occurred.
From an NLP standpoint, this could be used as a seed to perform sentiment or bias analysis. As there are only 393 unique expressions denounced a total of 570 times, this can probably mostly be used as an evaluation set or to bootstrap a few shot algorithms to detect similar expressions like insults, threats, etc.

5. Quantitative Analysis

In order to give an overview of the quantity of data available in the ANQ debates, three statistical representations are shown in Figure 4. The graphics respectively illustrate the distribution of spoken words, utterances and sentence for each year with transcribed debates. It is important to note that the statistics reflected in the graphs only cover direct or reported speech in the transcriptions, thus excluding texts from summaries, topic mentions, title, vote reports, etc. The corpus currently contains a total of 1,27 billion sentences spread across 282,57 millions utterances.
The words and sentences distributions look similar throughout the length of the corpus, while the utterance trend is showing a progressive decrease in number. This seems to indicate that the MNAs would speak for a longer period each time they talk. Other hypothesis can point to more scripted interactions or to less dynamic debates. A more in-depth analysis on the nature and dynamics of verbal interactions would be required to verify these hypothesis.
This new corpus also enables deeper analysis using the metadata compiled on each MNAs by projecting the data on other dimension like sex, region, political party, etc. For instance, the first woman was elected MNA in 1961 among a total of 95 members and was granted the management of a minister the following year.
As shown in Figure 5, apart from the missing years between 1960 and 1963, there is a growing proportion of words spoken by female members (in red) compared to males (in blue) since this first occurrence. Clearly, the last two represented years contain much less exchanges as the debates were affected by the global pandemic.
The "*% Elected*" line is projected onto this data to reflected the ratio of male versus female MNAs in proportion to the total number of words spoken by either one for each year. For an easier comparison with the proportion of words spoken by female MNAs, the ratio of elected female MNAs is relative to the top of the bars. As an example, the ratio of elected female MNAs was 44.0% in 2019 (third bar from the right) while the proportion of their spoken words was 37%.
While the representation of women grew steadily from 1% in 1961 to 44% in the last election of 2018, we can see in the same figure that the ratio of transcribed words attributed to female speakers does not follow the same growth rate. This is evidently not a complete analysis by any means, as other variables might influence this ratio like if a MNA is responsible for a minister, if they represent a large city versus a distant region, the attendance rate, etc.

6. Conclusion

This paper presented the creation of a TEI-formatted version of the ANQ online corpus. The process to convert source content into a fully standardized corpus was

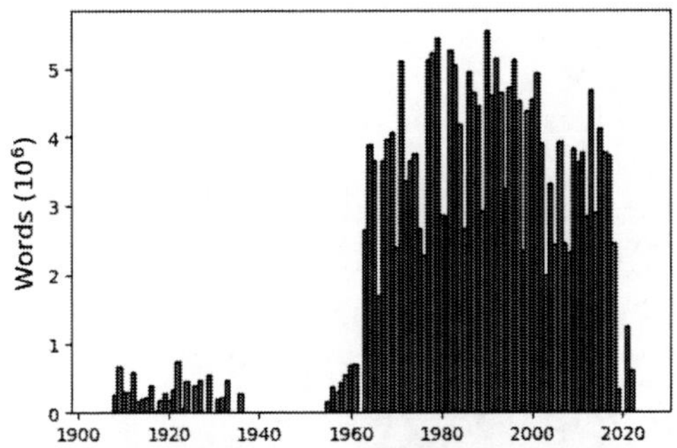

(a) Speech turns' words per year.

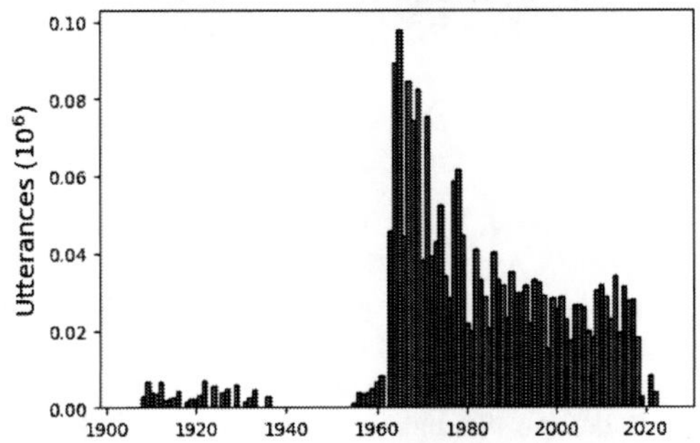

(b) Utterances per year.

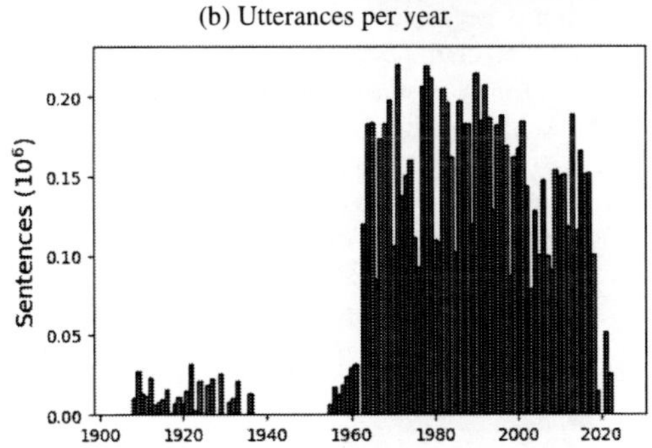

(c) Sentences per year.

Figure 4: Statistical overview of the ANQ corpus.

detailed, as were the data integration tasks needed to enrich it.

Future work would include adding other available but still unprocessed information like topics, named entities, and so on. Other transcriptions will also be added like parliamentary committees' transcriptions which are classified by domain of activity such as education, health, economy, justice, etc. Other levels of annotations could also be added to facilitate the analysis of the discourse's flow such as speakers hesitations, interjections, insults, topics, etc. In addition, complementary annotations could be provided by linking the videos with the transcriptions of the debates and analysing physical communicative phenomenon, like gestures, facial expressions, etc. This would require the integration of tags in Parlamint standard like the *<kinesic>* used in the TEI format of Parla-Clarin, as well as a significant manual or automated annotation effort.

This large dataset of regionalized expressions of a language also enables researchers to train or fine-tune large scale language models to improve natural language processing tools. The annotations and enriched information of the corpus could also help to study the impact of such data on automated tasks like named entities recognition, sentiment analysis, topic modeling, and so on. Improving these tools and resources could support the study of other research hypothesis in academic fields in addition to linguistics and natural language processing. .

7. Acknowledgements

The authors would like to thank the Assemblée Nationale du Québec for their effort, collaboration and access to their data.

8. Bibliographical References

Abercrombie, G. and Batista-Navarro, R. (2020). Sentiment and position-taking analysis of parliamentary debates: a systematic literature review. *Journal of Computational Social Science*, 3(1):245–270, jan.

Andrej Pančur, M. S. and Erjavec, T. (2018). SlovParl 2.0: The Collection of Slovene Parliamentary Debates from the Period of Secession. In Darja Fišer, et al., editors, *Proceedings of the Eleventh International Conference on Language Resources and Evaluation (LREC 2018)*, Paris, France, may. European Language Resources Association (ELRA).

Conneau, A., Khandelwal, K., Goyal, N., Chaudhary, V., Wenzek, G., Guzmán, F., Grave, E., Ott, M., Zettlemoyer, L., and Stoyanov, V. (2019). Unsupervised Cross-lingual Representation Learning at Scale. *CoRR*, abs/1911.02116.

Dorte Haltrup Hansen, C. N. and Offersgaard, L. (2018). A Pilot Gender Study of the Danish Parliament Corpus. In Darja Fišer, et al., editors, *Proceedings of the Eleventh International Conference on Language Resources and Evaluation (LREC 2018)*, Paris, France, may. European Language Resources Association (ELRA).

Eide, S. R. (2020). Anföranden: Annotated and Augmented Parliamentary Debates from Sweden. In *PARLACLARIN*.

Erjavec, T., Ogrodniczuk, M., Osenova, P., Ljubešić, N., Simov, K., Grigorova, V., Rudolf, M., Pančur, A., Kopp, M., Barkarson, S., Steingrímsson, S., van der Pol, H., Depoorter, G., de Does, J., Jongejan, B., Haltrup Hansen, D., Navarretta, C., Calzada Pérez, M., de Macedo, L. D., van Heusden, R., Marx, M., Çöltekin, Ç., Coole, M., Agnoloni, T., Frontini, F., Montemagni, S., Quochi, V., Venturi, G., Ruisi, M., Marchetti, C., Battistoni, R., Sebők, M., Ring, O., Darģis, R., Utka, A., Petkevičius, M., Briedienė, M., Krilavičius, T., Morkevičius, V., Diwersy, S., Luxardo, G., and Rayson, P. (2021). Multilingual

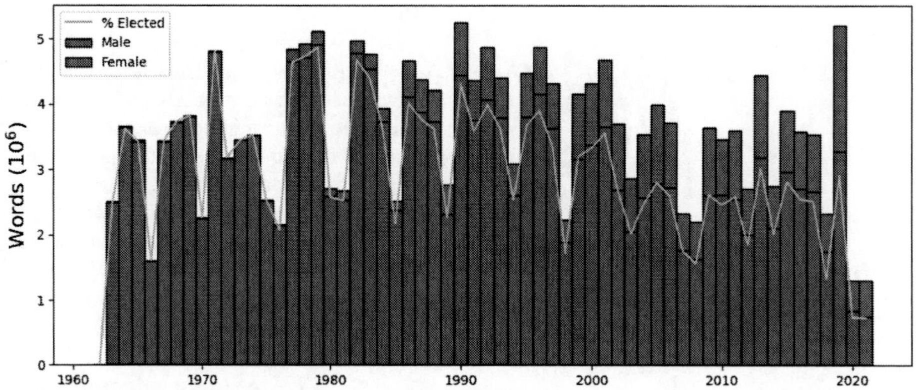

Figure 5: Number of words spoken by sex from 1963 to 2021.

comparable corpora of parliamentary debates ParlaMint 2.1. Slovenian language resource repository CLARIN.SI.

Gallichan, G. (1988). Les débats parlementaires du Québec (1792-1964) et la mémoire des mots. *Papers of The Bibliographical Society of Canada*, 27(1).

Gallichan, G. (2004). Le Parlement « rapaillé »: la méthodologie de la reconstitution des débats. *Les Cahiers des dix*, (58):273–296.

Naderi, N. and Hirst, G. (2018). Automatically labeled data generation for classification of reputation defence strategies. In Darja Fišer, et al., editors, *Proceedings of the Eleventh International Conference on Language Resources and Evaluation (LREC 2018)*, Paris, France, may. European Language Resources Association (ELRA).

Nguyen, M. V., Lai, V., Veyseh, A. P. B., and Nguyen, T. H. (2021). Trankit: A Light-Weight Transformer-based Toolkit for Multilingual Natural Language Processing. In *Proceedings of the 16th Conference of the European Chapter of the Association for Computational Linguistics: System Demonstrations*.

Nivre, J., de Marneffe, M.-C., Ginter, F., Goldberg, Y., Hajič, J., Manning, C. D., McDonald, R., Petrov, S., Pyysalo, S., Silveira, N., Tsarfaty, R., and Zeman, D. (2016). Universal Dependencies v1: A Multilingual Treebank Collection. In *Proceedings of the Tenth International Conference on Language Resources and Evaluation (LREC'16)*, pages 1659–1666, Portorož, Slovenia, May. European Language Resources Association (ELRA).

Onur Gungor, M. T. and Çağıl Sönmez. (2018). A Corpus of Grand National Assembly of Turkish Parliament's Transcripts. In Darja Fišer, et al., editors, *Proceedings of the Eleventh International Conference on Language Resources and Evaluation (LREC 2018)*, Paris, France, may. European Language Resources Association (ELRA).

Richardson, L. (2007). Beautiful soup documentation. *April*.

Saint-Pierre, J. (2003). La reconstitution des débats de l'Assemblée législative du Québec, une entreprise gigantesque de rattrapage historique. *Bulletin d'histoire politique*, 11(3):12–22.

Steingrímsson, S., Helgadóttir, S., Rögnvaldsson, E., Barkarson, S., and Gudnason, J. (2018). Risamálheild: A Very Large Icelandic Text Corpus. In Nicoletta Calzolari (Conference chair), et al., editors, *Proceedings of the Eleventh International Conference on Language Resources and Evaluation (LREC 2018)*, Miyazaki, Japan, May 7-12, 2018. European Language Resources Association (ELRA).

Vaswani, A., Shazeer, N., Parmar, N., Uszkoreit, J., Jones, L., Gomez, A. N., Kaiser, L., and Polosukhin, I. (2017). Attention is all you need. *CoRR*, abs/1706.03762.

Proceedings of ParlaCLARIN III @ LREC2022 pages 33–34
Marseille, 20 June 2022

Parliamentary Corpora and Research in Political Science and Political History

Luke Blaxill
University of Oxford
https://www.lukeblaxill.com
luke.blaxill@hertford.ox.ac.uk

Abstract

This keynote reflects on some of the barriers to digitised parliamentary resources achieving greater impact as research tools in political history and political science. As well as providing a view on researchers' priorities for resource enhancement, I also argue that one of the main challenges for historians and political scientists is simply establishing how to make best use of these datasets through asking new research questions and through understanding and embracing unfamiliar and controversial methods than enable their analysis. I suggest parliamentary resources should be designed and presented to support pioneers trying to publish in often sceptical and traditional fields.

The two decades since the millennium have witnessed a 'data deluge' of digitised sources for research. Scholars working with political texts are amongst the most fortunate beneficiaries, with the digitisation of parliamentary proceedings providing an invaluable resource both for traditional qualitative scholarship and large-scale quantitative text-mining approaches. And yet the impact of the release of digitised datasets in directly inspiring new research in political science and political history has been smaller than might have been hoped for, especially given the publicity generated by generalist exemplar studies (Lansdall-Welfare et al., 2017). Indeed, in the 1970s it was widely believed that computational analysis would come to dominate the humanities and social sciences as the range of resources increased and technology developed (Shorter, 1971). And yet, even in the richly-supported realms of political science and history, remarkably few books and articles have appeared which feature digitised resources such as parliamentary proceedings at their analytical core. This paper looks at some of the reasons for this and suggests some potential solutions.

In political science and political history, researchers tend to be less concerned with language itself, but in language as discourse, and discourse as a means of studying (for example) political change, power, identities, institutions, and cultures. They study parliamentary proceedings with this in mind. This makes the addition of contextual data to parliamentary debates vital to maximising their utility as research tools. Expanding coverage of metadata concerning speakers themselves (e.g. party; seniority; gender); the type of proceedings; who else is in the chamber; speaker interactivity; and other variables, are all extremely welcome. For large scale text mining analyses, classifying topics of debates (which enable large-scale diachronic and international comparisons) has often revolved around the Comparative Agendas Project (Baumgartner et al., 2019) but this has largely focussed on post-1945 data, and many historians and political scientists work on nineteenth century proceedings where the Comparative Agendas topic classifications are much less reliable. Other crucial determinants of the 'real meaning' of what is happening in Parliament relate to uncaptured subtleties: speakers often use irony, jokes, vary their tone, make oblique references to current or previous events in the chamber, and respond to unrecorded heckles. All of these escape (or at least partially escape) the textual record. Reconstructing this discursive context helps scholars (and citizens) interpret proceedings more readily.

The challenge of ensuring digitised parliamentary proceedings achieve the maximum research impact in political history and political science runs deeper than resource optimisation. Partly, resource creators and enhancers have been so successful and industrious that the digital provision and enhancement of parliamentary proceedings often runs ahead of the needs of the majority of the history and political science research communities. This means that enhanced digital resources – which allow new research questions to be asked and methods to be used – are published before the community has formulated these new research questions or developed these new methods. The challenge for digitally-inclined political researchers attempting to act as a scholarly vanguard is thus to devise new and interesting research questions that could not have been asked without these datasets and (particularly) to develop analytical methods which will be accepted and impactful in traditional fields such as History, where even rudimentary text mining and linguistic classification are controversial (Guldi and Armitage, 2014; Blaxill, 2020). I will give some thoughts on how parliamentary corpora can be constructed and presented so as to best assist researchers attempting pioneering computer-led analysis in traditional and sceptical fields.

1. References

Baumgartner, F. R., Breunig, C., and Grossman, E. (2019). *Comparative policy agendas: Theory, tools, data*. Oxford University Press.

Blaxill, L. (2020). *The War of Words: The Language of British Elections, 1880-1914*. Boydell Press.

Borgman, C. L. (2010). The digital archive: The data deluge arrives in the humanities.

Guldi, J. and Armitage, D. (2014). *The history manifesto*. Cambridge University Press.

Lansdall-Welfare, T., Sudhahar, S., Thompson, J., Lewis, J., Team, F. N., and Cristianini, N. (2017). Content analysis of 150 years of british periodicals. *Proceedings of the National Academy of Sciences*, 114(4):E457–E465.

Partington, A. (2013). Corpus analysis of political language.

Shorter, E. (1971). *The Historian and the Computer*. Prentice Hall, Englewood Cliffs, N. J.

Proceedings of ParlaCLARIN III @ LREC2022 pages 35–38
Marseille, 20 June 2022

Error Correction Environment for the Polish Parliamentary Corpus

Maciej Ogrodniczuk, Michał Rudolf, Beata Wójtowicz, Sonia Janicka

Institute of Computer Science, Polish Academy of Sciences
Warsaw, Poland

maciej.ogrodniczuk@ipipan.waw.pl, michal@rudolf.waw.pl,
beata.wojtowicz@ipipan.waw.pl, s.janicka@student.uw.edu.pl

Abstract

The paper introduces the environment for detecting and correcting various kinds of errors in the Polish Parliamentary Corpus. After performing a language model-based error detection experiment which resulted in too many false positives, a simpler rule-based method was introduced and is currently used in the process of manual verification of corpus texts. The paper presents types of errors detected in the corpus, the workflow of the correction process and the tools newly implemented for this purpose. To facilitate comparison of a target corpus XML file with its usually graphical PDF source, a new mechanism for inserting PDF page markers into XML was developed and is used for displaying a single source page corresponding to a given place in the resulting XML directly in the error correction environment.

Keywords: parliamentary data, error correction, Polish

1. Introduction

The Polish Parliamentary Corpus[1] (Ogrodniczuk, 2018; Ogrodniczuk and Nitoń, 2020) contains proceedings of the Polish parliament from the last 100 years of its modern history, currently of over 800M tokens. The process of adding data to the XML corpus has been heterogeneous, ranging from almost-direct inclusion of newest born-digital data already available in clean formats (such as HTML) to tedious correction of automatically OCR-ed image-based PDF files containing older materials (before 1990).

Even though the latter have already been manually verified by human proof-readers at the time of their OCR, the process still resulted in many problems of various types, including structural errors (such as retained unnecessary header information) or typographical errors (e.g. corresponding to words present in dictionary but invalid in the given context). This motivated another correction round in a new environment, developed especially for detection and correction of errors in the corpus. Below we describe the process of analysing corpus texts, present the correction environment and various add-ons improving the proofreading work.

2. Error Candidate Detection

Two experiments have been carried out before the decision was made about the target method of error candidate detection in the corpus. Since precision of error detection seems to be the most important factor of such task, two models were tested. The language model-based, intended to verify how the newest transformer models for Polish can cope with a straightforward task requiring considerable precision, was compared to a simple rule-based model, long known for its precision.

[1]Pol. Korpus Dyskursu Parlamentarnego, see `clip.ipipan.waw.pl/PPC`.

2.1. Language Model-Based Error Candidate Detection

Language models have been successfully used for OCR post-correction for Polish e.g. at PolEval 2021 (Kobyliński et al., 2021)[2]. One of the submitted solutions, ranked second best (Wróbel, 2021), was tested in an experiment to find error candidates in the Polish Parliamentary Corpus. The solution was based on a sequence to sequence model using T5 architecture (Raffel et al., 2020) and a publicly available PLT5 LARGE language model for Polish[3]. Unfortunately, even though the model was successful in discovering and correcting such cases as two words glued together, missing or excessive spaces and several types of grammatical errors, the number of false positives (most likely caused by a different training domain) rendered its use impractical.

2.2. Rule-Based Error Candidate Detection

To eliminate excessive false positives, a rule-based solution was implemented. It consists of several modules intended to detect various classes of errors.

Structural errors are mostly merged enumerations or speaker names treated as normal text, leading to assigning utterances to a wrong speaker. In some cases supposed speaker labels are in fact standard text.

Comments and metadata were marked in original texts with simple brackets (e.g. *Thank you. (Applause)* which led to many conversion errors as sometimes the brackets were also used in the text, usually containing numbers or statistics, for example *(about 98%)*. This

[2]See also `http://2021.poleval.pl/tasks/task3`.

[3]`https://huggingface.co/allegro/plt5-large`

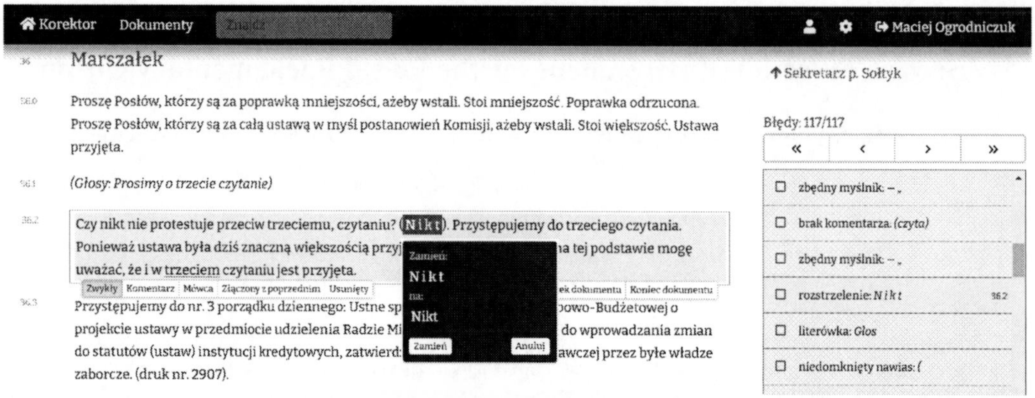

Figure 1: Interface of the error correction environment: replacement suggestion for a spaced-out word

problem was solved by adding the rules concerning common comment phrases.

Punctuation errors made a separate category with many subclasses such as wrong or unmatched quotation marks or brackets, wrong types of hyphenation (minuses vs. n- or m-dashes etc.), excessively hyphenated words etc.

Broken or unfinished paragraphs mostly resulted from conversion errors but could also denote missing content.

Misspellings resulting in out-of-vocabulary strings were also quite common, particularly in older sessions which were often printed on low-quality paper. Such cases are detected using Morfeusz 2 (Kieraś and Woliński, 2017), the most efficient morphological analyser for Polish. Due to a high number of proper names, this step was limited to lowercase tokens[4].

Common OCR errors or typos corresponding to highly improbable in-dictionary words were also detected with a set of special rules. This included low-frequency words having a high-frequency orthographic neighbour, e.g. *glosowanie* (*glossing*) instead of *głosowanie* (*voting*) or rare grammatical cases, e.g. *sytemu* (*satiated* $_{\text{DAT}}$) instead of *systemu* (*system* $_{\text{GEN}}$) or *tyko* (*beanpole* $_{\text{VOC}}$) instead of *tylko* (*only*).

Other types of errors included missing or redundant spaces, remains of non-textual elements such as tables or footnotes (which were to be removed from the proceedings), characters outside the common character set or spaced-out words.

3. Error Correction Process

Annotations produced by the rule-based system were distributed to human proofreaders in a newly implemented Web-based error correction environment[5]. After logging in and selecting a text allocated for verification, they were supposed to read the text in the left/center pane (see Figure 1), consult the list of detected potential errors displayed in the right pane and correct or discard them. Apart from resolving hinted problems the proofreaders were also asked to assign speeches to speakers, distinguish the speeches from extra-textual events, mark the opening and closure of the sitting, correct annotations of misidentified comments, mark undelivered speeches etc.
The following three-step procedure was used, starting from the most to the least important issues:

1. correcting the structure of the text (distinguishing between speaker information, comments and spoken text, divided into paragraphs); errors in this layer can disrupt search results for large blocks of text so they are the most painful
2. correcting the structure of the sentence (typos, punctuation errors, hyphenation etc.): these types of errors can spoil the analysis of the sentence and cause misinterpretation of ambiguous words
3. checking the consistency of the corrections throughout the text; obviously different terms of office had different stenographers and slightly different conventions; some of them change even within a single sitting.

The interface of the error correction environment offers several functions facilitating the task such as opening the source PDF, adding general comments to the document or searching for a phrase or a certain identifier in

[4]Different spelling conventions used in pre-war texts may also result in false positives (since corpus creators decided to retain the original spelling from the official parliamentary proceedings). For the correction process it means that the proofreaders have to consult the rules prevailing at the time of the sitting.

[5]`https://korektor.rudolf.waw.pl`, authorized access only.

the document. Sections of text selected for correction are marked in colour.

After clicking the highlighted text, a pop-up may appear with a correction suggestion (see the dark box in Figure 1). The proofreader might select to accept the proposed change or discard it. Even when there is no suggestion available, the proofreader may edit the content in place or change the structure of the text using one of the buttons (under the yellow box in Figure 1):

- Zwykły (*Plain*), i.e. the content of the speech
- Komentarz (*Comment*), used for fragments which relate to non-textual events, such as the beginning/end of the meeting, applause etc.
- Mówca (*Speaker*), marks a given passage as an identifier of the person speaking (usually their name and position)
- Złączony z poprzednim (*Merged with previous paragraph*), joins the current paragraph with the preceding one into a single, continuous text
- Usunięty (*Deleted*), deletes the paragraph.

Changes can be cancelled by clicking on the back arrow icon that appears to the right of the modified paragraphs.

The right pane provides a list of all automatically detected errors in the document. Clicking an item displays its corresponding paragraph in the center pane. Once the error has been corrected, the line is marked with a tick. Suggestions can also be ignored.

Apart from just looking at suggestions, the proofreaders were instructed to read the whole text and correct erroneous words, typos, spelling mistakes, unnecessary punctuation marks and other similar issues not detected by the rule-based system. When not certain, they were supposed to refer to the original text in the PDF file (using the integrated mechanism for locating a given text in a PDF document, see Section 5.) and keep the original spelling.

4. Inserting Page Markers into XML

In some cases the correction process requires looking into the graphical PDF source. Without knowing which page to look on, it might pose an enormous difficulty to locate the exact occurrence of the word on phrase in a multi-page, non-searchable document. This situation motivated a sub-project based on the assumption that the results of any (even considerably dirty) OCR could be, with a reasonable accuracy, compared with the clean XML text to insert page boundary markers.

In order to perform OCR, the PDF files needed to be converted into JPG format first. Then, the open source optical character recognition engine Tesseract[6] (Smith, 2007) was used to extract strings consisting of last five words of each page, which identified this page boundary. Those identifiers were subsequently stored in a list covering all the pages in a given document.

At this point, the actual procedure of inserting page boundary markers could start and each string on the list was searched for in the corresponding XML TEI file. In order to counteract possible errors resulting from imprecise text recognition, the search was fuzzy and allowed for the Levenshtein distance of six between the extracted string and the XML TEI file. When the given string was found, a page boundary marker with the page number was inserted, and the next string was searched for, starting where the previous one was found.

The XML TEI files in the Polish Parliamentary Corpus omit some parts of the original PDF files, such as tables or indices, and sometimes include blank pages. This had to be taken into account in order to maintain correct page numeration, and was successfully implemented. Moreover, pages in the PDF files frequently end with word breaks marked with a hyphen. The goal of the project was to avoid splitting words with the markers and insert them either before or after the words in question. Therefore, the need to establish whether a page ended with a whole or split word arose. In this respect, the OCR results turned out to be unreliable, as the hyphens often remained undetected in the recognized text. Therefore, the text in XML TEI files needed to be examined and the index to insert page boundary marker adjusted. As a result, the markers were effectively inserted following the word partially relegated to the next page in the PDF files.

The results of inserting page boundary markers proved satisfactory in the case of documents consisting of long chunks of text. The quality of OCR performed by Tesseract generally sufficed to detect the appropriate spot for page boundary markers. Occasional problems occurred for files of worse quality, but such an issue arising on one page did not prevent the next marker from being inserted correctly.

The following issues, however, remained unresolved:

Extremely short paragraphs In the Polish Parliamentary Corpus, the text spoken by each person is located in a different tag. Consequently, in the case of a page ending with an extremely short paragraph (e.g. a one-word statement preceded by a statement made by another person), the string identifying page boundary consists of words belonging to two different tags; it may also include the elements classified as a tag attribute in an XML TEI file rather than its content (e.g. the name of the person speaking). As the strings identifying page boundaries were searched for inside one tag at a time, in such particular cases markers with page numbers could not be inserted.

Repetitive phrases Another problem was posed by documents with numerous repetitive phrases, such as names of decrees or laws. Such files, however, were limited in length and number, and presumably do not amount to a high percentage in the whole corpus.

[6] `https://github.com/tesseract-ocr/tesseract`

5. Current Findings

The process of correcting errors in the corpus has been running for several months now so we can try to analyze its effectiveness. First of all, Table 1 presents the number of errors of various categories discovered in the subset of the corpus already assigned to proofreaders. It contains the proceedings of Sejm (lower house), with 2898 texts dated between 1919 and 2019. The vast majority of errors are related to punctuation which may result from different typing conventions (of quotation marks or brackers) but also OCR problems (hyphenation). However, the most important (from the perspective of corpus users) are structural errors, resulting in assigning utterances to wrong speakers or treating comments as spoken data.

Structural errors	71 790
unmarked speakers	32 481
enumerations	20 857
Comments and metadata	18 452
Punctuation errors	427 830
wrong quotation marks	314 772
hyphenation errors	102 103
bracket problems	6175
other punctuation problems	4780
Broken or unfinished paragraphs	121 182
Misspellings	113 170
Common OCR errors and typos	3827
Other errors	40 680
spacing problems	24 843
non-textual elements	15 720
spaced-out words	117
All errors	778 479

Table 1: Detected error counts, by class

Table 2 presents the effectiveness of rule-based error detection measured with proofreader reaction (accepted vs. ignored system suggestions). The number is a fraction of all detected errors since only approx. 30% of the assigned data is currently corrected. In our opinion the acceptance rate of errors discovered by the model seems reasonably high.

Accepted suggestions	195 416	87%
Ignored suggestions	28 486	13%
All suggestions	223 902	100%

Table 2: Error detection effectiveness

6. Looking to the Future

The environment was designed to integrate various error detection and text correction mechanisms so it inadvertently becomes the main corpus editing tool for Polish parliamentary data. One direction of its development are obviously improvements in the current error discovery, both in terms of its scope, e.g. to include detection of incomplete documents (without the formal end of the meeting) and technical capabilities, e.g. plugging in new methods of error detection capable of discovering other types of errors (e.g. syntactic errors, difficult misspellings etc.)

On the other hand, since the environment already proved to offer non-technical users the opportunity to edit corpus texts in a straightforward way, it is planned to be extended with new functions for adding longer fragments of text (confirmed to be missing) or marking up the formal structure of the meeting (agenda items).

Acknowledgements

The work reported here was financed under the 2014–2020 Smart Development Operational Programme, Priority IV: Increasing the scientific and research potential, Measure 4.2: Development of modern research infrastructure of the science sector, No. POIR.04.02.00-00C002/19, "CLARIN — Common Language Resources and Technology Infrastructure".

We would like to thank Krzysztof Wróbel for his language model-based error candidate detection experiment (see Section 2.1.).

Bibliographical References

Kieraś, W. and Woliński, M. (2017). Morfeusz 2 – analizator i generator fleksyjny dla języka polskiego. *Język Polski*, XCVII(1):75–83.

Kobyliński, Ł., Kieraś, W., and Rynkun, S. (2021). PolEval 2021 Task 3: Post-correction of OCR Results. In (Ogrodniczuk and Kobyliński, 2021), pages 85–91.

Ogrodniczuk, M. and Kobyliński, Ł., editors. (2021). *Proceedings of the PolEval 2021 Workshop*. Institute of Computer Science, Polish Academy of Sciences.

Ogrodniczuk, M. and Nitoń, B. (2020). New Developments in the Polish Parliamentary Corpus. In Darja Fišer, et al., editors, *Proceedings of the Second ParlaCLARIN Workshop*, pages 1–4. ELRA.

Ogrodniczuk, M. (2018). Polish Parliamentary Corpus. In Darja Fišer, et al., editors, *Proceedings of the LREC 2018 Workshop* ParlaCLARIN: Creating and Using Parliamentary Corpora, pages 15–19. ELRA.

Raffel, C., Shazeer, N., Roberts, A., Lee, K., Narang, S., Matena, M., Zhou, Y., Li, W., and Liu, P. J. (2020). Exploring the Limits of Transfer Learning with a Unified Text-to-Text Transformer. *Journal of Machine Learning Research*, 21(140):1–67.

Smith, R. (2007). An Overview of the Tesseract OCR Engine. In *Proceedings of the 9th International Conference on Document Analysis and Recognition, vol. 2*, pages 629–633. IEEE Computer Society.

Wróbel, K. (2021). OCR Correction with Encoder-Decoder Transformer. In (Ogrodniczuk and Kobyliński, 2021), pages 97–102.

Proceedings of ParlaCLARIN III @ LREC2022 pages 39–46
Marseille, 20 June 2022

Clustering Similar Amendments at the Italian Senate

Tommaso Agnoloni[1], Carlo Marchetti[2], Roberto Battistoni[2], Giuseppe Briotti[2]
[1]Institute of Legal Informatics and Judicial Systems (CNR-IGSG); [2]Senato della Repubblica
tommaso.agnoloni@igsg.cnr.it
{carlo.marchetti, roberto.battistoni, giuseppe.briotti}@senato.it

Abstract

In this paper we describe an experiment for the application of text clustering techniques to dossiers of amendments to proposed legislation discussed in the Italian Senate. The aim is to assist the Senate staff in the detection of groups of amendments similar in their textual formulation in order to schedule their simultaneous voting. Experiments show that the exploitation (extraction, annotation and normalization) of domain features is crucial to improve the clustering performance in many problematic cases not properly dealt with by standard approaches. The similarity engine was implemented and integrated as an experimental feature in the internal application used for the management of amendments in the Senate Assembly and Committees. Thanks to the Open Data strategy pursued by the Senate for several years, all documents and data produced by the institution are publicly available for reuse in open formats.

Keywords: bills, amendments, text similarity, near-duplicates detection, clustering

1. Background and Motivation

As part of its daily activities the staff of the Italian Senate collects and organizes amendments presented by Senators on proposed laws assigned for discussion to Parliamentary Committees or for plenary discussion in the Assembly.

The Information Technology Office of the Senate develops and provides document management automation tools to speed up the process and improve the service. Application needs include assisting the operator in identifying similar amendments in a dossier in order to group them for simultaneous voting. Similar amendments can be scattered along the dossier and include those applying the same modification to different parts of the law.

Ideally, similar amendments are those producing the same effect on a proposed law. In practice, similar amendments are near duplicate texts differing in a few words in their formulation.

2. Amendments in the Legislative Process

In the lawmaking process, amendments are proposals for modification of the text of a bill, *i.e.* a proposed law under discussion within (a branch of) the Parliament. They contain proposals to change, remove or add to the existing wording of bills in order to modify their effect, allowing for bills to be improved or altered as they progress through the Parliament. Amendments are submitted in writing, to the Committee and/or to the Assembly, by the individual Senators, by the Committee that examined the bill in the referring seat, by the rapporteur or by the Government and are usually printed and distributed at the beginning of the discussion. The President decides whether they are feasible (*i.e.* related to the subject) and admissible (*i.e.* having a real modifying effect and not in contrast with resolutions already adopted). Amendments examining and voting proceed according to a precise order, starting with those that make the most radical changes to the original text, gradually reaching those that are less distant from it. Moreover, proposals of similar content must be placed and discussed simultaneously, if possible. Amendments to an amendment may also be tabled, so-called sub-amendments, which must be voted on before the amendment itself. When voting on amendments, some of them may be absorbed (when the meaning of the amendment is included in the broader meaning of another amendment already voted and approved) or precluded (when the amendment conflicts with amendments already approved). Members of parliament can then decide to support or oppose the amendment when it is time to vote. Amendments do not need to be passed to have an effect. Non-government amendments may be proposed for other reasons: to make a political point MPs, particularly those from opposition parties, may propose amendments with the aim of advertising alternative policies or challenging the Government. These will often have little chance of succeeding but are a means of debating concerns in Parliament. Obstructionistic technique (to propose a huge number of amendments differing in few words) sometimes practiced by oppositions in order to slow down the legislative process, is one of the most notable case where the automated analysis of amendment content and similarity detection would ease the work of the Senate staff.

3. Open Documents Dataset

Since 2016 the Senate of the Republic publishes all legislative documents in standard Akoma Ntoso XML format[1] with Open license CC BY 3.0. Documents are timely published via automated scripts in the

[1]`http://www.akomantoso.org/`

GitHub repository `AkomaNtosoBulkData`[2], (Senato, 2016). This makes it easier to massively download texts for researchers, journalists, or anyone interested in accessing them automatically.

This is part of the wider Open Data strategy pursued by the Italian Senate through its data portal *dati.senato.it*[3]. The main purpose of such project is to make available, in open and freely reusable formats, most of the data already published on the institutional website of the Senate[4] concerning every aspect of the political and institutional activity: bills with their process, electronic voting of the Assembly, Committees, Parliamentary Groups, Senators. This in order to ensure greater transparency on the work of the institution and encourage the concrete participation of citizens in the decision-making process.

In the `AkomaNtosoBulkData` document repository, data are structured following the same logical organization of the Senate website: for every Legislative term every bill has its own web page named "*Scheda DDL*" where it is possible to view the parliamentary phases with all related documents (presented and approved bills, reports, amendments, etc.)

The first level of the bulk data is composed of the Legislative terms. Any of them contains folders of bills in the Italian Senate. These folders contain the bills' text organized by type : proposed, debate, approved. More in detail each folder contains:

> *ddlpres*: the text of the proposed bill or transmitted from the other branch of the Parliament;
>
> *ddlcomm*: the text of the bill proposed by the Committee;
>
> *ddlmess*: the text of the bill approved by the Italian Senate;
>
> *emend*: the amendments discussed in the Assembly;
>
> *emendc*: the amendments discussed in the Committees.

In this experimentation we focused on the *emendc* dataset of amendments presented and voted in the Committees. Amendments presented in the committees for the modification of a bill are collected in *dossiers*. Amendments are grouped by article of the bill they aim to modify. The information on the affected article is available among the amendment's metadata but not reported in its text. Metadata in the Akoma Ntoso structuring include signatories of the proposed amendment linked via persistent URIs to RDF metadata in the Open Data portal. The amendment content is structured in HTML for presentation on the website. For the purpose of similarity analysis amendments are treated as plain text.

4. Document Similarity and Clustering

The problem of clustering (grouping by similarity) is a classical problem studied extensively in the scientific literature in statistics and data analysis (Leskovec et al., 2020), (Manning et al., 2008).

The study of the clustering problem precedes its application to the textual domain. Traditional methods for clustering have generally focused on the case of quantitative data.

In a nutshell, any document clustering approach requires a vector representation of texts with features selection and weighting, the choice of a similarity metric between pairs of vectors, and a clustering strategy.

There are different types of clustering algorithms which differ in the strategy followed to group the elements and in the various a priori assumptions (Leskovec et al., 2020). The choice of which approach to adopt depends on the characteristics of the problem under consideration.

In our case, the goal is to obtain a *partial clustering* of the elements (amendments in a *dossier*). In fact, not all amendments must be included in a cluster, but only those that have at least one *"similar"*.

Furthermore, the clusters we aim to must be composed of elements that are very close to each other in their textual formulation (near duplicate texts) and not, for example, of texts that simply deal with the same topic. Our main goal a this stage is therefore to assess *lexical similarity* among texts rather than their *semantic similarity*. Moreover, in our case the number of clusters to be created is not known a priori and depends on the characteristics of the amendments in the dossier under examination. Finally, the algorithm must not be based on any a priori information or manually annotated dataset but only on the analysis of the elements (unsupervised approach).

4.1. Hierarchical Agglomerative Clustering

The most appropriate approach to clustering in this scenario is Hierarchical Agglomerative Clustering (*HAC*) (Manning et al., 2008), (Aggarwal and Zhai, 2012). Its application to amendments was previously experimented in (Notarstefano, 2016). The general concept of agglomerative clustering is to iteratively group together elements on the basis of their mutual similarity. At the beginning, each element is seen as a cluster of size 1 (*singleton* cluster). Subsequently, each element is searched for its closest element according to the chosen similarity measure and they are grouped into a cluster. At the next iteration, the process is repeated between the clusters formed in the previous step and the singleton clusters. The procedure is repeated until all the elements are grouped into a single cluster.

The process of merging the elements into successive ever larger levels of clusters creates a hierarchy, typically displayed in a dendrogram. The dendrogram

[2] `https://github.com/SenatoDellaRepubblica/AkomaNtosoBulkData`

[3] `http://dati.senato.it`

[4] `http://www.senato.it/`

shows in a tree view the order and distance of the mergers during the hierarchical clustering process. At the lowest level, leaf nodes correspond to the individual elements. Internal nodes correspond to clusters created at each iteration. When two documents or two clusters are merged, a new node is created in the tree corresponding to the largest cluster that contains them. The process ends with the creation of a single cluster that gathers all the clusters previously created and therefore contains all the documents, corresponding to the root node of the tree.
Clusters are those groups obtained by cutting the dendrogram at a certain threshold T. The elements that have not yet been merged with any cluster at the cut-off threshold will remain in their *singleton* clusters, thus giving rise to a partial clustering. Hierarchical clustering algorithms differ by the strategy to establish grouping of clusters created at each iteration (*linkage strategy*).
We chose *complete linkage* where the similarity among two clusters amounts to the similarity of their *most distant* elements. This is equivalent to choosing the pair of clusters whose merging produces a new cluster with the minimum diameter.

4.2. Parameters Configuration

In this experiment we tested typical choices for document clustering in order to establish a baseline for further more advanced configurations:

- *tokenization* of texts around typical words separators (whitespace, tabs, carriage returns) and punctuation marks;
- token normalization using the *Snowball Stemmer* for Italian;
- removal of standard *stop-words* for the Italian language (*Python NLTK stop-words*). All other textual and numerical tokens are kept in the vector representation;
- vectorization with TF (*term-frequency*) weights and L_2 normalization to account for documents of different length;
- cosine similarity as a measure of distance between vector representations of texts. Cosine similarity is normalized between 0 and 1 (identical texts). The chosen minimum similarity threshold for grouping two texts in the same cluster is 80% (0.8);
- the criterion chosen for the HAC algorithm for clusters larger than two is the *complete-linkage* described above. With the chosen configuration, the HAC algorithm produces a normalized dendrogram with distances ranging between 0 (each element in its *singleton cluster*) and 1 (a single cluster that contains all the elements). In this way, the value on the dendrogram at the intermediate nodes represents the maximum distance between the elements that make up the clusters that are formed at each iteration. For example, with a value of the cut-off threshold T equal to 0.2, the produced clusters will be composed of elements whose mutual distance will be *at most* equal to 0.2 and therefore *at least* 80% similar (similarity ≥ 0.8);
- we indicate this value as "*cluster compactness*" and include it among the attributes of the formed clusters.

The choices for the algorithm parameters is also driven by the application scenario where we want to use our similarity engine (see Sect. 7).
In fact, in order to simplify user interaction, we don't want to use the algorithm for exploratory analysis where the user can adjust the parameters, but we want to use fixed parameters valid independent on the document corpus that the algorithm is applied to (the dossier of amendments in our case). In particular we aim to a fixed cut-off threshold.
This is the reason why we chose TF vectorization and not TF.IDF. The IDF component of TF.IDF weighting in fact, introduces a dependency of the document vectors on the corpus and therefore a dependency on the corpus of their distances and ultimately of the cut-off threshold. Moreover, experiments using TF.IDF weighting did not show a significant performance improvement, particularly in the problematic cases (Sect. 5.3).
For the same reason of portability among different dossiers without further tuning, we chose the *complete-linkage* criterion which gives an easily interpretable cluster distance as the pairwise-distance of their most distant elements. The fixed minimum pairwise similarity threshold of 0.8, empirically established as optimal, corresponds to a 0.2 dendrogram cut-off threshold in the complete linkage case.
HAC is not very computationally efficient, as it requires at least comparing each pair of texts and doing it several times later with the resulting groups. In its most efficient implementation using *priority queues* the computational complexity is $O(N^2 LogN)$.
This type of algorithm is therefore not applicable to large datasets. In our case this is not a problem since the size of the dataset is relatively small (in the order of thousands of amendments per dossier).

5. Experiments and Evaluation

The algorithm was tested and evaluated on two dossiers, respectively:

- the dossier relating to Senate Act n. 1248[5] composed of 1247 amendments treated in the 8th

[5]https://www.senato.it/leg/18/BGT/Schede/Ddliter/testi/51685_testi.htm

Committee (Public works, communications) and 13th (Territory, environment, environmental assets). The presented text of the amended bill is made up of 30 articles.

- the dossier relating to Senate Act n. 2272[6] composed of 659 amendments treated in the 1st Committee (Constitutional Affairs) and 2nd (Justice). The presented text of the amended bill is made up of 19 articles.

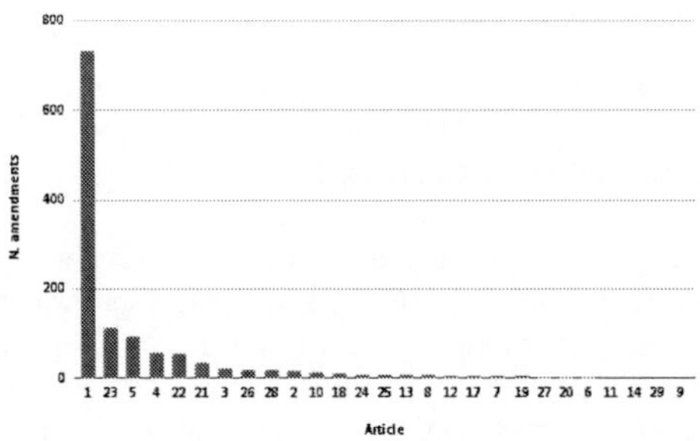

Figure 1: Act n. 1248 - distribution of number of amendments for bill article.

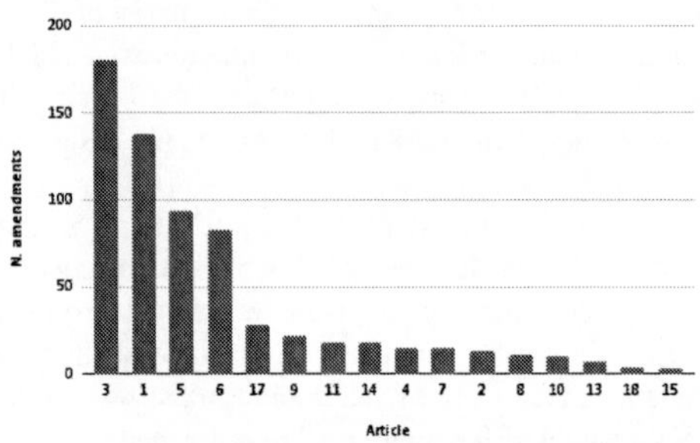

Figure 2: Act n. 2272 - distribution of number of amendments for bill article.

5.1. "Gold Standard"

A dataset with the expected "real" clustering was produced by the committees' staff for the selected dossiers. For each of the two dossiers, each amendment was manually annotated with the *label* of the cluster to which it should be assigned or with no label in the case of an amendment without similar (*singleton*).
For the dossier of Act n. 1248, manual labeling produces groupings with the following characteristics:

- 485 of the 1247 amendments (39%) have no similar and are not clustered (*singleton*);

- 762 of the 1247 amendments (61%) are grouped into 266 clusters (of size greater than or equal to 2). The minimum cluster size is 2, the maximum size is 12, the average size is 2.8. In fact, most clusters (82%) have size 2 (56%) or 3 (26%).

For the dossier of Act n. 2272:

- 246 of the 659 amendments (37%) have no similar and are not clustered (*singleton*);

- 413 of the 659 (63%) amendments are grouped into 139 clusters (of size greater than or equal to 2). The minimum cluster size is 2, the maximum size is 13, the average size is approximately 3 (2.97). In fact, most clusters (74%) have size 2 (54%) or 3 (20%).

The validation and evaluation process is in general the most difficult part of the application of a clustering algorithm since it is not generally possible to define a single "real" clustering (in principle it is correct to merge similar elements either in several small homogeneous clusters or in a single less homogeneous cluster).

5.2. Evaluation

There are several metrics used to measure the agreement between two clusterizations. The most common are ARI (Adjusted Rand Index) and AMI (Adjusted Mutual Information).
RI (Rand Index) can be seen as a percentage of correct decisions made by the algorithm. It can be calculated using the formula:

$$RI = \frac{TP+TN}{TP+FP+FN+TN}$$

The ARI variant measures the similarity between the assignment of elements to clusters provided by the algorithm and the real one ignoring the permutations and normalized with respect to random assignment (for the random assignment of elements to clusters the value of ARI is 0).
AMI is based on Shannon's Information Theory and measures the MI (*Mutual Information*) of the algorithm assignments and the "real" ones always normalized with respect to the hypothesis of random assignment (Adjusted for Chance). AMI is equal to 1 when the two partitions are identical and is equal to 0 when the MI between two partitions is equal to the expected value for the random assignment.
Which is the most correct measure to use for the comparison between two clusterizations is an open problem. The rule of thumb (Romano et al., 2016) is:

- Use ARI when "real" clustering is made of large, homogeneously sized clusters.

- Use AMI when "real" clustering is unbalanced and there are small clusters.

[6] `https://www.senato.it/leg/18/BGT/Schede/Ddliter/testi/54162_testi.htm`

Being in the second case (unbalanced clustering and small clusters) we will prefer AMI to evaluate the agreement between the cluster assignment proposed by the algorithm and the "real" one, but both measures will be reported.
With the configuration of the *HAC* algorithm described above the comparison between the clusters produced by the algorithm and the "real" ones produces the AMI and ARI scores reported in Table 1

	AMI	ARI
Act n. 1248	0.71476	0.34511
Act n. 2272	0.95248	0.95469

Table 1: Evaluation against gold with AMI and ARI scores. Algorithm configuration: TF vectorization *cosine distance*; *cut-off* T=0.2; *complete linkage*.

5.3. Error Analysis

While for Act n. 2272 there is a good agreement between the grouping produced by the algorithm and the "gold" clusters (about 95%), for Act n. 1248 the results are not as good. An analysis of the assignment errors, in particular for Act no. 1248, reveals that a significant part of the wrong assignments concern amendments whose texts only differ in the identification of the subdivision affected by the modification (for example, suppression of letters or numbers):

Cluster E.1
Al comma 1, sopprimere la lettera s).
Al comma 1, lettera s), sopprimere il numero 1).
Al comma 1, lettera s) sopprimere il numero 1).
Al comma 1, lettera s), sopprimere il numero 2).
Al comma 1, lettera s), sopprimere il numero 3).
...
Al comma 1, lettera s) , sopprimere il numero 4).

Another source of errors relates to amendments dealing with the deletion of an entire article . In fact, the information on the article affected by the suppression is external and is not part of the text.

Cluster E.2
Sopprimere l'articolo.
Sopprimere l'articolo.
Sopprimere l'articolo.
Sopprimere l'articolo.
...

In all previous cases, the limit of a purely lexical comparison among texts is evident. In fact, texts are actually almost identical from the lexical point of view but the meaning and effect of the modifications are completely different.
The better evaluation scores obtained for Act n. 2272 is actually due to the almost complete absence, in the relative dossier, of these types of amendments.

Other sources of error concern the similarity between larger texts and contained texts (marked as similar in the *gold* but not always captured by the similarity measure used with the chosen threshold).
For example:

Cluster E.3
Al comma 3, apportare le seguenti modificazioni: a) sopprimere le parole: «possono essere abilitati ad assumere direttamente le funzioni di stazione appaltante e»; b) sostituire le parole: «in deroga alle disposizioni di legge in materia di contratti pubblici, fatto salvo il» con le seguenti: «nel rispetto delle disposizioni di legge in materia di contratti pubblici e nel».

Al comma 3, sostituire le parole: «e operano in deroga alle disposizioni di legge in materia di contratti pubblici, fatto salvo il rispetto» con le seguenti: «e operano nel rispetto delle disposizioni di legge in materia di contratti pubblici e».

There are other sources of error, less systematic, generally due to similarities that are difficult to grasp automatically, at least with the lexical measures used.

6. Exploiting Domain Features

Amendments are actually a very peculiar kind of technical and domain specific text. They are required to express not only the type (suppression, insertion, replacement) and the content of the modification to apply, but also to identify as accurately as possible the structural division of the bill (paragraph, letter, number..) where to apply it.
As seen in the error analysis in previous section, textual citations to legislative subdivisions are among the major sources of similarity errors when treated purely lexically. For this reason we experimented how the preprocessing of texts with the annotation and normalization of legislative citations affects the clustering performance .
We applied *Linkoln*[7], (IGSG-CNR, 2018), a tool we previously developed for the automatic detection and linking of legal references contained in legal texts written in Italian (Bacci et al., 2019). *Linkoln* is able to detect references to entire acts, and hierarchical divisions therein, including multiple references.

6.1. Experiments with Domain Features Annotation

The following pre-annotations of texts in input to the clustering algorithm were tested and evaluated:

- **artemd** - an indivisible token (e.g. *ARTEMD1*) is added to the text in order to include the information on the amended article (information available among the metadata of the amendment);

[7] `https://gitlab.com/IGSG/LINKOLN/linkoln`

- **div** - texts are pre-processed (via a customization of the *Linkoln* annotation pipeline) in order to detect and normalize citations to legislative subdivisions. The text of the citation is replaced by an indivisible normalized token, e.g.:

  Al comma 1, lettera a), numero 2), sostituire..
  $\longrightarrow$
  Al DIVCOM1LETAITEM2, sostituire..

- **urn** - texts are pre-processed (via *Linkoln*) in order to recognize and normalize legislative citations. The text of citations is replaced by an indivisible normalized token derived from the *urn* standard identifier (Spinosa et al., 2022) of the detected reference, e.g.:

  Dopo il comma 5, inserire il seguente: « 5-bis. L'articolo 1, comma 166, della legge 30 dicembre 2018, n. 145, è sostituito dal seguente: "A valere sui contingente di personale...
  $\longrightarrow$
  Dopo il DIVCOM5, inserire il seguente: «5-bis. L'STATOLEGGE20181230145ART1COM166, è sostituito dal seguente: "A valere sui contingente di personale...)

The idea is that the replacement of citations (either to legislative acts or subdivisions) with a single normalized token allows to reduce the noise and the ambiguity in the comparison of texts.

type	annotation	AMI	ARI
0	no-annotation	0.71476	0.34511
1	artemd	0.71394	0.33288
2	artemd-div	0.85999	0.77947
3	**div**	**0.87381**	**0.83304**
4	urn-div	0.87325	0.83073
5	(full) artemd-urn-div	0.87069	0.81691

Table 2: Act n. 1248 - clustering evaluation with pre-annotations.

type	annotation	AMI	ARI
0	**no-annotation**	**0.95248**	**0.95469**
1	artemd	0.95131	0.95713
2	artemd-div	0.94706	0.95151
3	div	0.94969	0.95431
4	urn-div	0.94138	0.94576
5	(full) artemd-urn-div	0.94024	0.94381

Table 3: Act n. 2272 - clustering evaluation with pre-annotations.

Tables 2 and 3 show the results of the experiments with different pre-annotation configurations:

Type 0: *(no-annotation)* no pre-annotation of the texts;

Type 1: *(artemd)* - a token is added to the text indicating the article of the bill that is affected by the amendment;

Type 2: *(artemd-div)* - like Type 1 plus replacement of detected legislative subdivisions with normalized token;

Type 3: *(div)* - like Type 2 but without adding the token indicating the article being amended;

Type 4: *(urn-div)* - in addition to legislative subdivisions, legislative citations are detected and replaced with a normalized token derived from their *urn* standard identifier;

Type 5: *(artemd-urn-div)* texts are pre-annotated with all *features* (amended article, subdivisions and normalized legislative citations).

Results show a significant improvement (up to 16% in AMI) in clustering performance with pre-annotations of type 2 to 5 over the purely lexical tokenization (type 0). In the overall evaluation on the entire dossier, type 1 annotation does not improve the evaluation scores but in practice, it solves the issue for wrong clusters like Cluster E.2 reported in sect. 5.3
The improvement of evaluation results for Act n. 1248 only, can be explained by the fact that Act n. 2272 includes only few amendments whose textual content is mainly made of legislative references (e.g. suppressive of entire subdivisions) as also shown by the fact that clustering performance without annotation is already high. When dealing with noisy textual content introduced by the ambiguous and repetitive textual tokens of legislative citations, reference annotation and normalization has a beneficial effect in reducing wrong similarities while being neutral in all other cases.

7. Integration with the Amendments Management Application

Along their workflow, amendments are managed by Senate clerks within the application *Gestore Emendamenti* (GEM), an amendments management system developed by the IT office of the Senate.
Similis[8], the service for clustering of similar amendments, was recently integrated in production as an additional experimental functionality within the GEM application.
The algorithm for similarity analysis and clustering is implemented in *Python 3.9* using the well-known *Nltk* and *SciKit* libraries. This algorithm is then included in a microservice also implemented in *Python* using the *Flask* library and exposed with a ReST interface and

[8] `https://github.com/SenatoDellaRepubblica/Similis`

JSON input/output data format. The microservice documentation is in the *OpenApi* standard.
The new functionality allows to compute the similarity clusters of a dossier of amendments and to obtain a visualization of the cluster they belong to in a column of the amendment display grid in GEM. Fig. 3 shows part of the complete dossier of amendments to Act n. 2448 of the 18th legislature (about 6665 amendments) discussed in the 5th Permanent Committee.

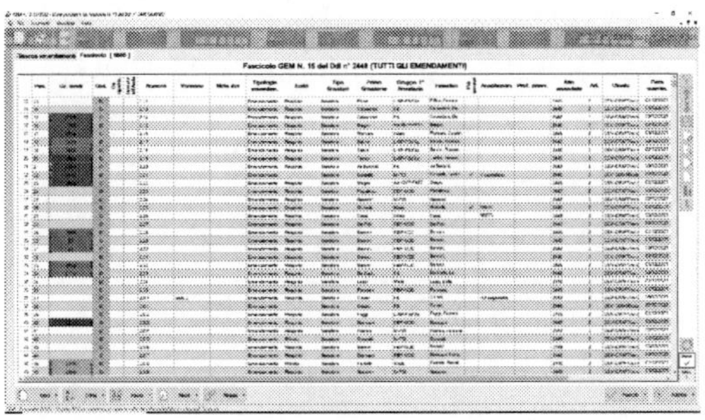

Figure 3: *GEM - amendments management application with cluster visualization.*

In the new "Similar Groups" column of the grid view (Fig. 4), for each amendment belonging to a cluster it is shown:

- the cluster ID with a unique cell color background assigned to the cluster;
- a compactness indicator (showing how close the elements of the cluster are to identical) displayed as a white bar with a shade of red (as a percentage);
- a symbol, on the right of the cell, indicating whether the amendment is at the beginning, in the middle, or at the end of the cluster in the column representation;
- a contextual menu which allows to navigate the elements of the cluster, especially useful for clusters scattered in the column.

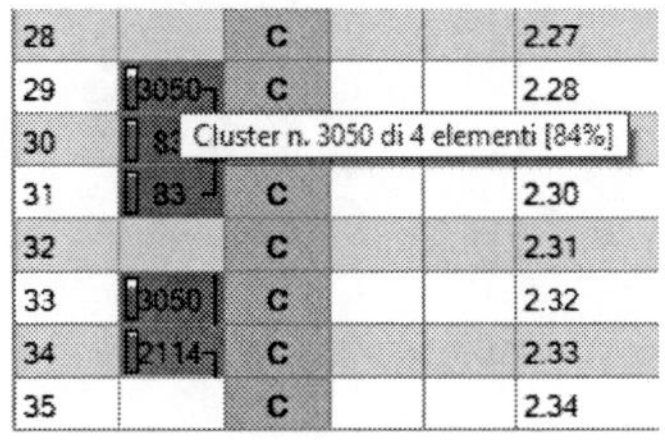

Figure 4: *GEM - detailed view of the cluster column visualization.*

It is also possible to apply a filter to each cluster in order to show in the dossier grid only the amendments belonging to it.

8. Conclusions and Future Work

We experimented standard lexical similarity measures and document clustering algorithms on dossiers of legislative amendments. Preliminary results show that the extraction and annotation of domain features, in particular legislative citations within texts, allow to significantly improve the performance evaluation against manually annotated cluster assignments.
We provided an implementation of the clustering engine exposed as an internal web service within the Italian Senate IT infrastructure. The service is invoked from the application for the management of amendments in use for the Committees' and Assembly's activities. The User Interface of the application was evolved in order to include functionalities for the detection, visualization and navigation of clusters of similar amendments in the examined dossiers. The new functionality is now implemented in production and ready to be made available as an experimental feature to Senate clerks for testing and feedbacks.
Legislative amendments are a peculiar type of text, constrained by drafting rules and having several structural properties and domain features. We plan to automatically extract more of such features in order to further experiment and evaluate the effects of integrating domain knowledge in their automatic similarity analysis.
By making available this experimental functionality to final users we expect to gain a more in-depth evaluation of the quality of detected clusters, report of problematic cases and an overall evaluation of the user experience, including the effectiveness of the visualization in the User Interface, when dealing with incoming amendments dossiers on new proposed laws.

9. Acknowledgements

The authors wish to thank Paola Di Marco, Lucia Pasquini and Stefano Marci for their support in building the gold standard and for the testing efforts of Similis in the Italian Senate committees.

Bibliographical References

Aggarwal, C. C. and Zhai, C. (2012). A Survey of Text Clustering Algorithms. In Charu C. Aggarwal et al., editors, *Mining Text Data*, pages 77–128. Springer US, Boston, MA.

Bacci, L., Agnoloni, T., Marchetti, C., and Battistoni, R. (2019). Improving Public Access to Legislation Through Legal Citations Detection: The Linkoln Project at the Italian Senate. *Knowledge of the Law in the Big Data Age*, pages 149–158. Publisher: IOS Press.

Leskovec, J., Rajaraman, A., and Ullman, J. D. (2020). Chapter 7 - Clustering. In *Mining of Massive Datasets*. Cambridge University Press, New York, NY, 3° edizione edition, January.

Manning, C. D., Schütze, H., and Raghavan, P. (2008). Hierarchical clustering. In *Introduction to Information Retrieval*, pages 346–368. Cambridge University Press, Cambridge.

Notarstefano, J. (2016). Automated Clustering of Similar Amendments. Cern IT Lightning Talks: session 10, Jun.

Romano, S., Vinh, N. X., Bailey, J., and Verspoor, K. (2016). Adjusting for Chance Clustering Comparison Measures. *Journal of Machine Learning Research*, (17):1–32, August.

Spinosa, P., Francesconi, E., and Lupo, C. (2022). A Uniform Resource Name (URN) Namespace for Sources of Law (LEX). Internet Draft draft-spinosa-urn-lex-15, Internet Engineering Task Force, March. Num Pages: 56.

Language Resource References

IGSG-CNR. (2018). *LINKOLN 2.0: the software for the automatic detection and linking of legal references contained in legal texts written in Italian.* https://gitlab.com/IGSG/LINKOLN/linkoln.

Senato. (2016). *Akoma Ntoso - Bulk Data - Senato della Repubblica.* https://github.com/SenatoDellaRepubblica/AkomaNtosoBulkData.

Proceedings of ParlaCLARIN III @ LREC2022 pages 47–55
Marseille, 20 June 2022

Entity Linking in the ParlaMint Corpus

Ruben van Heusden, Maarten Marx, Jaap Kamps
University of Amsterdam
Science Park 904, 1098XH
r.j.vanheusden@uva.nl, maartenmarx@uva.nl, kamps@uva.nl

Abstract

The ParlaMint corpus is a multilingual corpus consisting of the parliamentary debates of seventeen European countries over a span of roughly five years. The automatically annotated versions of these corpora provide us with a wealth of linguistic information, including Named Entities. In order to further increase the research opportunities that can be created with this corpus, the linking of Named Entities to a knowledge base is a crucial step. If this can be done successfully and accurately, a lot of additional information can be gathered from the entities, such as political stance and party affiliation, not only within countries but also between the parliaments of different countries. However, due to the nature of the ParlaMint dataset, this entity linking task is challenging. In this paper, we investigate the task of linking entities from ParlaMint in different languages to a knowledge base, and evaluating the performance of three entity linking methods. We will be using DBPedia spotlight, WikiData and YAGO as the entity linking tools, and evaluate them on local politicians from several countries. We discuss two problems that arise with the entity linking in the ParlaMint corpus, namely inflection, and *aliasing* or the existence of name variants in text. This paper provides a first baseline on entity linking performance on multiple multilingual parliamentary debates, describes the problems that occur when attempting to link entities in ParlaMint, and makes a first attempt at tackling the aforementioned problems with existing methods.

Keywords: entity linking, multilingual, ParlaMint

1. Introduction

The ParlaMint corpus was created by CLARIN[1] in order to facilitate multilingual research on parliamentary proceedings, with the original project concerning four countries, which was later increased to seventeen countries and counting (Erjavec et al., 2021). The goal of the ParlaMint project is the unification of parliamentary debates across European countries, facilitating research of these documents by researchers across various disciplines. The ParlaMint subcorpora consist of both 'plain text' and annotated versions, with the annotated versions containing automatically annotated Part-of-Speech tags, lemmas, Named Entities, as well as a variety of other linguistic features. These Named Entities can be of particular interest to researchers, as they provide them with a landscape of actors and objects present in the dataset, as well as the relationships between these entities.

Although a wide variety of entity linkers is available today, the case of linking Named Entities in the ParlaMint corpus to an existing knowledge base is of a different nature than most other Entity Linking (EL) tasks. Not only are the entities in four different alphabets, some languages lack solid coverage by the EL systems, and many countries have different morphologies and are rich in inflections. Moreover, we are dealing with real world data, and as such some of the entities might be misspelled or ambiguous, or strings that are not a Named Entity are mistakenly tagged as Named Entity. Such mistakes mostly consist of strings being tagged that are too generic, for example 'Mr Speaker', complicating the linking process, or entities being tagged with the incorrect entity type. Although the parliamentary proceedings of the countries in ParlaMint are carefully curated, spelling mistakes do occur on rare occasions. For example in the Dutch subcorpus, several names containing the 'ö' character are written with 'oe' instead, or vice versa, or the name 'pechtold' is reported as 'pechtol'. This is amplified by a problem that is quite specific to spoken text and by extension parliamentary debates, best described as *aliasing* or the existence of name variants. The problem of aliasing occurs when actors are not mentioned with their full name, but for example only their surname, or a nickname. For example 'Joe Biden' might be referred to as 'Mr. Biden', which complicates the linking process, as not having the first name to work with significantly increases ambiguity.

In this research, we evaluate three existing Entity Linking systems, namely **DBPedia-spotlight**, **WikiData** and **YAGO** on the ParlaMint dataset, investigating the aforementioned problems.

Our research questions are as follows:

- **How well do three existing Entity Linking systems (DBPedia, WikiData, YAGO) work on parliamentary actors, such as those present in ParlaMint?** For this research question we extracted members of local parliaments from WikiData and extracted the unique *Q-item* identifiers to obtain gold standard data for individual countries, and provide a fair comparison across countries by having names without inflections and possible spelling errors. We evaluate the accuracy

[1] `https://www.clarin.eu/content/parlamint-towards-comparable-parliamentary-corpora`

of all three systems on the dataset and report the main differences between the three systems, while also focusing on the difference in performance of the linkers across languages. Hereby we extend on the works of Pillai et al. (2019) and Färber et al. (2015) by analysing the Entity Linking component of these three knowledge bases.

- **How much does lemmatization help with improving the performance on languages with a high number of inflections?** For languages such as Polish, Named Entities are inflected quite often, making the Entity Linking process more difficult. In this research question, we make use of the provided lemmas of the Entities in ParlaMint to investigate whether lemmatization can help improve the performance of Entity Linking systems, and when lemmatization is less effective.

- **How can the phenomenon of aliasing be counteracted?** One of the peculiarities of the ParlaMint dataset is the phenomenon of *aliasing*, where names are either abbreviated or nicknames are used. For example in the case of 'Joe Biden' and 'President Biden' or 'Biden'. In this research question we investigate two simple methods of counteracting the phenomenon. The first method works by searching for variants of the name at various levels, for example in debates in the same week, or debates in the same month. The other method uses the speaker metadata present in the ParlaMint corpora to match entities with members of parliament and other speakers.

2. Related Work

Regarding the case of Entity Linking in multiple languages, there have been several papers that address this issue (De Cao et al., 2021; Sil et al., 2018; Botha et al., 2020; McNamee et al., 2011; Pappu et al., 2017). Sil et al. (2018) introduce a neural method for performing entity linking in multiple languages. Their approach is to link entities from different languages to their corresponding entities in the English version of Wikipedia. To achieve this, they train a neural network that makes use of multilingual word embeddings to compare the contexts of entities and candidates, as well as using features such as the number of overlapping words. The model is trained on English entities, and tested on different languages to see how well this zero-shot setting works for the entity linking case. In their work they found that the model is able to achieve state-of-the-art performance on both the monolingual case and the multilingual case, given that multilingual embeddings are available for those countries.

De Cao et al. (2021) makes a clear distinction between the tasks of *Cross Lingual Entity Linking* (XEL) and *Multilingual Entity Linking*(MEL). In the case of Cross Lingual Entity Linking, candidates from different languages are all mapped to entities in a monolingual knowledge base. In the case of Multilingual Entity Linking, candidates from different languages are mapped into a multilingual knowledge base. In their paper they describe their MEL system, which consists of an auto-regressive seq2seq model for computing the context similarity between the entities in text and the candidate entities in the knowledge base.

Our work attempts to bypass the issues associated with language specific knowledge bases, by using the Q-items provided by WikiData as the means of verifying links from entities to the knowledge base. By using these items, entities in a specific language could be linked to the Q-ID of that item, even if the item is represented in another language.

The problem of aliasing, or the usage of name variants and partial names for different types of entities has been studied previously. One study that addressed this problem is Gottipati and Jiang (2011), which attempts to tackle, among other things, the problem of name variants. This is done by query expansion, where both knowledge from the query itself and external knowledge are used to resolve entities. To resolve entities using local knowledge, other named entities in the same document as the query entity are checked to see whether they contain the query entity as a substring. If so, then this entity is added to the query as an alternative variant. The algorithm used in our paper is quite similar to the method for adding local knowledge used in Gottipati and Jiang (2011), with the exception that our method is not limited to one document, but rather includes multiple documents based on the time window.

There have been a multitude of papers that compare different knowledge bases on various aspects, such as consistency and timeliness of information. (Färber et al., 2015; Pillai et al., 2019). Färber et al. (2015) compare several knowledge bases including WikiData, DBPedia and YAGO on a variety of aspects. These aspects include the number of languages included in the knowledge base, which domains are covered, the number of relations in the knowledge base and the whether or not correctness constrains are enforced in the knowledge base, among other criteria. They found that there are various differences between knowledge bases, mostly regarding the amount of information present for facts (such as a description or a source of the fact), but argue that the exact requirements needed for a knowledge base can vary depending on the specific task it is being used for.

3. Method

3.1. Q-Items

Q-items or Q-IDs are the identifiers used in WikiData for identifying unique entities and concepts in the WikiData knowledge base.[2]. These identifiers are cross

[2]`https://www.wikidata.org/wiki/Wikidata:Glossary`

lingual, meaning that for example 'Angela Merkel' will have the same Q-ID, whether the entity is searched in the English or German WikiData. Besides entities, Q-IDs are also given to attributes or properties of entities. For example 'Member of the European Parliament', which has Q-ID $Q27169$. These Q-IDs thus allow for the comparison of entities in different languages and different knowledge bases, given that the knowledge base in question also reports Q Numbers. For both DBPedia and YAGO this is true at least up to a degree, and for entities that do not have this Q-ID, the Q-ID can often be discovered through a WikiPedia link present for the entity.

3.2. Systems

We evaluate three Knowledge Bases / Entity Linking systems: **DBPedia**, **WikiData** and **YAGO**. Below we describe them briefly.

3.2.1. DBPedia

The API from *DBPedia spotlight* (Mendes et al., 2011) is used to detect and link entities in text to the DBPedia knowledge base. In the API the 'candidates' call is used to retrieve candidates for the entity, and the default parameters are used. To link entities from DBPedia with WikiData, we retrieve the Q-items from the entities in DBPedia using the $< owl : SameAs >$ property. If the entity does not have a Q-item, we retrieve the link to the Wikipedia page and retrieve the Q-item through an API call to the WikiMedia API. DBPedia supports less languages than WikiData and YAGO, and the information of an entity is not always present in all languages. To ensure that the maximum performance by DBPedia is achieved, a fallback mechanism is implemented, where if an entity is not encountered in the local DBPedia version, an attempt to retrieve the English version is made. This significantly improved the scores of the model. Ideally, we would want to input entities into the system and bypass the entity recognition system, as we know the inputs are entities. Although DBPedia has this functionality, it is only available for English and works very poorly when applied to other languages. Therefore, the entity recognition component is used but a simple string matching filter is used to ensure no completely inaccurate guesses are made by the system due to language coverage issues.

3.2.2. WikiData

WikiData is a knowledge base created by the WikiMedia foundation, containing roughly 97 million entities in more than 300 languages.[3] For querying WikiData we use the SPARQL endpoint for the WikiData API, using the 'EntitySearch' feature and retrieve the Q-items for the returned entities. We only retrieve the first entity from a list of responses, and set the language for each of the queries, depending on the language of the entity.

[3]https://www.wikidata.org/wiki/Wikidata:Statistics

3.2.3. YAGO

YAGO (Suchanek et al., 2007) is another knowledge base that builds on Wikidata, with the latest version ,YAGO4, containing roughly 64 millions entities at the time of writing. YAGO stores facts in RDF format and uses logical constraints to increase the coherence of the knowledge base, for example by making sure entities can not be persons and places at the same time. [4] For querying YAGO, a similar approach to the one used for WikiData is used, using the SPARQL endpoint of YAGO for querying, providing the language of entities depending on the language the entities are in.

3.3. Comparison

As the ParlaMint corpus is a very large corpus that consists of multiple languages and alphabets, annotating a large set of entities for entity linking is not very feasible. In order to obtain a proxy for the performance of the models on Parlamint, and evaluate their performance on different languages, a baseline test was performed on the names of local politicians from ten countries, extracted from WikiData using membership querying. (Query can be found in Appendix 1). This method of obtaining gold standard for the entity linking process was chosen over manual annotation of ParlaMint entities, as it provides us with high quality Named Entity names that do not contain the noise discussed previously, such as aliasing. However, as the Named Entities used are all members of parliament in their respective countries, we feel that these entities provide an accurate representation of (part of) the ParlaMint corpus and therefore the results obtained for the samples of local politicians should provide a good proxy on the results of the entity linkers on the real ParlaMint data, albeit an ideal case.

For the comparison experiment, we collected 100 members of parliament from ten countries together with their Q-item through a membership query performed on WikiData. We then ran all three systems on the 100 members from parliament, and reported their accuracy for the countries respectively. For the politicians, only people that started in office from 01-01-2014 onward were selected, to be in line with the time period of the ParlaMint project.

This test was conducted to obtain scores of the systems in 'ideal' conditions, with correctly written full names and with minimal ambiguity. This allows us to later manually 'distort' these entities to investigate the effect of aliasing while maintaining gold standard links. It also provides us with a means of comparing the performance of the entity linking systems across different languages, allowing us to analyse whether the performance differs between different languages or language families.

[4]https://yago-knowledge.org/getting-started

3.4. Lemmatization

In order to study the effect of lemmatization on the performance of the three systems, we measure the amount of inflection for all entity types by comparing how many times the original string is equal to the lemma, to get in indication of the amount of inflection for different countries. To gain a more detailed understanding, we selected twenty frequent entities such as Angela Merkel and Donald Trump from the ParlaMint corpus and selected inflections by finding entities that contain these entities as substring. Thus for each entity we obtain a list of variants of that name. For each of these variants, we run WikiData, as this was the best performing model in the comparison, and calculate the overall precision by weighting the scores of each variant by the amount of times they occur, to get a more realistic indication of the effect of lemmatization when applied to individual entities.

3.5. Aliasing

Because entities are often unambiguous within a local context, aliasing can occur, following Grice's Maxim of quantity. That is, given a situation in which an entity is known to the participants in for example a debate, referencing this person by surname provides the appropriate amount of information to successfully disambiguate that person in that context, without the superfluous addition of the first name when this is not required. However, when attempting to link individual terms, this phenomenon becomes problematic, as it increases the ambiguity of an entity.

To study the effect of aliasing on the performance of the three models, we set up an experiment where we only use surnames for the entity linking process. We use the local politicians collected for the 'ideal' scenario here, as these can be easily changed and we can readily generate the gold standard for them. We decided to limit the experiment to five countries, namely The Netherlands, Belgium, France, Poland and the United Kingdom. For each of these countries, we select 10 entities and remove their first names. For example 'Margaret Thatcher' becomes 'Thatcher'. We then evaluate the performance of the three models on these lists of surnames and report the scores.

3.5.1. Temporal De-Aliasing Algorithm

The method used in this paper is similar to the method used in Gottipati and Jiang (2011). We start with an entity E and a list of discovered variants V. At the start, this record only contains E itself, $V = \{E\}$. Now we find all other Named Entities in the document with the same type as E, and if they contain E as a substring, they are added to V. To maximise the number of discovered variants, we also introduce a temporal parameter in the algorithm, which determines how many debates 'around' the mention of the entity we consider for discovering variants. After this procedure, we obtain the variant v^* from V that occurred the most in the considered documents (excluding E itself). This entity v^* is then used as the query to the knowledge base.

3.5.2. Restricting Considered Entities

Apart from the temporal based approach, we also experiment with the usage of the metadata available for the ParlaMint corpora. In this version we make use of the lists of members of parliament available for a specific country. For a named entity found in the text, we compare it to the database of parliamentary members of that country using a simple cosine similarity score between character n-grams of the surnames of the target entity and the knowledge base. We use character two and three grams for encoding the entities into vectors. As some entities might not be present in the metadata of that particular country (such as ministers from different countries) we also consider ministers from other countries if no compatible match is found within the metadata of the country itself. If no entity has a high enough similarity threshold, we report it as a NIL entity. Because the performance of this method partly relies on the entities selected for the linking (i.e. only selecting local entities will prevent the step of using metadata from different countries to have an effect), we take a balanced sample of local politicians and entities referenced in multiple countries (the 'international entities'), instead of using the names from local politicians from the WikiData membership query. For both categories, we select ten entities at random.

3.6. Code

Our code is available at `https://github.com/RubenvanHeusden/LRECMultilingualEntityLinkingCode`

4. Results

In this section the results to the experiments posed in Section 3 are presented in the order that they are discussed above.

4.1. Comparison

Table 1 shows the results of running DBPedia, WikiData and YAGO on the automatically retrieved local politicians. One thing that can be noticed immediately is the high performance of the WikiData system on the task. One obvious reason for this is the fact that the entities were extracted from the WikiData knowledge base, and therefore the system is more likely to get the entities correct. However, some mistakes are still made by the WikiData system. Further inspection of the results showed that this was almost entirely due to ambiguous names, which caused WikiData to link with incorrect entities, for example 'James Morris' being linked to a researcher instead of a politician for the United Kingdom, or 'Sophie Hermans' being linked to a researcher instead of the correct politician for the Netherlands.

For DBPedia, the scores are on par with WikiData for a few countries such as NL and FR, but fall behind for

Country	DBPedia	WikiData	YAGO
NL	0.97	**0.98**	0.56
DE	0.58	**0.94**	0.60
FR	0.95	**0.97**	0.95
CZ	0.31*	**0.95**	0.87
HU	0.75	**0.90**	0.73
EN	0.74	**0.87**	0.78
IT	0.18*	0.95	**0.97**
IS	0.67*	**1.00**	0.85
DK	0.69	**0.96**	0.79
TR	0.52	**0.97**	0.71
Mean	0.74	**0.94**	0.73

Table 1: Accuracy of DBPedia, WikiData and YAGO on 100 local politicians from 8 countries. (* signifies that the model either did not support the language, or the language was not properly recognized. These countries were also not considered for the mean of the system performance).

most other countries. There are several reasons for this lower performance, the main reason being the inability of the system to recognize entities. If an entity is not recognized or only partially recognized, a correct link cannot be made. To eliminate the effect of mistakes in the recognition of DBPedia, we have also used the 'search' API. However, this API is only available in English, and although it can sometimes link entities in other languages, this is by no means guaranteed. Furthermore, although Czech and Italian are reportedly supported by DBPedia, the API was not able to retrieve resources in those languages. For YAGO the main problem is also that the system does not recognize the entity present, and thus returning a NIL result.

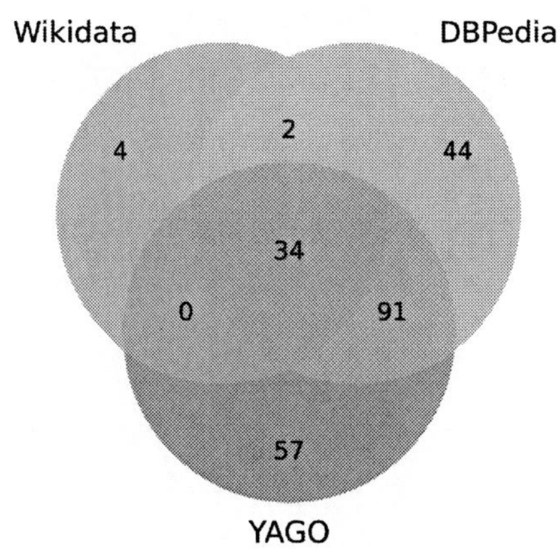

Figure 1: Venn diagram showing the overlap between the mistakes of the 3 systems (excluding IT, IS and CZ).

Figure 1 shows the distribution of errors between the three systems. The first observation that can be made is that there are only a few instances in which WikiData makes a mistakes that the other two systems did not make. However, we do see that in the cases of both DBPedia and YAGO, the system makes mistakes that the others two systems do not make, more often. DBPedia and YAGO also overlap on a large number of cases, showing that these systems are quite similar not only in scores (as seen in Table 1) but also in the type of mistakes they make. The overlap between all three systems shows that when WikiData makes a mistake, the other two systems almost always also make that mistake. In the majority of cases where all three systems made the same mistake, this concerned the miss classification of an entity, rather than the system outputting a NIL prediction.

If we compare the performances of the systems across different languages, we can see that WikiData is quite stable across different languages, with English being the worst performing language. This can be partially explained by the fact that English is the most prevalent language on WikiPedia, and thus more cases of ambiguity arise than for other languages, a hypothesis supported by the types of mistakes made by WikiData. For DBPedia and YAGO there is a bit more variance across languages, with YAGO scoring relatively low on NL and DE, as well as on TR. DBPedia scores higher on NL, but also scores relatively low on DE and TR, suggesting a gap in the coverage of entities in those languages for the two systems. However, these results are on ideal cases in which the name is in canonical form, and the full name is used. It does give as an indication of the relative performances of the systems on the languages in ParlaMint. Next we will investigate what happens when these ideal conditions are not met, in the cases of the presence of inflections name variants.

4.2. Lemmatization

In this section, the results of lemmatization are presented, with several examples being given, and a detailed analysis of lemmatization being made for the PER entities of seven countries. In Table 2 several examples of the names of people being inflected are shown. Inspection of the lemmas found that among the countries that inflect words most often are Polish, Czech and Latvian. With for example Dutch and English having virtually no inflections, something that is in line with the intuition about the morphologies of these languages.

Entity	Inflections
Angela Merkel	Angeli Merkel Merkelova
Donald Tusk	Donaldem Tuskiem Donaldzie Tusku Donaldowi Tuskowi

Table 2: Examples of inflections of popular entities in different languages in the Polish language.

As can be seen from Table 3, the amount of lemmatization various greatly from country to country, as well as from type to type. Especially the MISC entity type is often changed after lemmatization. This is not unexpected, as the MISC entity type can contain a great variety of entities, and thus these might be lemmatized more often.

	LOC	MISC	ORG	PER
LV	-	-	0.87	0.60
TR	0.52	-	0.72	0.45
IS	0.67	0.80	0.64	0.41
CZ	0.77	0.38	0.65	0.41
PL	0.87	-	0.76	0.36
HR	0.62	0.91	0.69	0.36
SI	0.76	0.91	0.75	0.34
IT	0.06	-	0.13	0.26
FR	0.40	0.18	0.35	0.24
BE	0.09	0.42	0.26	0.15
HU	-	0.26	0.18	0.15
LT	0.24	0.50	0.88	0.05
DK	0.12	0.61	0.41	0.04
NL	0.04	0.41	0.10	0.03
ES	0.01	0.08	0.04	0.02
BG	0.09	0.73	0.68	0.01
GB	0.00	0.06	0.01	0.00

Table 3: Fraction of the unique entities in each subcorpus of ParlaMint that changed after lemmatization. NaN values indicate the category was not present in that subcorpus. Sorted on the PER entity type.

Surprisingly, organisations also get lemmatized frequently. Examples of this include 'Partij voor de Dieren' being lemmatized to 'Partij voor de Dier' in The Netherlands, and 'east midlands trains' being lemmatized to 'east midlands train' in the United Kingdom, removing the plural 's'. This suggests using the lemmatized version of organisations might actually be harmful to the performance entity linking models on those entities. Investigating the PER entity type it can be seen that countries such as Latvia, Turkey and Icelandic have entities that are lemmatized often, and thus we expected these countries to benefit most from using lemmas for entity linking.

In Table 4, the results of lemmatization are shown on the names of twenty international PER entities for seven countries when linked using WikiData. It can be seen that for PL, CZ, HR and IS, the lemmatization has a clear positive effect on the scores of the EL system, showing that for these languages lemmatization is beneficial. For NL and BG however, the usage of lemmatization has a negative effect on performance, especially for BG. This is most likely due to the fact that these languages do not inflect words often, and thus lemmatization might 'correct' entities that do not need to be corrected. An example of this for NL would be the lemmatization of 'Edith Schippers' into 'Edith Schipper', where a correct entity is lemmatized into an incorrect one.

Country	Percentage of entities recognized	
	Before lemmatization	After lemmatization
PL	0.33	0.53
CZ	0.37	0.67
HR	0.29	0.74
IS	0.67	0.75
LV	0.16	0.24
BG	0.77	0.40
NL	0.91	0.89

Table 4: Accuracy of the WikiData system on a set of 20 entities, before and after lemmatization.

To conclude this research question, the usage of lemmatization has a significant positive impact on several languages with a large number of inflections, such as PL, CZ and HR. For languages with a low number of inflections, such as BG and NL, the lemmatization has no effect, and for BG, the performance is actually severely hampered by the unnecessary use of lemmatization.

4.3. Aliasing

When evaluating the systems on the manually aliased names, it was found that all three systems failed to recognize persons only mentioned by their surname, achieving a score of zero for all tested countries. However, it is important to mention that in the case of DBPedia, the system does not return any entity, while in the case of WikiData and YAGO, the systems often returned a 'family name' entity for the surname or a reference to a disambiguation page.

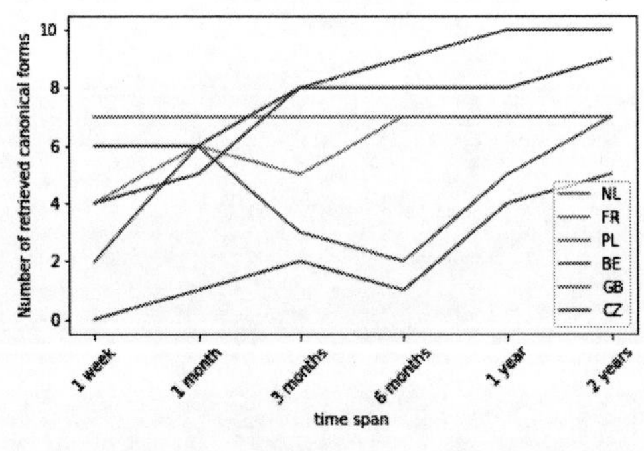

Figure 2: Results of applying the aliasing algorithm with various time spans for six countries (the time span is from both sides, so '1 month' means 1 month earlier and 1 month later).

In Table 2 the results of applying the time-based dealiasing algorithm with various settings for the temporal granularity are shown. The y-axis represents the total number of entities that was correctly resolved, out of a maximum of ten entities. For most countries, the amount of correctly de-aliased mentions increases as the time span parameter is increased with the exception of Poland, for which the number of resolved entities remains the same. The drops in the number of resolved entities can be explained by the fact that over a certain time period, for ambiguous entities, another incorrect variant might be more popular than the correct variant, causes a drop that is later resolved as the time span is increased. This will largely depend on the chosen entity, as less ambiguous names will not have this problem to the same extent.

4.3.1. Constricted Entity Disambiguation

Below are the results of applying the disambiguation method that only considers entity present in the speaker metadata of the specific country, or the speaker metadata of the other countries. As can be seen from Table 5, the performance of a simple EL system using string similarity performs relatively poor when considering only local entities. This is not surprising, as the samples are a mix of local and international figures. However, for some countries the scores for using only local politicians are also low for the local politicians group. This is the case in Belgium, where it was found that most entities from the sample were in fact not parliamentary actors. In the case of using speaker metadata from multiple parliaments, the performance of the simple model on all countries is increased, suggesting this approach definitely has some merit over the approach only using local entities.

Country	Only local	Multiple Parliaments
NL	0.55	0.80
FR	0.45	0.60
PL	0.35	0.60
BE	0.20	0.35
GB	0.40	0.55
CZ	0.35	0.45

Table 5: Results of applying the de-aliasing approach based on ParlaMint speaker metadata, with using only metadata from the country itself, and metadata on members of parliament from other countries. For each country, 20 entities were evaluated.

To conclude this research question, we found that the simple time based de-aliasing method we used is already quite effective for some cases in the de-aliasing of names, although the limitations of the method are also clear. This does provide us with some insights into the problem of aliasing, and possibilities for future work on more complicated methods. One interesting possibility could be to extend the idea of the constricted entity linking method, and incorporate the usage of the linked metadata present in some of the corpora, with links to Wikipedia, Twitter or other external sources. These sources can then be used to provide more context surrounding the entity, to provide a model with more information in the case of ambiguous entities, a method often used within the field of Entity Linking.

5. Discussion & Future Work

In future work, the approaches used for alleviating the effects of aliasing could be refined, by for example using context from debates for the surnames and using methods such as BERT other Transformer based models to score entities. For the analysis of the lemmatization effects, the lemmatizers that each country employed themselves were used. Without detailed knowledge of the language and the software used, there is no way of assessing the quality of these lemmatizers. This might cause differing results for the lemmatization of certain countries. Although this work only deals with the PER entities present in the ParlaMint corpus, it can also be extended to the other entity types present in the corpus. The problems of lemmatization and aliasing also exist for these entity types, albeit in slightly different forms and severities. For organization names, aliasing will most likely take the form of abbreviations of names, which could be resolved through the usage of local context, possibly combined with a list of abbreviations for large organisations. In the case of locations, the main challenge in linking the entities (apart from lemmatization) is the ambiguity arising from different locations having the same name. This could possibly be resolved by only considering locations within the country of the parliamentary debate, or giving higher weights to locations within that country.

6. Conclusion

In this paper we investigated the performance of three entity linking systems on data from the ParlaMint corpus, and we found that the WikiData system performed the best overall for the local politicians, although all systems performed relatively well. Through investigation of the ParlaMint dataset, we found that for certain languages, entities are often inflected or entities are referred to by aliases. These phenomena create noise in the dataset, and are problematic for creating entity links for all entities in ParlaMint. We investigated the effect of lemmatization on the entities in the dataset by using the automatically generated lemmas of the entities and comparing the performance of WikiData on entities before and after lemmatization. We found that for PL, CZ and HR, lemmatization had a big effect, while in particular for BG and NL the effects were negligible or it actually hampered performance, in the case of BG. Thus for some languages, lemmatization can have a profound positive effect on the performance of entity linking systems, although one must be careful in choosing which languages to use it for, as to not harm the performance of the model by lemmatizing unnecessarily. Finally, we investigated the effect of aliasing on the ability of models to properly link entities, by manually aliasing ten ground truth politicians for five languages. We found that it severely inhibited the models from finding the correct entities. Through the usage of a simple heuristic using corpus statistics and term occurrence in files, a significant portion of names could be resolved, although the simplicity of the heuristic also introduces errors concerning ambiguity, leaving an interesting opportunity for future work.

7. Language Resource References

Erjavec, Tomaž and Ogrodniczuk, Maciej and Osenova, Petya and Ljubešić, Nikola and Simov, Kiril and Grigorova, Vladislava and Rudolf, Michał and Pančur, Andrej and Kopp, Matyáš and Barkarson, Starkaur and Steingrímsson, Steinhór and van der Pol, Henk and Depoorter, Griet and de Does, Jesse and Jongejan, Bart and Haltrup Hansen, Dorte and Navarretta, Costanza and Calzada Pérez, María and de Macedo, Luciana D. and van Heusden, Ruben and Marx, Maarten and Çöltekin, Çağrı and Coole, Matthew and Agnoloni, Tommaso and Frontini, Francesca and Montemagni, Simonetta and Quochi, Valeria and Venturi, Giulia and Ruisi, Manuela and Marchetti, Carlo and Battistoni, Roberto and Sebők, Miklós and Ring, Orsolya and Darģis, Roberts and Utka, Andrius and Petkevičius, Mindaugas and Briedienė, Monika and Krilavičius, Tomas and Morkevičius, Vaidas and Bartolini, Roberto and Cimino, Andrea and Diwersy, Sascha and Luxardo, Giancarlo and Rayson, Paul. (2021). *Linguistically annotated multilingual comparable corpora of parliamentary debates ParlaMint.ana 2.1.*

8. Bibliographical References

Botha, J. A., Shan, Z., and Gillick, D. (2020). Entity linking in 100 languages. *arXiv preprint arXiv:2011.02690.*

De Cao, N., Wu, L., Popat, K., Artetxe, M., Goyal, N., Plekhanov, M., Zettlemoyer, L., Cancedda, N., Riedel, S., and Petroni, F. (2021). Multilingual autoregressive entity linking. *arXiv preprint arXiv:2103.12528.*

Färber, M., Ell, B., Menne, C., and Rettinger, A. (2015). A comparative survey of dbpedia, freebase, opencyc, wikidata, and yago. *Semantic Web Journal*, 1(1):1–5.

Gottipati, S. and Jiang, J. (2011). Linking entities to a knowledge base with query expansion. Association for Computational Linguistics.

McNamee, P., Mayfield, J., Lawrie, D., Oard, D. W., and Doermann, D. (2011). Cross-language entity linking. In *Proceedings of 5th International Joint Conference on Natural Language Processing*, pages 255–263.

Mendes, P. N., Jakob, M., García-Silva, A., and Bizer, C. (2011). Dbpedia spotlight: shedding light on the web of documents. In *Proceedings of the 7th international conference on semantic systems*, pages 1–8.

Pappu, A., Blanco, R., Mehdad, Y., Stent, A., and Thadani, K. (2017). Lightweight multilingual entity extraction and linking. In *Proceedings of the Tenth ACM International Conference on Web Search and Data Mining*, pages 365–374.

Pillai, S. G., Soon, L.-K., and Haw, S.-C. (2019). Comparing dbpedia, wikidata, and yago for web information retrieval. In *Intelligent and Interactive Computing*, pages 525–535. Springer.

Sil, A., Kundu, G., Florian, R., and Hamza, W. (2018). Neural cross-lingual entity linking. In *Thirty-Second AAAI Conference on Artificial Intelligence.*

Suchanek, F. M., Kasneci, G., and Weikum, G. (2007). Yago: a core of semantic knowledge. In *Proceedings of the 16th international conference on World Wide Web*, pages 697–706.

A. Appendix

SPARQL query to retrieve local politicians

```
SELECT ?item ?itemLabel ?group ?groupLabel
?district ?districtLabel ?term ?termLabel ?start ?end
WHERE
{
  ?item p:P39 ?statement .
  ?statement ps:P39/wdt:P279* wd:%s ; pq:P580 ?start .
  OPTIONAL { ?statement pq:P2937 ?term }
  OPTIONAL { ?statement pq:P582  ?end }
  OPTIONAL { ?statement pq:P768  ?district }
  OPTIONAL { ?statement pq:P4100 ?group }
  FILTER((!BOUND(?end) || ?end > NOW())
  && (?start > "2014-01-01T00:00:00+00:00"^^xsd:dateTime) )
  SERVICE wikibase:label { bd:serviceParam wikibase:language "[AUTO_LANGUAGE],en". }
}
ORDER BY ?start ?end
```

Listing 1: Example of Named Entity XML tag

Trump
Macron
Salvini
Putin
Kennedy
Berlusconi
Merkel
Juncker
Cameron
Obama
Blair
Thatcher
Stalin
Barnier
Hitler
Johnson
Tusk
Churchill
Timmermans
Hollande

Table 6: Entities used for the lemmatization Research Question

Proceedings of ParlaCLARIN III @ LREC2022 pages 56–60
Marseille, 20 June 2022

Visualizing Parliamentary Speeches as Networks: The DYLEN Tool

Seung-bin Yim[1], Katharina Wünsche[1], Asil Cetin[1], Julia Neidhardt[2], Andreas Baumann[3], Tanja Wissik[1]
[1]Austrian Academy of Sciences,[2] TU Wien,[3] University of Vienna
Vienna, Austria
[1]{seung-bin.yim, katharina.wuensche, asil.cetin tanja.wissik}@oeaw.ac.at
[2]julia.neidhardt@tuwien.ac.at, [3]andreas.baumann@univie.ac.at

Abstract

In this paper, we present a web based interactive visualization tool for lexical networks based on the utterances of Austrian Members of Parliament. The tool is designed to compare two networks in parallel and is composed of graph visualization, node-metrics comparison and time-series comparison components that are interconnected with each other.

Keywords: parliament data, lexical networks, network visualisation, diachronic comparison

1. Introduction

Analyzing and visualizing the dynamics of language change is of interest to a broad field of studies including linguistics, natural language processing, digital humanities (DH) and computer science. In the project Diachronic Dynamics of Lexical Networks (DYLEN), we investigated lexico-semantic change based on two large corpora and how this change can be measured and visualized (Baumann et al., 2019). In this paper we will describe one component of the DYLEN tool[1] [2] that was developed within the DYLEN project, which visualizes lexical networks based on the utterances of the Austrian Members of Parliament (MPs) between 1996 and 2017 and enables diachronic comparison. The development of a new tool was necessary because no out of the box network-visualisation tool was specifically designed to allow diachronic network comparison and supported all the functions which were identified by potential users during a dedicated workshop. The tool adds a web based interactive visualization tool to the digital humanities toolbox that can be used to explore and compare different lexical networks over time and visualize related data.

2. Related Work

There are two common approaches for visualizing lexical networks: word clouds and graph-based visualizations. While word clouds (or collocation clouds) as for example described by Beavan (Beavan, 2008), Rayson (Rayson, 2008)), Heimerl et al. (Heimerl et al., 2014) and Xu et al. (Xu et al., 2016) display collocated words as a sorted list and represent statistical measures such as frequency or Mutual Information via a word's font size, color or brightness, graph-based visualizations usually show network graphs with a node for each word and edges representing collocations and/or semantic associations. Additional statistical information such as word frequency or the Mutual Information of two words can be encoded via the edge thickness or node size, whereas color is often used to represent a word's part-of-speech tag (cf. (Laußmann et al., 2011); (Lee and Jhang, 2013); (Brezina et al., 2015)). For the visualization of even more information like time series or multiple statistical values at once, (Rayson et al., 2017) propose multidimensional visualizations that combine multiple visualization components such as line charts, network graphs or tables. Network visualizations are not the only way of presenting linguistic, and in particular parliamentary, data: journalists of the German news magazine Zeit Online combine line charts, video snippets, pictograms and textual annotations in an online tool that allows users to analyze German parliamentary speeches from 1949 to 2019 (Zeit Online, 2019). For browsing and searching German political speeches from 1990 onward, (Barbaresi, 2018) provides the tool politische-reden.eu that offers basic visualizations for word-frequency distributions as well as the option to read full speeches containing a selected word.

3. Data

For analyzing and visualizing the lexical repertoire of MPs in the Austrian parliament in the DYLEN tool we used lexical networks (Marakasova et al., 2022). The constructed networks are based on the ParlAT Corpus, containing the proceedings of the Austrian Parliament from 1996 to 2017 (Wissik and Pirker, 2018). The ParlAT data was split into 376 subcorpora, containing all utterances of a single MP, out of which networks were constructed. Not all the MPs had enough utterance data to construct networks. Thus, not all MPs are searchable in the tool. Here, nodes represent lexical words (nouns, proper nouns, verbs and adjectives). Two nodes are

[1]The DYLEN tool is available at https://dylen-tool.acdh.oeaw.ac.at/

[2]Source code is available at https://github.com/acdh-oeaw/dylen-tool and https://github.com/acdh-oeaw/dylen-backend

linked if they share similar contexts (based on pairwise similarities between the respective word embeddings). For the general networks of parties, the subcorpora of grouped MPs according to their party affiliation were created. In such a general network nodes stand for the most frequent words that constitute the selected corpus of an MP or party.

4. Use Case and Tool Description

The objective of the DYLEN tool was to support diachronic comparison of lexical networks. In the following, we will present a use case for the application of the tool, describe the tool development process and its components.

4.1. Use Case

Does the general content of MPs' speeches remain stable or does it change over time? Quantitative analysis on different levels have shown that changes in governing coalitions have an impact on the lexical usage of parties in the Austrian parliament (e.g. (Hofmann et al., 2020), (Kern et al., 2021)). Can these dynamics also be seen via the visualization and comparison of lexical networks of single MPs? As an example we have chosen an MP of the SPÖ (Social Democratic Party of Austria) who was MP from 1983 to 2017: Dr. Josef Cap. The available data visualisations are covering the period from 1996 to 2016. We will look in more details at the network of the year 2003, where SPÖ was in opposition and at the network of the year 2014, where the SPÖ was in governing coalition with the ÖVP (Austrian People's Party). In the chosen time period, the MP had similar roles, in 2003 he was chairman of the parliamentary group and in 2014 he was deputy chairman of the parliamentary group.

4.2. Tool Development Process

The features of the tool were derived from user stories identified in a workshop that was conducted at the beginning of the project (Knoll et al., 2020). The dual track agile approach (Sedano et al., 2020) was followed for the development of the tool, two usability test rounds were conducted to improve the user experience. Vue.js and d3.js were used for the frontend, a Java Spring boot backend service was developed and made available for query via GraphQL interface.

4.3. Tool Components

When the user selects the network to explore and clicks on the submit button, a dashboard appears with three visualization components (Fig. 1), namely network-graph visualization, node-metrics comparison and time-series components. The network-graph visualization component visualizes networks of words used by a certain MP or party. The node-metrics comparison component lets users compare different networks based on their metrics [3] (e.g., degree centrality or betweenness centrality). The time-series component shows the change in difference in similarity measures relative to specific years (first, last, previous). The visualizations can be used to explore different aspects of the lexical networks. Each of the components were designed to let users compare two networks in parallel. In this paper, we will focus on the description of the network graph visualization and the node-metrics comparison based on the use case example.

4.3.1. Network Graph Visualization

Network-graph visualizations consist of nodes and edges that connect the nodes. Different information can be encoded using the size, thickness, colors of nodes and edges. In the DYLEN tool, nodes are most frequently occurring words within the selected corpus (i.e. single MP or party), and two nodes are connected by an edge if they share similar contexts. The similarity between the nodes are calculated by first training word embeddings with skip-gram model, then applying pairwise cosine similarity function. The size of nodes are determined by word frequency, while the thickness of edges represent contextual/semantic similarity of the words. The colors of the labels represent different part-of-speech tags.

A major aspect to consider when visualizing network data is the size of the network and visualization performance. Theoretically, a lexical network can have as many nodes as the size of the vocabulary and all the connections between them, such large graphs can be hard to explore and inefficient to visualize. Different graph filtering algorithms exist to tackle these issues (Hu and Lau, 2013), which can be divided into two groups, stochastic and deterministic graph filtering algorithms (Von Landesberger et al., 2011). Early user tests have shown that the lexical networks of parliamentary data are too large for visualization. The tool provides a deterministic graph filter based on eight different network metrics, such as betweenness centrality. In addition to the graph filter, a timeout mechanism is implemented to prevent users from unpleasant user experience when they select a large range of filter values. Another problem that makes interpretation and exploration of large graph visualizations difficult is edge cluttering. To account for this issue, the tool provides an option to change the visibility of edges with a slider based on similarity values alongside with Pan, Zoom in/out functionalities. Since the tool is designed for diachronic comparison, it allows to visualize two networks at the same time. There is a year slider to select a specific year to be visualized. For example, the lexical networks of Dr. Josef Cap in two different years are quite different in size. Based on this, one could hypothesize that speakers of the opposition party

[3]Detailed descriptions about the metrics can be found on the *Technical Details* page of *Node Metrics Comparison* tab at the start page of the tool

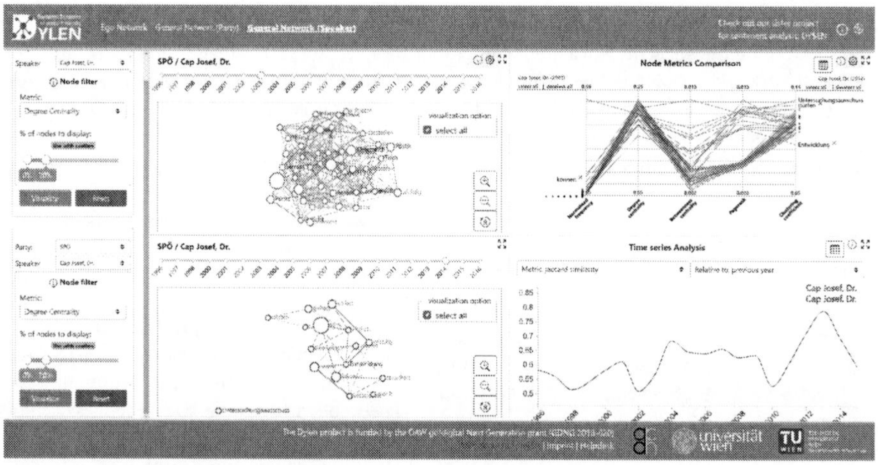

Figure 1: Dashboard view with all components.

might be more active in the parliament. Hypotheses like this can be then tested with a larger number of individuals. As demonstrated with the use case described above, network visualization can be useful for comparison of networks in their size and complexity over time, and for deriving hypotheses based on analyses like this.

4.3.2. Node Metrics Comparison

The node-metrics comparison component can be used to explore the network topology. For example, different centrality measures can be used to extract key phrases (Boudin, 2013). Parallel coordinates are used as the visualization technique. The visualization consists of n parallel axes, where n is the number of node metrics to be visualized. The chart allows visualization of all nodes of a network in one chart and facilitates the comparison of node metrics. Parallel coordinates can be used for identification of outliers, trends or clusters (Johansson and Forsell, 2015). Some challenges had to be addressed to increase the usability of the visualization. One issue was the labels of the nodes. Lots of nodes had metrics values within a small range, simply displaying the full labels would lead to overlapping labels. This issue is addressed by replacing the labels by the asterisk (*) character to denote that multiple labels are overlapping. When the user hovers over the asterisk characters, the full label is displayed. Another way to deal with the issue is to reorder the axes and put the metrics with more even distribution to the most left and right axis, respectively. In addition to the parallel coordinates view, the node-metrics comparison component offers a table view, with which the user can select/filter/sort nodes. This is useful if the network is too large and has to be reduced in size for proper visualization. An example application of keyword extraction using centrality metrics for our use case is shown in Table 1. It is extracted by sorting the nodes according to the two centrality metrics that have been demonstrated to be useful for keyphrase extraction (Boudin, 2013) and taking the ranks of the nodes. The extracted keywords are fairly different between the networks in the years 2003 and 2014 and could be a subject of further analysis.

4.4. Interactivity Between Components

One of the tool's main strengths is the interactivity between the individual visualizations, i.e., the network graphs, the parallel coordinates plot as well as the table view, which supports the Visual Information-Seeking Mantra defined by (Shneiderman, 1996): "overview first, zoom and filter, then details on demand". While the graphs provide a first overview of the network structure and highlight the most frequent words based on their node sizes, users who are interested in the network metrics and their distribution can take a look at the parallel coordinates plot and highlight words by hovering over them in either the graph or the parallel coordinates visualization. Moreover, users have the option to select and deselect words by clicking on their labels or (un)checking them in the table view, which can reduce the complexity by filtering out words that are of minor interest.

4.5. Challenges and Limitations

There are some remaining challenges and limitations. One aspect is the size of the network and the performance of visualization. This could be addressed by either increasing the efficiency of the visualization itself by different algorithms/libraries/APIs or by reducing the number of nodes and edges with sophisticated filtering algorithms, such as edge filtering. Another challenge is the visualization of multidimensional data in the case of node metrics comparison. Parallel coordinates are useful when the user is interested in analyzing patterns or outliers, but presenting the node labels within a limited screen size remains a challenge.

Network	Top 10 Keywords (nouns) - Closeness Centrality	Top 10 Keywords (nouns) - Degree Centrality
Cap Josef, Dr. (2003)	Wahrheit, Situation, Österreicher, Kritik Abfangjäger, Teil, Tag, Art, Möglichkeit, Haider	Wahrheit, Situation, Österreicher, Kritik, Abfangjäger, Art, Möglichkeit, Haider, Entwicklung, Gegengeschäft
Cap Josef, Dr. (2014)	Regierung, Österreich, Weg, Möglichkeit Jahr, Land, Modell, Diskussion, Russland, Union	Regierung, Land, Modell, Österreich, Weg, Möglichkeit, Jahr, Diskussion, Russland, Union

Table 1: Keyword extraction using centrality metrics.

5. Future Work

The practical contribution of our work, the interactive visual analysis tool, has the potential to be used with other similar corpora for exploratory analysis in the future. Even though the scope of our current project focused on the Austrian Parliament data, the detailed requirement analysis conducted with the users (Knoll et al., 2020) and the successful technical implementation present a solid basis for future work. Further development in the database layer of the tool to import data in different structures and customization possibilities for visualization components will be the primary tasks to achieve this. Another functionality that could be useful is to add filters for each of the metrics axes and combine with brushing (Martin and Ward, 1995). A feature that was planned but not yet implemented is keyword-in-context, which could improve the value of the tool, since it was requested by multiple usability testers.

6. Conclusion

We have introduced the DYLEN Tool, a web-based interactive visualization tool for lexical networks of Austrian Parliament proceedings. The tool can be used to explore and analyze lexical networks via three different visualization components, such as graph visualization, parallel coordinates and time series visualization and demonstrated to be useful for deriving hypotheses and gaining an overview of network topologies. However, some challenges remain such as performance issues related to the size of the networks and more effective visualization for multidimensional data for comparing node metrics.

7. Acknowledgements

This research was funded by the ÖAW go!digital Next Generation grant (GDNG 2018-02).

8. Bibliographical References

Barbaresi, A. (2018). A corpus of German political speeches from the 21st century. Proceedings of the Eleventh International Conference on Language Resources and Evaluation (LREC 2018), pages 792–797, Miyazaki, Japan. ELRA.

Baumann, A., Neidhardt, J., and Wissik, T. (2019). Dylen: Diachronic dynamics of lexical networks. In *LDK (Posters)*, pages 24–28.

Beavan, D. (2008). Glimpses through the clouds: collocates in a new light, June.

Boudin, F. (2013). A comparison of centrality measures for graph-based keyphrase extraction. In *International joint conference on natural language processing (IJCNLP)*, pages 834–838.

Brezina, V., McEnery, T., and Wattam, S. (2015). Collocations in context:a new perspective on collocation networks.

Heimerl, F., Lohmann, S., Lange, S., and Ertl, T. (2014). Word Cloud Explorer: Text Analytics Based on Word Clouds. In *2014 47th Hawaii International Conference on System Sciences*, pages 1833–1842, January. ISSN: 1530-1605.

Hofmann, K., Marakasova, A., Baumann, A., Neidhardt, J., and Wissik, T. (2020). Comparing lexical usage in political discourse across diachronic corpora. In *Proceedings of the ParlaCLARIN II Workshop*, pages 58–65.

Hu, P. and Lau, W. C. (2013). A survey and taxonomy of graph sampling. *arXiv preprint arXiv:1308.5865*.

Johansson, J. and Forsell, C. (2015). Evaluation of parallel coordinates: Overview, categorization and guidelines for future research. *IEEE transactions on visualization and computer graphics*, 22(1):579–588.

Kern, B. M., Hofmann, K., Baumann, A., and Wissik, T. (2021). Komparative zeitreihenanalyse der lexikalischen stabilität und emotion in österreichischen korpusdaten. *Proceedings of Digital Lexis and beyond at OELT*.

Knoll, C., Cetin, A., Möller, T., and Meyer, M. (2020). Extending recommendations for creative visualization-opportunities workshops. In *2020 IEEE Workshop on Evaluation and Beyond-Methodological Approaches to Visualization (BELIV)*, pages 81–88. IEEE.

Laußmann, J., Lux, M., Menßen, C., and Mehler, A. (2011). An online platform for visualizing lexical networks. In *Web Intelligence and Intelligent Agent Technology, IEEE/WIC/ACM International Conference on*, volume 1, pages 495–496, Los Alamitos, CA, USA, aug. IEEE Computer Society.

Lee, S.-M. and Jhang, S.-E. (2013). Visualization of Collocational Networks: Maritime English Keywords.

Martin, A. R. and Ward, M. O. (1995). High dimensional brushing for interactive exploration of multivariate data. In *Visualization Conference, IEEE*, pages 271–271. IEEE Computer Society.

Rayson, P. E., Mariani, J. A., Anderson-Cooper, B., Baron, A., Gullick, D. S., Moore, A., and Wattam, S. (2017). Towards interactive multidimensional visualisations for corpus linguistics. *Journal for language technology and computational linguistics*, 31(1):27–49.

Rayson, P. (2008). From key words to key semantic domains. *International Journal of Corpus Linguistics*, 13(4):519–549, January.

Sedano, T., Ralph, P., and Peraire, C. (2020). Dual-Track Development. *IEEE Software*, 37(6):58–64, November.

Shneiderman, B. (1996). The Eyes Have It: A Task by Data Type Taxonomy for Information Visualizations. In *Proceedings of the 1996 IEEE Symposium on Visual Languages*, VL '96, page 336, USA, September. IEEE Computer Society.

Von Landesberger, T., Kuijper, A., Schreck, T., Kohlhammer, J., van Wijk, J. J., Fekete, J.-D., and Fellner, D. W. (2011). Visual analysis of large graphs: state-of-the-art and future research challenges. In *Computer graphics forum*, volume 30, pages 1719–1749. Wiley Online Library.

Xu, J., Tao, Y., and Lin, H. (2016). Semantic word cloud generation based on word embeddings. In *2016 IEEE Pacific Visualization Symposium (PacificVis)*, pages 239–243, April. ISSN: 2165-8773.

Zeit Online. (2019). Darüber spricht der bundestag.

9. Language Resource References

Marakasova, A., Neidhardt, J., Baumann, A., and Wissik, T. (2022). Dylen: Diachronic dynamics of lexical networks.

Wissik, T. and Pirker, H. (2018). Parlat beta corpus of austrian parliamentary records. In *Proceedings of the LREC 2018 Workshop'ParlaCLARIN*, pages 20–23.

Proceedings of ParlaCLARIN III @ LREC2022 pages 61–70
Marseille, 20 June 2022

Emotions Running High? A Synopsis of the State of Turkish Politics through the ParlaMint Corpus

Gül M. Kurtoğlu Eskişar,[1] **Çağrı Çöltekin**[2]
[1]Department of International Relations, Dokuz Eylül University, Turkey
[2]Department of Linguistics, University of Tübingen, Germany
gul.kurtoglu@deu.edu.tr, ccoltekin@sfs.uni-tuebingen.de

Abstract

We present the initial results of our quantitative study on emotions (Anger, Disgust, Fear, Happiness, Sadness and Surprise) in Turkish parliament (2011–2021). We use machine learning models to assign emotion scores to all speeches delivered in the parliament during this period, and observe any changes to them in relation to major political and social events in Turkey. We highlight a number of interesting observations, such as anger being the dominant emotion in parliamentary speeches, and the ruling party showing more stable emotions compared to the political opposition, despite its depiction as a populist party in the literature.

Keywords: emotion, parliamentary corpora, Turkey

1. Introduction

Increasing polarization of politics (Enyedi, 2016; McCoy et al., 2018) and global rise of populism (Moffitt, 2016; Cox, 2018) can be counted among the main catalysts of the renewed interest in the role of sentiments in politics. At the same time, studying emotions in politics has traditionally remained a polarizing subject in political science literature (Marcus, 2000, p.221). On the one hand, there is the idea that emotions are "the expression of personal emotions," (Marcus, 2000, p.222) and that political issues ultimately carry sentimental value (Werlen et al., 2021, p.1). On the other hand is the rationalist approach, where emotions become handmaidens to the goals that actors pursue. However, recent studies increasingly problematize this Manichean outlook, and argue that "[i]nformal, affective manifestations of politics are enormously influential, profoundly shaping inter- and intra-national democracy." (Prior and van Hoef, 2018, p.48).

While exploring the relevance of sentiments in politics, parliaments in particular have remained at the center of attention as "[p]arliamentary and legislative debate transcripts provide access to information concerning the opinions, positions, and policy preferences of elected politicians." (Abercrombie and Batista-Navarro, 2020). Although parliaments exist in a variety of regime settings, ranging from democratic to autocratic, the existing literature almost exclusively consist of studies on democracies in the developed world to better understand their political processes (Diermeier et al., 2012; Kapočiūtė-Dzikienė and Krupavičius, 2014; Werlen et al., 2021; Rheault et al., 2016; Abercrombie et al., 2019). It creates a lacuna, as recent research suggests that parliamentary debates in non-democratic settings can be as nuanced and worth exploring as their democratic counterparts (Kurtoğlu Eskisar and Durmuşlar, 2021). Hence, any relevant input or data from non-democracies has the potential to significantly contribute to the study of emotions in politics.

The goal of our study is therefore threefold. First, we aim to analyze the Turkish parliamentary transcripts for their emotional content. Although there are some studies on the nature of parliamentary debates in Turkey (Elçi, 2019), including content analyses of the speeches of political leaders on specific issues (Devran and Özcan, 2016; Güngör, 2014) or linguistic analysis of emotions in Turkish (Toçoğlu and Alpkoçak, 2018), none of them exclusively focus on emotions in the Turkish parliament, or are as comprehensive in their coverage and findings as our study. Through an overview of emotions in the Turkish parliament, our second aim is to offer a preliminary discussion of their role in hybrid regimes, which is mostly overlooked in the relevant bodies of literature. Although the subject of this study naturally falls under the focus of political science, relatively few political scientists have done research on the topic using computational methods (Hopkins and King, 2010, p.230). Therefore, by adopting a multi-disciplinary (computational linguistics and political science) approach to the topic, this study also hopes to contribute to the growing number of such collaborative studies in the field.

We single out Turkey for further discussion for several reasons. First, as a country that has witnessed a regime shift (from democratic to hybrid or autocratic) in recent years, monitoring the leading emotions in Turkish politics can help to discover any existing linkage between regime types and emotions expressed in comparative parliamentary settings. An analysis on Turkish parliament is also a welcome addition to the existing literature, which has few comparative studies (Abercrombie et al., 2019, p.6). Methodologically speaking, it reduces measurement inconsistencies or bias by focusing on the same parliament under different regime settings.

2. Turkish Politics in Recent Years: A Synopsis

To explore our goals, we overview the prevailing emotions or sentiments in the Turkish parliament from June 2011 to April 2021. For our purposes, we focus on the following emotional states as markers in our study: Fear, anger, surprise, disgust and sadness and happiness.[1]

Although ruled by the same political party (Adalet ve Kalkinma Partisi, AKP) since 2002, Turkish politics has experienced many ups and downs. During the period studied, Turkey experienced a number of significant social and political events, some of which include the following: Gezi protests (28 May 2013-30 August 2013), "bribery and corruption operations" (17-25 December 2013), ban on access to social media (Twitter) on (20 March 2014-3 April 2014), local elections (30 March 2014), Soma mining accident where 301 miners lost their lives (30 May 2014), presidential elections (10 August 2014), Kurdish refugee inflow (approximately 150000 people) from Kobani, Syria in September 2014, general elections (7 June 2015, 1 November 2015), series of terrorist attacks that resulted in 862 deaths (7 June 2015–1 November 2015),[2] restart of negotiations with EU since 5 November 2013 (14 December 2015), coup d'etat attempt (15 July 2016), announcement of the state of emergency (20 July 2016), referendum for constitutional changes (16 April 2017), ban on access to Wikipedia (29 April 2017), presidential elections (24 June 2018), removal of the state of emergency (19 July 2018), local elections (31 March 2019), annulment of local election results for Istanbul (6 May 2019), local election for Istanbul (23 June 2019).

3. Method

We investigate the research questions outlined above using data-driven, quantitative methods on parliamentary corpora. In particular, we use machine learning methods to detect emotion in parliamentary speeches, and base our analyses on changes in emotions in the parliamentary discourse through time.

[1]Both choices, the date range and the emotions studied, are motivated by practical reasons. The range covers the complete range available from the Turkish section of the current version of the ParlaMint corpus (Erjavec et al., 2021), and the emotions are the ones studied by the Turkish emotion corpus TREMO (Toçoğlu and Alpkoçak, 2018).

[2]"Haber analiz: Davutoğlu ne demek istedi, 862 insanın hayatını kaybettiği 7 Haziran ve 1 Kasım seçimleri arasında neler oldu?" `https://t24.com.tr/haber/haber-analiz-davutoglu-ne-demek-istedi-862-insanin-hayatini-kaybettigi-7-haziran-ve-1-kasim-secimleri-arasinda-neler-oldu,836288` (accessed on 15 March 2022).

Country	Period	Segments	Avg. Length
TR	2011–2021	357 726	108.58
UK	2014–2021	505 490	212.65

Table 1: Basic statistics of the parliamentary corpora used. The last column lists the average number of words in each speech segment.

3.1. Data

Parliamentary data The main source of data we use is from the ParlaMint corpora collection (Erjavec et al., 2021; Erjavec et al., 2022). ParlaMint is a multilingual, multiple-country collection of parliamentary corpora, mainly consisting of the transcriptions of the speeches delivered in the main proceedings of the parliaments of the respective countries. The ParlaMint project currently publishes parliamentary corpora of 17 countries in a unified format. We use the section of the Turkish corpus (ParlaMint-TR) for our main analysis. Although our focus is analyzing emotion in the Turkish parliament, we also run a similar analysis on ParlaMint-GB to verify the validity of our analysis. We note, however, that this only serves as a general sanity check. The differences in the parliamentary debates in two countries as well as the methodology we use makes a detailed comparison difficult.

For Turkish parliament, we include the top five parties based on number of speeches in the given period, and take the `segments` in the TEI-encoded corpus which are uninterrupted speech segments by the speakers. This leaves *Adalet ve Kalkinma Partisi* (AKP, 'Justice and Development Party'), *Cumhuriyet Halk Partisi* (CHP, 'Republican People's Party'), *Milliyetçi Hareket Partisi* (MHP, 'Nationalist Movement Party'), *Halkların Demokratik Partisi* (HDP, 'Peoples' Democratic Party'), and *İYİ Parti* (IYIP, 'Good Party') from Turkish parliament. For comparison with the UK parliament, we followed a similar approach, considering the most active four parties: *Conservative Party* (CON), *Labour Party* (LAB), *Liberal Democrats* (LD), *Scottish National Party* (SNP). The most outspoken fifth group in the ParlaMint-GB corpus was the '*Crossbencher*'s of the British House of Lords, which we left out in our data. Table 1 presents basic statistics on the parliamentary corpora used in this study.

Emotion corpora To train the machine learning methods for emotion classification, we make use of the TREMO data set for Turkish (Toçoğlu and Alpkoçak, 2018). TREMO is a corpus of sentences annotated manually for six emotion classes (Anger, Disgust, Fear, Happiness, Sadness and Surprise). Toçoğlu and Alpkoçak (2018) follow well-known ISEAR data set (Scherer and Wallbott, 1994), where a large number of participants are asked to describe experiences associated with each emotion. The texts provided by participants were further checked by experts, filtering out the

Corpus	Class	Instances	Avg. Length
TREMO		25 989	7.02
	Anger	4723	7.14
	Disgust	3620	6.15
	Fear	4393	6.51
	Happy	5229	7.14
	Sadness	5021	7.10
	Surprise	3003	8.26
ISEAR		5395	24.49
	Anger	1079	27.54
	Disgust	1066	23.92
	Fear	1076	26.71
	Joy	1092	22.00
	Sadness	1082	22.33

Table 2: Basic statistics of the emotion-annotated corpora used in this study.

conflicting texts and labels. The TREMO data set differs from the original ISEAR data, leaving 'Shame' and 'Guilt' emotions out, introducing a new emotion class 'Surprise', and using the label 'Happiness' instead of 'Joy'. For uniformity, we use the ISEAR data for English. ISEAR is available in a few slightly different versions on the Internet. We use the version from Bostan and Klinger (2018), but remove the instance belonging to 'Shame' and 'Guilt' classes. The statistics of the data sets as we use in this study are presented in Table 2.

3.2. Machine Learning Model

On both data sets, we use one-vs-rest SVM classifiers, with sparse character and word n-grams. SVM classifiers have been a common and successful choice for similar classification tasks (see Abercrombie and Batista-Navarro (2020) for a recent review). The n-gram features from both the characters and words are combined to a single feature matrix before applying TF-IDF weighting. We do not apply any preprocessing, except considering case normalization as a hyperparameter along with the maximum character and word n-grams included in the features and the SVM regularization parameter 'C' (the hyperparameter ranges and optimum values are documented in Appendix B). To find the optimum hyperparameters we perform a random search with 3000 iterations and pick the hyperparameter setting with the highest mean F1 score (macro-averaged) over 10-fold cross validation. We use the Python scikit-learn library (Pedregosa et al., 2011) for all machine learning experiments.

The macro averaged F1-scores of the respective models are 90.51% (sd=0.77 over 10 cross validation folds) on the TREMO data set, and 71.53% (sd=1.51) on the ISEAR data set. Although not directly comparable because of metrics reported and/or slight differences in the classes used in the experiments, these scores indicate substantially better models than the state-of-the-art scores reported in Toçoğlu and Alpkoçak (2018) and Bostan and Klinger (2018) (86% accuracy, and 62.2% macro-averaged F1 score, respectively).

3.3. Assigning Emotion Scores

The models with the best set of hyperparameters are re-trained using the complete data and used for assigning scores to each speech segment in the parliamentary data. Since we are not interested in assigning a single label to each segment, but detect the 'amount of a particular emotion' in text, we take the distance to the decision boundary of each one-vs-rest classifier, and take the sigmoid of each distance value to normalize the scores between 0 and 1. In the scores presented in the rest of this paper, a value of 1 is a confident estimate of the expression of a particular emotion, while a value 0 is a confident estimate that the given emotion is not expressed in a particular speech. A value close to 0.5 indicates that the classifier is rather uncertain.

In time-based visualizations displayed in the next section, each data point refers to the average emotion scores over a moth starting at the indicated date. We are interested in the change in the scores over time. An approximate interpretation of an absolute value at a particular date is similar to above. However, a value close to 0 means most speeches are non-emotional, 'rational'; a value close to 1 would mean that most speeches are emotionally loaded, and a value of 0.5 would indicate an equal number of emotional and non-emotional speeches.

4. Results

We summarize the overall emotional landscape of Turkish politics in Figure 1, which presents the average emotion scores for five largest parties in the Turkish parliament. The scores presented in the figure are averaged over all speeches during a month, and smoothed to show long-term trends more clearly. It is possible to divide our observations into general and party-specific findings. Due to the almost constant flow of political crises and issues experienced at home and abroad since 2011, and in line with earlier observations on Turkish foreign policy (Oran, 2010, p.3) and the populist character of the main political parties in Turkey (Baykan, 2018; Elçi, 2019), prior to conducting our research, we expected a relatively high variability of emotions in the parliament (cf. Figure 5 and 6 in the Appendix A, presenting a similar display of the UK parliament, where the scores seem more stable, despite the fact that the period also covers a rather volatile period of British politics due to Brexit).

Despite the series of volatile political events and populist characteristics attributed to Turkish politics in the literature, however, in Figure 1, the average scores remain below 0.5, indicating relatively non-emotional, rational speeches delivered in the parliament. More specifically, contrary to our expectations, political parties such as AKP have displayed less emotions than expected. We believe that this finding directly chal-

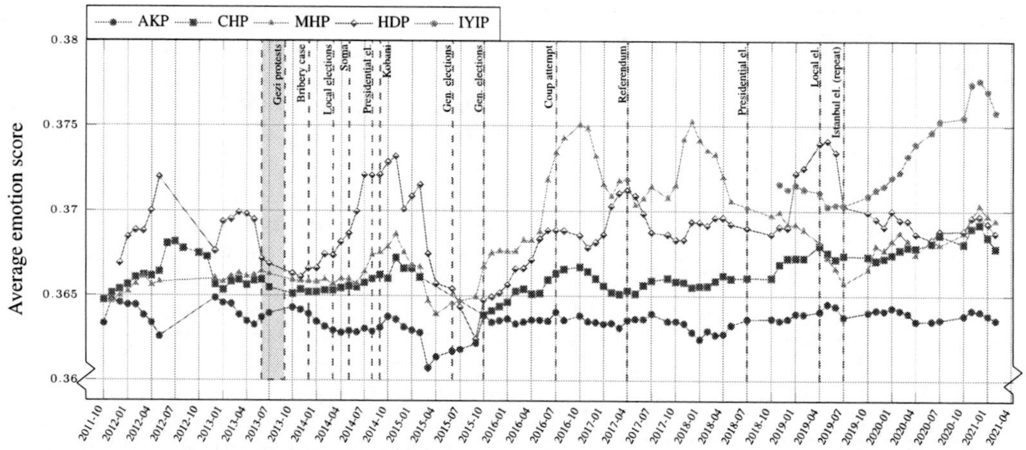

Figure 1: Average emotion scores for five parties in Turkish parliament throughout the period available from ParlaMint. The scores are averages of all emotion scores of speeches of all members of a party for a month. To display of longer-term trends, each data point represents an average of five-month window centered on the indicated month. Approximate dates of the periods of some of the events noted in Section 2 are indicated with vertical lines or shaded regions.

lenges the existing arguments in the literature on populism. Although more in-depth analysis is required to arrive at conclusive results, some possible factors behind this outcome are worth a mention: First, as an extension of the Weberian ideal type of a modern state, it is possible that discussions in a parliamentary setting are more 'rational' than 'emotional.' The second explanation is based on a rational choice approach: Since parliamentary debates are rarely followed closely and consistently by the public, politicians may have little incentive to adopt a sentimental speech style – for any political bargaining process, their immediate address, after all, is other politicians and not the public. Another reason for relatively stable and low emotion scores displayed by AKP could be attributed to its governing role. It may be a general tendency for the governing parties to express less emotion, in particular anger, in comparison to the opposition parties in the same parliament. This explanation is also supported by the emotion scores of the Conservative Party shown in Figure 5.

To display the particular emotions expressed in the parliament, Figure 2 presents the average emotion scores for all speakers during the period investigated. Averaging emotions across all parties seems to hide the variability of them in this figure. A clear finding here is that anger is the leading emotion in parliamentary speeches. Furthermore, there is a slight increase in anger, surprise and sadness, and a drop in happiness scores in time.

Since anger is the emotion that is displayed most frequently by all parties in the parliament, we present the anger scores per party in Figure 3. Detailed plots showing other emotions in a similar manner are provided in Figure 4.

Another interesting general finding is the relative persistence of emotional traits in the Turkish parliament in time. For instance, despite the new presidential system adopted in 2018, the outlook of parliamentary speeches has not drastically changed or decreased. This continuity may be due to a lag effect of the habits of political actors. If this assumption is valid, we would expect this effect to be measurably less in a follow up research.

A third general finding for the Turkish parliament has been the relatively constant, or unchanging emotions of all parties toward certain political events, such as the July 15 2016 coup attempt. Even parties that exist on the opposite sides of the political spectrum (e.g., ultranationalist MHP vs pro-Kurdish HDP) have displayed similar emotions during that time period. Whether this relative homogeneity of emotions is unique to the Turkish parliament, or can be traced in other parliamentary settings or not is probably worth exploring in another research.

In addition to these general findings, we also obtained a few counterintuitive results concerning the ruling party and the opponent parties in Turkey. First, HDP seems to have displayed more emotions compared to other political parties in our study. Moreover, it has also shown more anger compared to other political parties during the given time period. One possible reason behind this finding can stem from the party's identity: As the latest representative of a long chain of pro-Kurdish political parties in Turkish politics, HDP has frequently experienced repression, threat of prosecution or even party closure throughout its existence. Therefore, ceteris paribus, these conditions might have led it to display more anger compared to other political parties in the parliament.

HDP's overall level of display of emotions is followed by MHP–its polar opposite in terms of ideological and identity disposition. Unlike HDP or other parties, how-

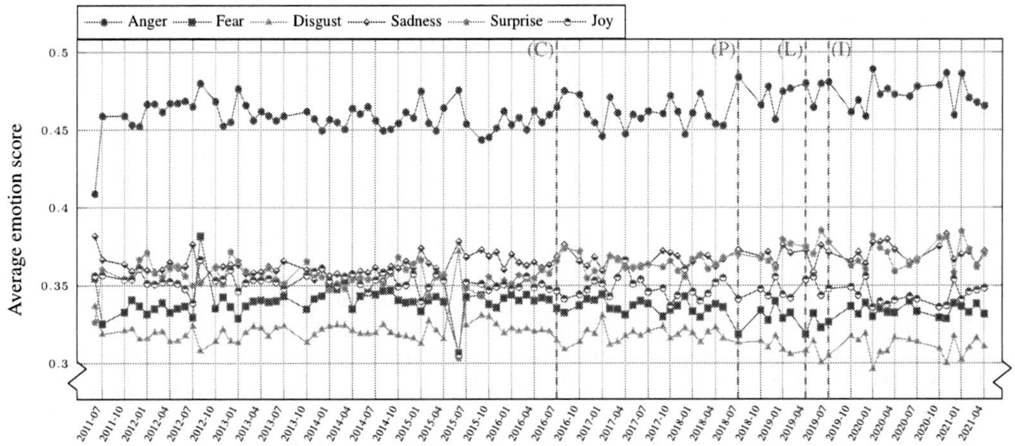

Figure 2: Average emotion scores for five parties in the Turkish parliament throughout the period available from ParlaMint. The scores are averages of all emotion scores of speeches of all members of a party for a month. Unlike the other figures, the scores are not smoothed in this figure. The marked horizontal lines correspond to 2016 military (C)oup attempt, 2018 (P)resedential elections after constitutional change to the 'presidential system', 2019 (L)ocal elections, and repeated local elections in (I)stanbul.

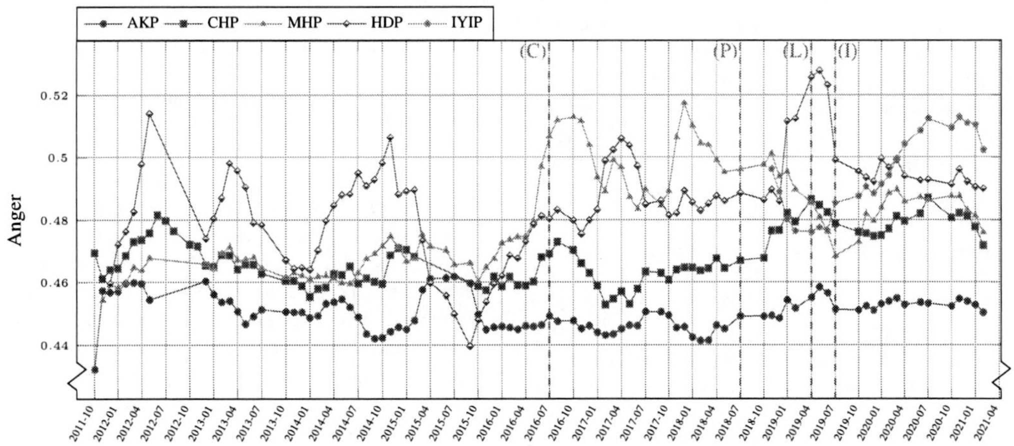

Figure 3: Average anger scores for five parties in Turkish parliament throughout the period available from ParlaMint. The scores are averages of all emotion scores of speeches of all members of a party for a month. To display of longer-term trends, each data point represents an average of five-month window centered on the indicated month. The marked horizontal lines correspond to 2016 military (C)oup attempt, 2018 (P)resedential elections after constitutional change to the 'presidential system', 2019 (L)ocal elections, and repeated local elections in (I)stanbul.

ever, MHP's display of anger (second highest after HDP) starts to decrease after 2018. The small but noticeable drop in anger levels in MHP can be explained with the political alliance it formed with the ruling AKP, whose anger levels have remained surprisingly low throughout the time period under focus. Although AKP–MHP rapprochement dates back earlier (Kurtoğlu Eskisar and Durmuşlar, 2021), the impact of their alliance became clear to all political players without any doubts in 2018 presidential elections. As a result of joining powers with the ruling party, MHP's display of emotions can be expected to run parallel to AKP, which has displayed low levels of anger compared to other political parties in time. A second possible explanation for the drop of anger level in MHP can be explained by the emergence of IYIP – a splinter party from MHP. IYIP may have taken over the anger level of MHP due to its initial identity as the primary nationalist/right wing opposition party filling the vacuum of MHP.

Among the political parties that are included in our study, IYIP has the shortest history. It formed a group in the Turkish parliament on 22 April 2018, and is thus, arguably, the most difficult party to discuss here. Albeit on a lower level, and for a shorter time period, similar to HDP, IYIP's overall anger level seems higher than other political parties, such as CHP or AKP. Yet, on average, we also observe that the speeches of IYIP have wavered in a way that cancels out those speeches with emotions with those that have remained mostly devoid of emotions. One possible explanation for this emotional oscillation may be due to the party's brief past: As a new party that splintered from MHP, which has put its mark on Turkish politics for decades, IYIP politicians may feel the need to prove their credentials and show themselves as a viable alternative to MHP. During its establishment, both MHP and AKP targeted IYIP, which may have also led it to adopt a more defensive tone and increase its anger levels. At the same time, however, IYIP has also tried to position itself as a center-right political party, which is the default stance of almost all political parties that have managed to come into power in Turkish politics for decades. As a result, the initial tendency to try to take over the place of MHP may have been replaced by the goal to establish itself as a center-right party in Turkish politics, which can also explain the variance.

CHP displays overall lower levels of anger compared to the other opposition parties, but nevertheless, they are still elevated compared to the AKP. Although CHP has been an opposition party for decades now, it is also the oldest political party of Turkey. Its relatively stable position in Turkish politics can explain its overall lower levels of anger compared to other political opposition parties in time. Another factor may also rise from its identity as a secular, rational party at the center of the political spectrum in Turkey. At the same time, despite its lower levels of anger compared to MHP, the second oldest political party in the parliament, the anger levels of both parties intersect in April 2019, following the local elections on 31 March 2019, when AKP lost in several major cities, including Istanbul to CHP. After the rejection of election results in Istanbul by the Supreme Electoral Council (Yüksek Seçim Kurulu), the election in Istanbul was repeated on 23 June 2019, where CHP won again, but this time by a far greater margin. The repetition of elections in Istanbul was regarded as unfair by CHP, which can also explain their highest anger level in the observed time period.[3]

Among all parties that are mentioned so far, the results concerning AKP are possibly the most counterintuitive: An initial overview of anger levels in AKP shows that although it may have displayed more anger prior to 2013, it decreased after 2013 and has remained consistently low in time. The initial change in the anger level and relative stability afterwards may arise from their self confidence in imagining themselves to be the ruler of the state. As the political party that has ruled Turkey since 2002, and in charge of all main state institutions, AKP has not been concerned with political survival in a long time, which can explain its low anger levels compared to other parties in the opposition.

Before wrapping up this section, due to its importance as a political event, a brief overview of the general reactions of all parties to the coup attempt on 15 July 2016 is useful.[4] Overall, the general reactions of political parties to this major event has ranged from spikes observed in anger, followed by surprise and sadness (see Figure 4). At the same time, their feelings of happiness, fear and (interestingly) disgust took a dip. For AKP, although anger levels have remained fairly consistent in time, during the coup attempt surprise and sadness took the front seat for emotions, instead of anger. Meanwhile, CHP has shown surprise and sadness along with anger, and, notwithstanding the presence of anger for HDP, surprise and sadness also seemed to prevail. For MHP, it was sadness and surprise that came out as a more prominent feeling, followed by anger against the coup.

5. Discussion

Although this study is based on initial observations and findings from the Turkish parliamentary corpus, it is still possible to draw some tentative conclusions and hypotheses for further in-depth research. One such assumption would involve the relationship between the regime type and the display of emotions in parliamentary corpus: As a regime displays more authoritarian traits, one can expect the parliamentary speeches of the dominant party to display less anger than the parties representing the opposition, possibly due to its diminished accountability for its actions. However, parties under existential threat (party closure or other forms of repression or threat against their identity) can be more inclined to display more anger in their speeches. In an authoritarian setting, ceteris paribus, one can expect more emotional display by opposition parties, as doing so may help increase their credentials as a political opponent for potential supporters. At the same time, loyal opposition in authoritarian settings are likely to display similar emotions to the ruling party. Although emotions are frequently associated with populism, our study suggests that this assumption requires further inquiry: Contrary to such expectations, display of emotions in a parliamentary corpus may also signify a more democratic setting, where actors with different political leanings are free to express their thoughts and ideas without fear of persecution. Although increased polarization can lead political actors to adopt a more aggressive or angry tone in their speeches to consolidate their followers, our initial findings do not seem to support

[3]"İstanbul seçim sonuçları: YSK kararı bekleniyor, iptal dahil kulislerde hangi ihtimaller konuşuluyor?," `https://www.bbc.com/turkce/haberler-turkiye-47861165` (accessed on 23 March 2022).

[4]Since IYIP was established after this event, it is left outside our discussion here.

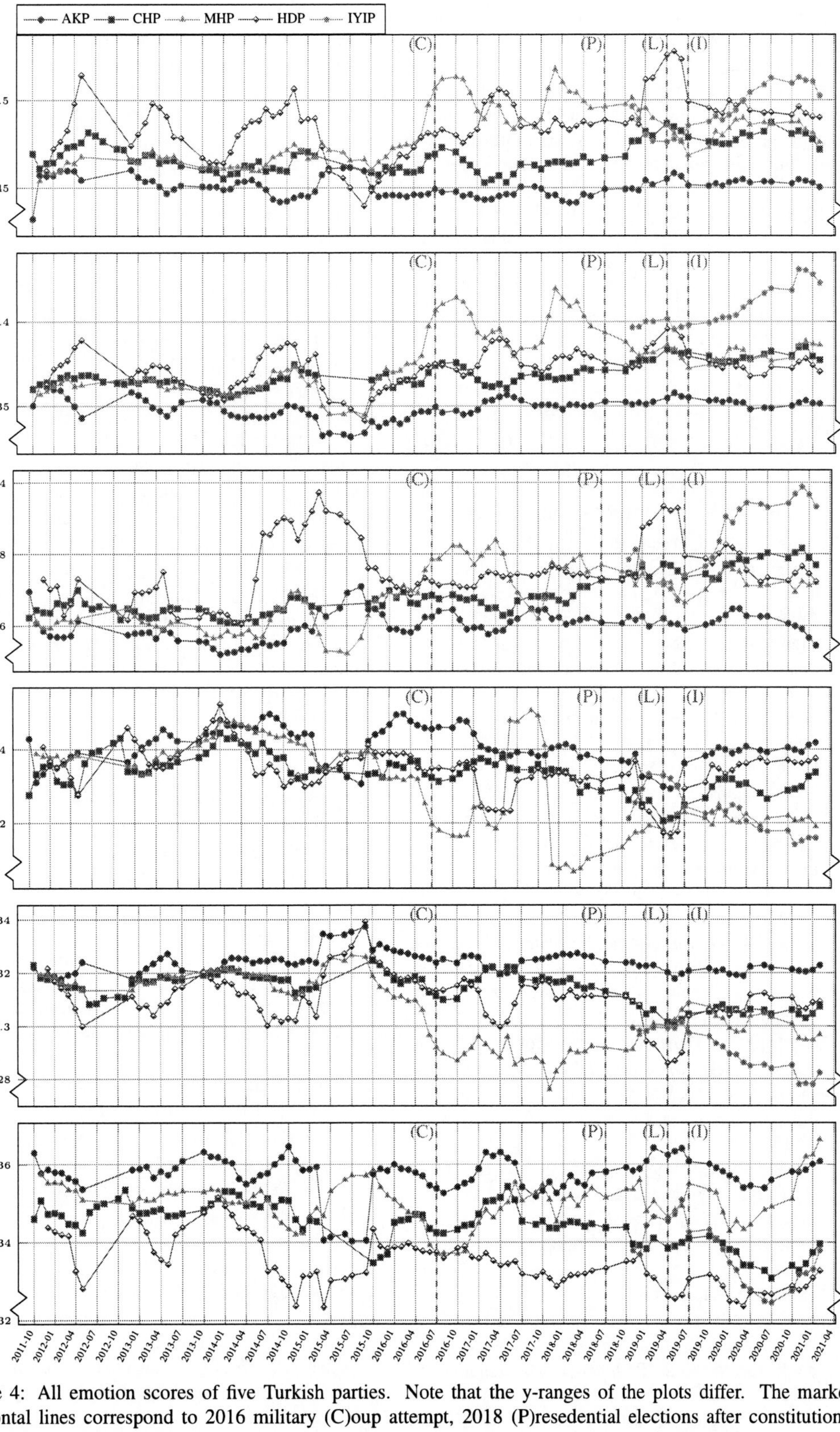

Figure 4: All emotion scores of five Turkish parties. Note that the y-ranges of the plots differ. The marked horizontal lines correspond to 2016 military (C)oup attempt, 2018 (P)resedential elections after constitutional change to the 'presidential system', 2019 (L)ocal elections, and repeated local elections in (I)stanbul.

this assumption. Still, more in-depth analyses can reveal conclusive results on this issue later.
Methodologically, our study is based on descriptive visualizations of emotion scores of parliamentary speeches measured by a machine learning method. Although we believe that the trends we discuss are clear, to test specific hypotheses, use of proper hypothesis testing mechanisms as well as validating the scoring method (e.g., by testing it on multiple parliamentary corpora, and manually checking the quality of emotion assignments) is necessary. Furthermore, to gain insight into specific events, focusing more on the relevant time period, and supporting the findings with other data sources (e.g., social media, political speeches outside the parliament) would be beneficial.

Acknowledgements

We would like to thank the anonymous reviewers for their insightful comments and suggestions.

6. Bibliographical References

Abercrombie, G. and Batista-Navarro, R. (2020). Sentiment and position-taking analysis of parliamentary debates: a systematic literature review. *Journal of Computational Social Science*, 3(1):245–270.

Abercrombie, G., Nanni, F., Batista-Navarro, R., and Ponzetto, S. P. (2019). Policy preference detection in parliamentary debate motions. In *Proceedings of the 23rd Conference on Computational Natural Language Learning (CoNLL)*, pages 249–259, Hong Kong, China, November. Association for Computational Linguistics.

Baykan, T. S. (2018). *The Justice and Development Party in Turkey: Populism, personalism, organization*. Cambridge University Press.

Bostan, L.-A.-M. and Klinger, R. (2018). An analysis of annotated corpora for emotion classification in text. In *Proceedings of the 27th International Conference on Computational Linguistics*, pages 2104–2119, Santa Fe, New Mexico, USA. Association for Computational Linguistics.

Cox, M. (2018). Understanding the global rise of populism. *Strategic Update, LSE Ideas*.

Devran, Y. and Özcan, Ö. F. (2016). Söylemlerin dilinden Suriye sorunu. *Marmara İletişim Dergisi*, 25:35–52.

Diermeier, D., Godbout, J.-F., Yu, B., and Kaufmann, S. (2012). Language and ideology in congress. *British Journal of Political Science*, 42(1):31–55.

Elçi, E. (2019). The rise of populism in Turkey: a content analysis. *Southeast European and Black Sea Studies*, 19(3):387–408.

Enyedi, Z. (2016). Populist polarization and party system institutionalization: The role of party politics in de-democratization. *Problems of Post-communism*, 63(4):210–220.

Erjavec, T., Ogrodniczuk, M., Osenova, P., Pančur, A., Ljubešić, N., Agnoloni, T., Barkarson, S., Calzada Pérez, M., Çöltekin, c., Coole, M., Dargis, R., de Macedo, L. D., de Does, J., Depuydt, K., Diwersy, S., Kopp, M., Krilavičius, T., Luxardo, G., Morkevičius, V., Navarretta, C., Rayson, P., Ring, O., Rudolf, M., Simov, K., Steingrímsson, S., Magnússon, Á., Üveges, I., van Heusden, R., and Venturi, G. (2021). ParlaMint: Comparable corpora of European parliamentary data. In *Proceedings of the CLARIN Annual Conference 2021*.

Erjavec, T., Ogrodniczuk, M., Osenova, P., Ljubešić, N., Simov, K., Pančur, A., Rudolf, M., Kopp, M., Barkarson, S., Steingrímsson, S., Çöltekin, c., de Does, J., Depuydt, K., Agnoloni, T., Venturi, G., Pérez, M. C., de Macedo, L. D., Navarretta, C., Luxardo, G., Coole, M., Rayson, P., Morkevičius, V., Krilavičius, T., Dargis, R., Ring, O., van Heusden, R., Marx, M., and Fišer, D. (2022). The ParlaMint corpora of parliamentary proceedings. *Language Resources and Evaluation*.

Güngör, S. (2014). Türk siyasetinde dil kullanımı: siyasal parti liderlerinin TBMM grup konuşmalarında siyasal söylem analizi. *Yasama Dergisi*, 26:65–88.

Hopkins, D. J. and King, G. (2010). A method of automated nonparametric content analysis for social science. *American Journal of Political Science*, 54(1):229–247.

Kapočiūtė-Dzikienė, J. and Krupavičius, A. (2014). Predicting party group from the Lithuanian parliamentary speeches. *Information Technology and Control*, 43(3):321–332.

Kurtoğlu Eskisar, G. M. and Durmuşlar, T. (2021). Responses of far right parties to refugees in hybrid regimes: the case of MHP in Turkey. *Journal of Ethnic and Migration Studies*, pages 1–22.

Marcus, G. E. (2000). Emotions in politics. *Annual review of political science*, 3(1):221–250.

McCoy, J., Rahman, T., and Somer, M. (2018). Polarization and the global crisis of democracy: Common patterns, dynamics, and pernicious consequences for democratic polities. *American Behavioral Scientist*, 62(1):16–42.

Moffitt, B. (2016). *The Global Rise of Populism: Performance, Political Style, and Representation*. Stanford University Press.

Baskın Oran, editor. (2010). *Turkish Foreign Policy, 1919–2006: Facts and Analyses with Documents*. Utah Series in Middle East Studies. University of Utah Press.

Pedregosa, F., Varoquaux, G., Gramfort, A., Michel, V., Thirion, B., Grisel, O., Blondel, M., Prettenhofer, P., Weiss, R., Dubourg, V., Vanderplas, J., Passos, A., Cournapeau, D., Brucher, M., Perrot, M., and Duchesnay, E. (2011). Scikit-learn: Machine learning in Python. *Journal of Machine Learning Research*, 12:2825–2830.

Prior, A. and van Hoef, Y. (2018). Interdisciplinary

approaches to emotions in politics and international relations. *Politics and Governance*, 6(4):48–52.

Rheault, L., Beelen, K., Cochrane, C., and Hirst, G. (2016). Measuring emotion in parliamentary debates with automated textual analysis. *PLOS ONE*, 11(12):1–18, 12.

Scherer, K. R. and Wallbott, H. G. (1994). Evidence for universality and cultural variation of differential emotion response patterning. *Journal of personality and social psychology*, 66(2):310.

Toçoğlu, M. A. and Alpkoçak, A. (2018). TREMO: A dataset for emotion analysis in Turkish. *Journal of Information Science*, 44(6):848–860.

Werlen, E., Imhof, C., and Bergamin, P. (2021). Emotions in the parliament: Lexical emotion analysis of parliamentarian speech transcriptions. In *Proceedings of the Swiss Text Analytics Conference 2021*.

A. Additional Plots

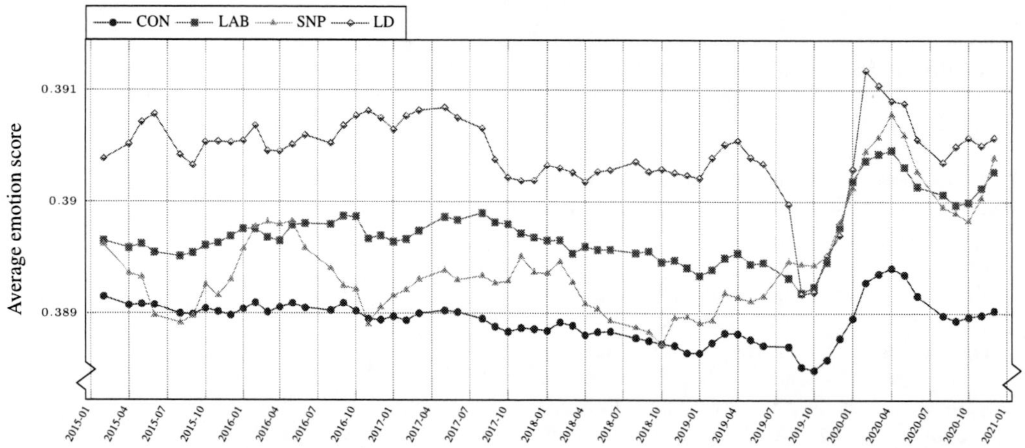

Figure 5: Average emotion scores for four most-active parties in the UK parliament throughout the period available from ParlaMint. The scores are averages of all emotion scores of speeches of all members of a party for a month in both houses in UK parliamentary system. To allow display of longer-term trends, each data point represents an average of five-month window centered on the indicated month.

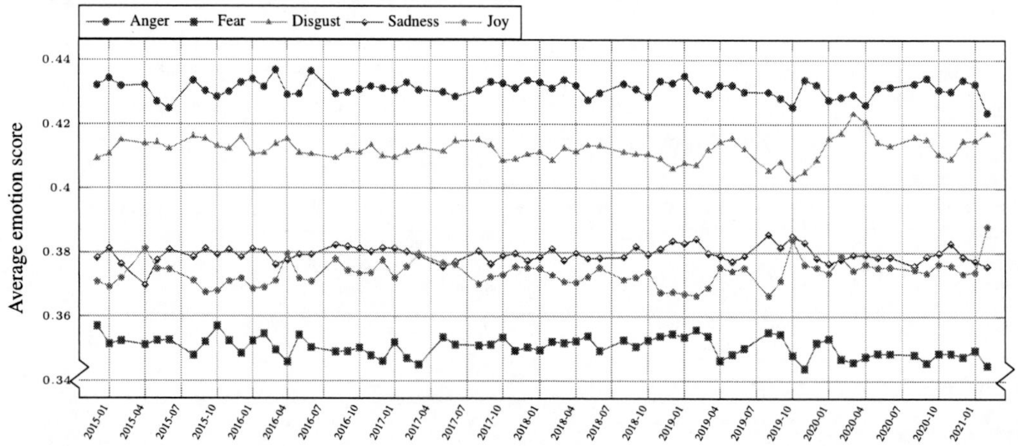

Figure 6: Emotion scores averaged over all parties in the UK parliament throughout the period available from ParlaMint.

B. Details of Model Tuning

For the classifiers used in this study, we use one-vs-rest support vector machines. The classifiers for both languages are first tuned on the respective data sets described in Section 3.1. We used a random sample of 3000 hyperparameter configurations from the hyperparameter space defined in Table 3, and picked the best hyperparameter configuration that yielded highest average macro F1-score in 10-fold cross validation.

Hyperparameter	range	sampling	best (EN)	best (TR)
Maximum order of character n-grams	1–8	uniform	6	7
Maximum order of word n-grams	1–4	uniform	4	2
The SVM regularization parameter ‘C’	0.001–5.0	uniform	0.94	0.91
Case normalization	word, char, both, none	categorical	word	word

Table 3: Hyperparameter space and best values for each language.

Proceedings of ParlaCLARIN III @ LREC2022 pages 71–80
Marseille, 20 June 2022

Immigration in the Manifestos and Parliament Speeches of Danish Left and Right Wing Parties between 2009 and 2020

Costanza Navarretta, Dorte Haltrup Hansen, Bart Jongejan
University of Copenhagen
Emil Holms Kanal 2, 2300 Copenhagen S, DK
costanza@hum.ku.dk, dorteh@hum.ku.dk, bartj@hum.ku.dk

Abstract

The paper presents a study of how seven Danish left and right wing parties addressed *immigration* in their 2011, 2015 and 2019 manifestos and in their speeches in the Danish Parliament from 2009 to 2020. The annotated manifestos are produced by the Comparative Manifesto Project, while the parliamentary speeches annotated with policy areas (subjects) have been recently released under CLARIN-DK. In the paper, we investigate how often the seven parties addressed immigration in the manifestos and parliamentary debates, and we analyse both datasets after having applied NLP tools to them. A sentiment analysis tool was run on the manifestos and its results were compared with the manifestos' annotations, while topic modeling was applied to the parliamentary speeches in order to outline central themes in the immigration debates. Many of the resulting topic groups are related to cultural, religious and integration aspects which were heavily debated by politicians and media when discussing immigration policy during the past decade. Our analyses also show differences and similarities between parties and indicate how the 2015 immigrant crisis is reflected in the two types of data. Finally, we discuss advantages and limitations of our quantitative and tool-based analyses.

Keywords: parliamentary records, manifestos, immigration

1. Introduction

This paper investigates how immigration was addressed in the manifestos and parliamentary speeches of Danish left and right wing parties in the past decade, also taking into account eventual changes after the 2015 immigration crisis.

Immigration policy has divided parliaments as well as the public opinion in many countries, and this has certainly been the case in Denmark during the past years. Moreover, Denmark has been pointed out as one of the European countries that have adopted the most restrictive policy towards immigrants, see e.g. (Hagelund, 2021). Unfortunately, immigration is still a warm issue and has become even more actual after the recent Russian invasion of Ukraine. Recently, a special Danish law has opened the country to refugees from Ukraine, showing a change from previous attitudes towards immigrants who have moved to Denmark in order to avoid war and persecutions.

The present study accounts for how seven Danish parties have addressed immigration in a) their 2011, 2015 and 2019 manifestos, which were annotated in the Comparative Manifestos Project[1], and b) in their speeches in the Danish Parliament (*Folketinget*) from 2009 to 2020. More specifically, we analyse how often the seven parties have addressed the issue and in which way, supported by existing NLP tools. The various tools have been chosen taking into account the different size of and the various annotations available for the manifestos and the parliamentary speeches.

The seven Danish parties included in the study are the following[2]:

- Danish People's party (Dansk Folkeparti - DF): DF achieved popularity for its strong line against immigrants and it has supported right wing governments.
- The Red-Green Unity List (Enighedslisten - EL): EL resulted from the merge of three left wing parties and is the leftmost party in the parliament. It supports left wing governments.
- Conservative People's party (Konservative Folkeparti - KF): KF is the historical conservative party that supports and/or has been part of right wing governments.
- Danish Social Liberal party (Radikale Venstre - RV): RV is a centre right party that traditionally supported and was part of right wing governments. In the past decades, it has changed line and has supported and/or been part of governments headed by the Social Democratic party.
- Social Democratic party (Social Demokratiet SD): SD is the largest Danish party and has been leading the government in 2014-2016, and 2019- .
- Socialist People's party (Socialistik Folkeparti - SF): SF is a left wing party that supports and/or has been part of Social Democratic governments in the investigated period.
- The Liberal party (Venstre - V): V was placed to the left of the Conservative People's party in the

[1] `https://manifesto-project.wzb.eu/`.

[2] The abbreviations used are those provided by the Comparative Manifestos Project. They do not always correspond to the abbreviations used by the parties in Denmark.

parliament when it was created[3]. It has been leading two right wing governments in the investigated time (2009-2014, 2016-2019), but it started losing its central position in politics after the 2019 elections.

This paper is organised as follows. First, in section 2, we account for projects which have collected and annotated parties' manifestos and parliamentary speeches and we delineate studies investigating how immigration has been addressed by Danish politicians. In section 3, we introduce the data we have used, and in section 4, we present our analyses of how immigration was dealt with by the seven parties in their manifestos. In section 5, we account for our investigation of the parliamentary speeches addressing immigration. Finally, section 6 contains a discussion and presents future work.

2. Background

2.1. Party Manifestos and Parliamentary Debates

The interest in the position of left and right wing parties from different countries towards specific policy issues has increased over the past decades because of the digital availability of political data of various types. For example, large collections of national and multinational parliamentary debates have been released, e.g. the EuroParl corpus (Koehn, 2005; Hajlaoui et al., 2014) and the recent ParlaMint corpora (Erjavec et al., 2021b; Erjavec et al., 2021a; Erjavec et al., 2022). Also parties' manifestos and political agendas from different meeting types and from many countries have been continuously collected and enriched with annotations about policy areas in large international projects such as the Comparative Manifesto Project [4]. and the Comparative Agendas Project [5].

The Comparative Manifesto Project (CMP) is classifying the policy areas in party election programs (manifestos) from many countries, applying 560 categories. The data is freely downloadable and also comprises Danish manifestos (Burst et al., 2020).

The Comparative Agendas Project (CAP) aimed to extend the USA's Policy Agendas Project[6] (Baumgartner et al., 2011) and thus covers the policy areas in political agendas of more countries than the USA. The agendas are annotated using 21 main classes and 192 subclasses.

Researchers from political science at the University of Aarhus have annotated Danish political data from 1953 to 2007 in the Danish Policy Agendas Project[7]. They have classified their data, legislative hearings, parliamentary debates, debates in the city councils, manifestos, and speeches by the Danish prime ministers, applying a slightly modified version of the Policy Agendas codebook and of the CAP codebook.

2.2. Immigration Studies

Scholars from various countries have analysed immigration policies in right and left wing parties, since immigration is a subject that often divides electors and politicians. The opinions of both groups are influenced by numerous factors comprising socio-economical issues and party competition, e.g. (Grande et al., 2019; Natter et al., 2020). In this section, we focus on recent studies that have addressed immigration policy in Denmark.

Green-Pedersen and Krogstrup (2008) analyse various parties' positions towards immigration in Denmark and Sweden in the 1980s and 1990s looking at the role of party competition that makes parties concentrate on specific issues. The focus on immigration is measured by counting the number of relevant text segments (quasi-sentences) in the parties' manifestos annotated by the Comparative Manifestos Project, and the number of questions on immigration issues posed to the immigration minister in the parliament. This study shows that immigration got low attention in the 1980s, while the situation changed in the 1990s after the Social Liberals (RV) and other centre-right parties left the right wing coalition. To stay in power, the right wing parties sought support from the Progress Party (Fremskridtspartiet) and, after this party's demise, from the Danish People's Party. Both parties had critical positions against refugees and immigration as one of their central themes. According to Green-Pedersen and Krogstrup (2008), also the Social Democratic Party changed its position and rhetoric towards immigration during the analysed period in order to avoid losing votes to the Danish People's Party.

Alonso and da Fonseca (2012) compare the immigration policy positions of left and right wing parties in 18 West European countries, one of these being Denmark. They also use data from the Comparative Manifesto Project and investigate immigration policies from 1975 to 2005. Alonso and da Fonseca (2012) aim to prove that all mainstream parties make use of anti-immigrant sentiments in the population, and that also left wing parties have continuously used a more negative tone about immigration in this period.

Alonso and da Fonseca (2012) look at the effect of emerging right wing parties on parties' positions and what they call *the salience theory*. This theory refers to the phenomenon of parties competing with each other in taking the ownership of specific issues and positions towards them (Petrocik, 1996). Alonso and da Fonseca (2012) measure the salience of immigration in the same way as Green-Pedersen and Krogstrup (2008), that is counting the number of references to immigration re-

[3] The name of the party in Danish is therefore *Left*.

[4] https://manifesto-project.wzb.eu/

[5] https://www.comparativeagendas.net/

[6] https://liberalarts.utexas.edu/government/news/feature-archive/the-policy-agendas-project.php

[7] http://www.agendasetting.dk/.

lated issues in the manifestos. The authors find that the salience of immigration increases in the agenda of all parties in the 18 considered countries during the investigated period independently from the emerging of anti-immigrant right wing parties. They explain this by e.g. the influence of of immigration policy in other countries and in the EU.

Hagelund (2021) investigates immigration policy changes in Denmark, Norway and Sweden following the refugee crisis in 2015. The author concludes that the strategies adopted in the three countries are different, and that the main focus for Danish politicians has been to create political support for a range of measures that restrict immigration and to reduce the impact of different cultures on the Danish society.

3. The Data

In our work, we use two different datasets. The first dataset consists of three Danish manifestos from each of the seven parties in relation to the political elections in 2011, 2015 and 2019. The second dataset is a corpus of Danish parliamentary speeches from the period 2009-2020, annotated with subject information.

The manifestos were downloaded from the Comparative Manifesto Project's website[8]. The project provides the manifestos in PDF format, and CSV files containing the text of the manifestos divided into minimal units, which are called *quasi-sentences*. A quasi-sentence is defined as a single statement or message, and often corresponds to a sentence[9]. A quasi-sentence can also coincide with other linguistic categories, such as clauses, clause segments, or name entities, e.g. a film or book title.

The Danish parliamentary speeches are a version of *The Danish Parliament Corpus (2009-2017) v.2* released under the CLARIN-DK repository in 2021[10] and extended with speeches from 2018-2020. The data consists of the transcripts of parliamentary speeches of the Danish Parliament enriched with information about the speakers, the timing of the speeches and subject areas. The transcripts were downloaded from the Danish Parliament's website[11]. The subject area annotations were semi-automatically added to the speeches, using the manual annotation of the agenda titles (Navarretta and Hansen, 2022).

The subject annotation distinguishes 19 main classes, which are a subset of the CAP classification scheme corresponding to the responsibility areas of the Danish parliament's committees after a strategy proposed by Zirn (2014). The annotated subject classes are the following: *Agriculture, Business, Culture, Defence, Economy, Education, Energy, Environment, European Integration, Foreign Affairs, Health Care, Housing, Infrastructure, Immigration, Justice, Labour, Local and Regional Affairs, Social Affairs* and *Territories* (Navarretta and Hansen, 2022).

A small part of the annotations were manually checked by humans taking into account the speeches' content. The consistency of the annotations of the main subject areas in part of the corpus was assessed training classifiers on the lemmatised titles of the agendas and the speeches (Hansen et al., 2019). Similarly, the consistency of the annotations of two co-occurring subjects in the corpus was tested by running multi-label classifiers on BOW and TF*IDF values of the titles of the agendas and the lemmatised speeches. The contribution of information about the speakers to classification was also tested. The best results running the classifiers on the BOW of the agenda titles and speech information gave an F1-score= 0.997 while an F1-score near 0.7 was achieves by classifiers trained on the BOW of the lemmatised speech (Navarretta and Hansen, 2022).

Navarretta and Hansen (2020) analysed the content of the party programs and the parliamentary debates of two left- and two right wing Danish parties based on frequent and specific lemmas occurring in the data. The analyses confirmed previous research that successfully use word-based scores from party programs in order to distinguish the party's positions towards specific subject areas, e.g. (Laver et al., 2003; Slapin and Proksch, 2008). Experiments act to identify the party membership of speakers from their speeches in the parliament gave an F1-score of 0.57.

4. Immigration in the Danish Manifestos

The length of the three manifestos of the seven parties is shown in Table 1. The length of the manifestos of

Party	2011	2015	2019
The People's Party	5,581	546	1,742
Red-Green Unity List	8,367	1,576	4,787
Conservat. People's P.	1,754	587	14,690
Danish Social Liberal P.	1,939	438	10,089
Socialist People's P.	7,789	3,003	10,927
Social Democratic P.	2,061	6,088	37,076
Liberal Party	3,066	1,379	2,001

Table 1: Words in the 2011, 2015 and 2019 manifestos

each party changes during the years and varies from party to party. The shortest manifesto comes from the People's Party and consists of 546 words (the party's 2015 manifesto), while the longest one comes from the Social Democratic Party and contains 37,076 words (the party's 2019 manifesto).

In Table 2, the number of quasi-sentences in the manifestos are given. Also in this case the number of quasi-sentences varies from party to party and there is also a large variance between the manifestos of the same party in different years.

[8]https://manifesto-project.wzb.eu/

[9]https://manifesto-project.wzb.eu/down/papers/handbook_2021_version_5.pdf.

[10]https://repository.clarin.dk/repository/xmlui/handle/20.500.12115/44

[11]ftp://oda.ft.dk

Party	2011	2015	2019
The Danish People's Party	392	39	112
Red-Green Unity List	693	122	373
Conservative People's P.	151	47	1,131
Danish Social Liberal P.	149	35	707
Social Democratic P.	175	584	2,841
Socialist People's P.	621	216	719
Liberal Party	253	116	177

Table 2: Quasi-sentences in manifestos

Following the strategy proposed by Green-Pedersen and Krogstrup (2008) and then adopted by Alonso and da Fonseca (2012), we extracted the quasi-sentences annotated with the codes 601.2 (Immigration - negative), 602.2 (Immigration - positive), 607.2 (Integration - positive), and 608.2 (Assimilation - negative) in the 2011, 2015 and 2019 manifestos.

Since the manifestos have different length, we calculated the relative frequency of quasi-sentences on immigration, that is their number divided by the total of quasi sentences in each manifesto for the seven parties. The relative frequency is shown in Figure 1. No party addressed immigration in their manifestos in 2011, therefore the data from 2011 is not included in the figure. All parties, except the Conservative People's party (KF) and the Socialist People's party (SF), write about immigration in their 2015 manifestos, and all parties, without exception, address immigration in their 2019 manifesto. This is a clear indication that immigration has become a more actual theme in all manifestos after the 2015 immigrant crisis.

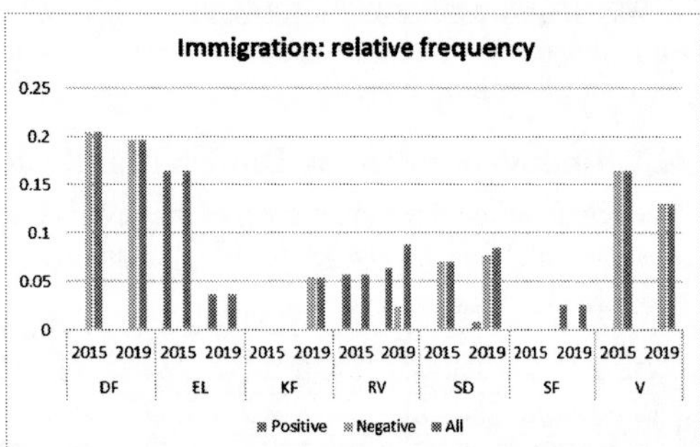

Figure 1: The relative frequency of quasi-sentences about immigration in the manifestos of the seven parties

The party with the highest relative frequency of quasi-sentences about immigration is the Danish People's Party (DF), and all their quasi-sentences are marked with negative codes by the Comparative Manifesto Project. Similarly, the Liberal party (V)' s manifestos contain relatively many negative quasi-sentences about immigration. Also the 2019 manifesto of the Conservative people's party (KF) addresses immigration exclusively with negatively marked quasi-sentences.

The left wing Red-Green Unity list (EL) addresses immigration relatively often in the 2015 manifesto, while the number of quasi-sentences related to immigration decreases in its 2019 manifesto. The quasi-sentences in both manifestos are annotated as being positive by the Comparative Manifesto Project. The 2019 manifesto of the Socialist People's party (SF) only contains positive quasi-sentences. Also the Social Liberals (RV)' 2015 manifesto only contains positive quasi-sentences, while the party's 2019 manifesto also contains few negatively marked quasi-sentences. Opposite to this, the 2015 and 2019 manifestos of the Social Democratic party (SD) contain relatively many negative quasi-sentence. However, the party's 2019 manifesto also contains few positively marked quasi-sentences.

We also counted the number of quasi-sentences annotated by the Comparative Manifesto Project with the codes 601 and 601.1, which indicate nationalism. Nationalism is often opposed to openness towards immigrants (Alonso and da Fonseca, 2012). The relative frequency of nationalism marked quasi-sentences in the manifestos of the seven parties is in Figure 2, in which only the manifestos where nationalism was addressed are included. The Danish People's party (DF) is the only party that has many nationalist quasi-sentences in all three manifestos, while the Conservative People's party (KF) has many nationalist quasi-sentences in the 2011 and 2019 manifestos. The manifestos of the Socialist People's party and the Red-Green Unity List do not contain nationalist quasi-sentences.

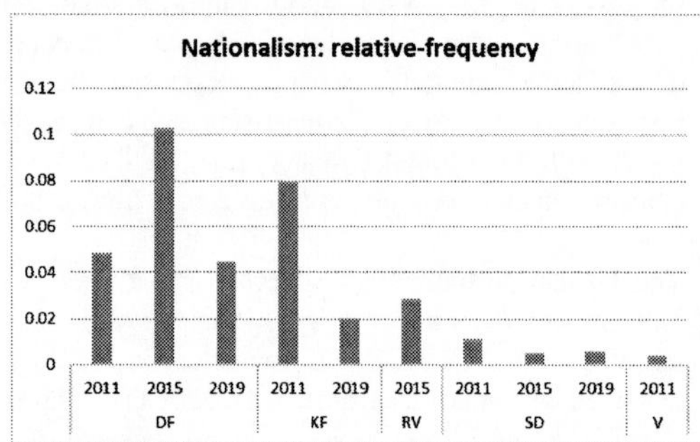

Figure 2: The relative frequency of nationalism quasi-sentences

4.1. Applying Sentiment Analysis to the Manifestos

Inspired by the work by Zirn et al. (2016), who applied sentiment analysis to German manifestos, we run a sentiment analysis tool, AFINN[12], on the immigration quasi-sentences . AFINN uses a sentiment lexicon and assigns weights to sentences based on the

[12] `https://github.com/fnielsen/afinn`

weights of the lemmas in the lexicon (Nielsen, 2011). We merged the AFINN lexicon with another larger lexicon, the Danish sentiment lexicon[13].

Before applying the modified AFINN lexicon on the manifestos' quasi-sentences, these were tokenised and lemmatised using the CLARIN-DK's workflow *Text Tonsorium*[14] (Jongejan, 2016). The AFINN tool assigns positive, negative or neutral (0.0) scores to each sentence (quasi-sentence in our case). The neutral scores are also given to a sentence if its words are not found in the lexicon.

Not surprisingly, the positive and negative scores provided by the tool do not always correspond to the positive and negative annotations of the Comparative Manifesto Project. The latter were assigned taking into account the context of quasi-sentences with respect to the addressed policy area, while the scope of the sentiment analysis tool is a (quasi-)sentence. It must also be noted that the AFINN tool was built to deal with social media texts and even if it is run with a larger lexicon, it does not cover many of the words contained in the manifestos. Finally, the tool does not take into account phenomena such as the scope of negation. Therefore, many quasi-sentences are marked as neutral (score 0.0), even when humans (the authors) judge them to be negative or positive. However, some interesting observations can be made based on the discrepancies and similarities between the annotations provided by the Comparative Manifesto Project and the scores marked by sentiment analysis tool.

Some parties present negatively marked quasi-sentences on immigration in a linguistically positive way. This is e.g. the case for the Danish People's Party (DF)'s manifestos, that uses a positive argument when proposing to help immigrants in their neighbouring areas instead of in Denmark.

From DF's 2015 manifesto:

1. *Flygtninge skal hjælpes i deres nærområder.*
   (Immigrants must be helped in their neighbouring areas.)
   (601.2 negative, Sent. analysis positive score)

2. *På den måde kan vi hjælpe langt flere.*
   (This way, we can help many more.)
   (601.2 negative, Sent. analysis positive score)

There are other cases in which two successive quasi-sentences are marked as positive by the Comparative Manifesto Project, while the sentiment analysis tools gives a negative score to the first quasi-sentence and a positive score to the second one. The reason for this difference is often that a negative argument precedes a statement about the necessity of helping refugees, as in the following example from the Red-Green Unity List (EL)'s 2015 manifesto:

3. *Danmark kan ikke tage imod alle flygtninge.*
   (Denmark cannot accept all immigrants)
   (602.2 positive, Sent. analysis negative score)

4. *Men vi kan og vi skal tage vores del af ansvaret.*
   (But we can and we must take our share of the responsibility.)
   (602.2 positive, Sent. analysis neutral score)

In other cases, the sentiment analysis's scores and the Comparative Manifesto Project's codes are similar, that is they are both positive or negative. An example of the latter is sentence 6 from DF's 2019 manifesto:

5. *Danmark har taget imod rigeligt med udlændinge igennem årene.*
   (Denmark has received an abundance of foreigners over the years.)
   (601.2 negative, Sent. analysis neutral score)

6. *Så vi skal have færre ind og flere ud!*
   (Therefore we must have fewer in and more out!)
   (601.2 negative, Sent. analysis negative score)

Concluding, comparing the two annotation types can help discovering various communicative strategies adopted by the parties in their manifestos.

5. Immigration in the Parliamentary Speeches

44,459 out of the 517,503 speeches from 2009-2020 (9%) address the policy subject *Immigration*. This is quite a large portion since the speeches are classified in 19 main policy subjects. The number of words in the speeches related to immigration is 4,308,165. The frequency of the subjects that were discussed together with immigration are shown in Figure 3. The subject

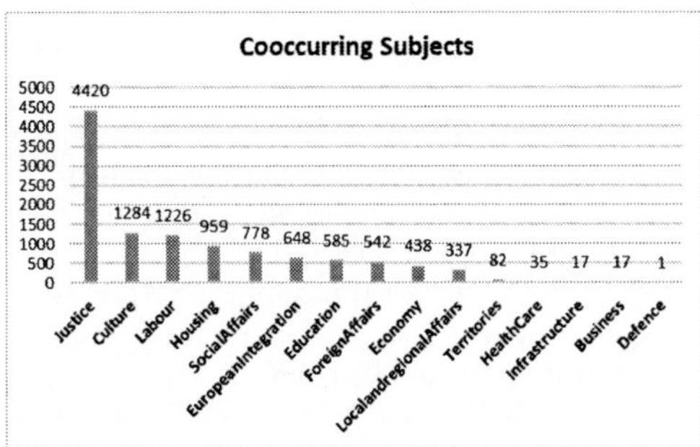

Figure 3: The policy subjects discussed with *Immigration*

that is discussed most frequently together with *Immigration* is *Justice*, which is not surprising. The other frequently co-occurring subjects in order of their frequency are *Culture, Labour, Housing, Social Affairs, European Integration* and *Education. Economy* is discussed together with *Immigration* only in 1% of the

[13] https://github.com/dsldk/danish-sentiment-lexicon.

[14] https://clarin.dk/clarindk/tools-texton.jsp

speeches, and this is less expected since *Economy* is an important factor in most policy subjects (Navarretta and Hansen, 2022). However, the low impact of economy on the immigration debate indicates that other factors play a more important role when parties and media address this subject.

Figure 4 gives the total time in hours during which immigration was debated in the parliament in 2009-2020. The figure shows that immigration is addressed

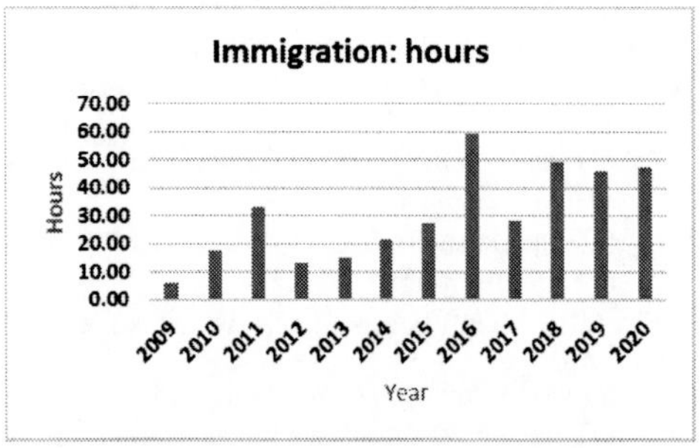

Figure 4: The hours during which *Immigration* is discussed every year

quite often in 2011, 2015, 2016 and then in 2018-20. In 2011, family reunion was a big issue, and that year the parliament voted strong restrictions towards it. These restrictions have also had consequences for Danish citizens married with citizens from non-EU countries or/and who have lived abroad for many years. After 2011, many mixed families moved to other European countries with less restrictive laws.

The increasing number of speeches about immigration from 2015 to 2020 is not surprising because of the immigration crisis, but they are probably also a consequence of what Green-Pedersen and Krogstrup (2008) call *party competition*. The Social Democrats and the Liberals have adopted some of the views of the Danish People's Party. Moreover, a new right party, The New Right (Nye Borgelige), has entered the parliament after the 2019 election presenting an even more restrictive line against immigrants than all other parties.

Figure 5 shows how many hours the seven parties spoke about the subject *Immigration* and the percentage of each party's total speaking time devoted to it. Politicians from the Danish People's Party (DF) use 11.57% of their speaking time addressing immigration, and this is in line with the focus on the subject in the party's manifestos. The Liberals (V) also devoted a lot of time to the subject (8.30% of their speaking time), which is not surprising since some of the most restrictive immigration laws were introduced under a liberal prime minister in this period. The Social Democrats (SD) used approx. 7% of their speaking time debating immigration. Also the politicians from The Red-Green Unity List (EL) discussed relatively often immigration (7.4% of their speaking time), and this is also in line

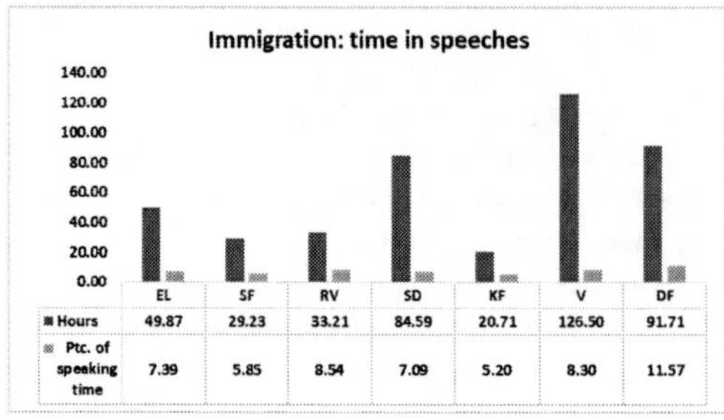

Figure 5: The time spent by the parties debating on immigration

with what they did in their manifestos. Surprisingly, the Social Liberals (RV) speak relatively much about immigration in the parliament (8.54% of their speaking time), even though their manifestos do not address the subject much. This might indicate that the party did not want to lose voters by underlying their positive line towards immigrants in the manifestos, On the opposite side, the Conservative People's party (KF) writes relatively much about immigration in the party's manifestos, but the conservative politicians contribute relatively little to the parliamentary debates on the subject (only 5.2% of their speaking time). The politicians from the Socialist People's party (SF) speak also less frequently about immigration than other parties, but this behaviour is in line with the content of its manifestos.

Figure 6 shows the speaking time devoted to immigration by the seven parties in their parliamentary speeches in the three years covered by the manifestos, that is 2011, 2015 and 2019. The figure confirms that there is not a one to one correspondence between the space given to immigration by the parties in their manifestos and the time they address on the same subject in their speeches even in the same year.

5.1. Extracting Immigration Topics from the Parliamentary Speeches

We used topic modeling to identify the main topics in the parliamentary speeches marked with the subject *Immigration*. Topic modeling has often been used to extract subtopics in text corpora, among many (Jelodar et al., 2019) and in political texts, e.g. (Greene and Cross, 2017).

The python 3 module scikit-learn was used in the experiments. First, we tokenised PoS-tagged and lemmatised the speeches with the Text Tonsorium tools available in CLARIN-DK. We used two datasets, one consisting of all lemmas, the second only comprising noun lemmas. Using noun lemmas for extracting topics in political texts has been proposed by e.g. (Martin and Johnson, 2015).

We extracted bag of words (BOW) and term frequency * inverse of document frequency (TF*IDF) values from

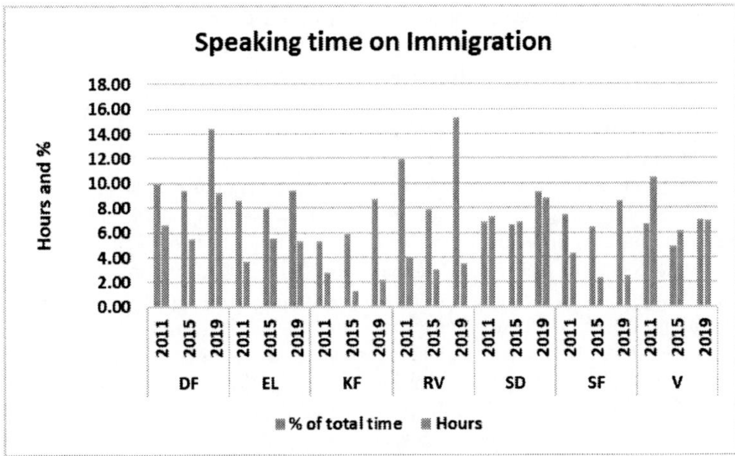

Figure 6: The time spent by the parties debating on immigration in the election years

the two datasets. Two topic modeling algorithms were trained on these two models: a) Latent Dirichlet Allocation (LDA) and b) Non-Negative Matrix Factorization (NMF). LDA is a probabilistic model (Blei, 2012) which has been extensively used for topic modeling in different domains while NMF is a matrix factorization and multivariate analysis technique, which can be used for topic modeling (Gillis and Vavasis, 2014).

We tested LDA and NMF on BOW and TF*IDF values calculated from the two datasets setting the number of topics to 10, 15 and 20. The most significant topic groups were obtained by the LDA algorithm run on BOW values of lemmas or noun lemmas when the number of topics was 15. The second best topic groups were obtained by NMF on TF*IDF values of noun lemmas.

Approximately one third of the topic groups returned by LDA identify grammatical categories, such as politicians' surnames, countries, party names or parts of party names. Three topic groups contained nearly the same lemmas, but in different order. The remaining topic groups are, however, interesting and help individuate some of the themes that were discussed not only in the parliament, but also in the news and media in the investigated period. The relevant topic groups suggested by LDA are listed below with titles suggested by the authors:

1. *Immigrants and naturalization*: handshake, ceremony, constitution ceremony, nationality, Grundtvig[15], the naturalization committee, naturalization office, naturalization, naturalization law, inequality, state pension, anti-democrat, Langballe[16], Denmark
2. *Immigration and local affairs*: municipality, crowns, working capacity, immigration, money, company, effort, job, solution, labour market, possibility, requirement, expense, work, millions
3. *Immigration and work*: municipality, immigrant, yield, labour market, money, work, housing, government, integration, expense, housing place, contribution, employment, million, welfare benefits
4. *Immigrant, culture differences, crime*: woman, man, constitution, person, law, security, crime, right, violence, prison, legislation, burka, security, minister of justice, person, people
5. *Refugees and legislation*: law case, rule, authority, limit, borders, border control, residence permit, police, law, usual practice, condition, verdict, government, legislation
6. *Religion*: Islam, Denmark, society, value, problem, religion, democracy, religious community, association, mosque, Muslim, opinion, country, religion freedom, Turkey, culture
7. *Integration*: camp, high school, parent, 10-years rule, Greenlander, quote system, lodging, room, bath, estimate of integration, number of refugees, burden, child-bride, Århus, Faeroese
8. *Family and conventions*: child, convention, parents, family, UN, Denmark, accommodation center, school, legislation, year, situation, re-education travel, responsibility, situation, interest
9. *Radicalization*: association, violence, mosque, courage, opinion, PET[17] supervision, police, environment, terrorist, radicalization, extremism, threat, encouragement, terror

[15]Grundtvig (1783-1872) was a Danish writer, politician and priest. He was the spiritual father of the folk high school tradition.

[16]One of the politicians of the Danish People's party

[17]Police intelligence service.

The first topic group is connected to one of the themes that were most debated in the considered period, the procedure for obtaining the Danish nationality. This also included the requirement that immigrants had to shake the hand of the official giving them the naturalization document during the naturalization ceremony. By shaking hands the immigrants were supposed to show that they followed the Danish culture. This requirement posed some problems under the COVID-19 pandemic when people could not meet in person and shake hands. Topic groups 2, 3 and 7 contain words related to the integration of immigrants, another theme that was often debated in the parliament and in the media in the past decade. Topic groups 4 and 9 indicate that immigration has been discussed together with crime and terrorism, while topic group 6 relates to religion and clothes[18]. Topic groups 5 and 8 indicate the connection between immigration policy, justice and international conventions. The topic modeling results confirm that Danish politicians have been mostly preoccupied with keeping the Danish society as it is, without being influenced by other cultures (Hagelund, 2021), and indicate the harshness of some of the immigration policy debates.

The NMF run on TF*IDF values also returns some other interesting topic groups, but more groups than those returned by LDA do not address semantically related words, but words that are related in different ways, e.g. being proper names, or abbreviations.

In order to extract interesting topics, both algorithms are useful and their results could be combined.

6. Discussion and Future Work

In this paper, we have investigated how immigration was dealt by seven Danish right and left wing parties in their manifestos and parliamentary speeches during the past twelve years (2009-2020) .

We have first followed the strategy of counting relevant quasi-sentences in the manifestos as proposed by researchers in political sciences (Green-Pedersen and Krogstrup, 2008; Alonso and da Fonseca, 2012) and we have extended the strategy to the parliamentary speeches. These quantitative analyses show that immigration has become even more a hot theme in the political scene over the past decade than it was in the preceding period studied in (Green-Pedersen and Krogstrup, 2008; Alonso and da Fonseca, 2012). Our work also confirms that some parties' positions towards immigration cannot only be explained by the fact that they belong to the right or left wing and that party competition and the world situation also play important roles (Green-Pedersen and Krogstrup, 2008; Alonso and da Fonseca, 2012; Hagelund, 2021).

We also found that the relative frequency of quasi-sentences on immigration in the manifestos indicates how the subject has been addressed as an important election theme by especially some parties. For example, right wing parties (DF, KF, and V) present restrictive views against immigration in their manifestos, while left wing parties (SF and EL) argue for helping immigrants. More complex is the situation for the center-left Social Democratic Party, which has got a position similar to that of the right wing parties with respect to immigration, and the center-right Social Liberal Party, which has kept its humanitarian and positive position towards immigrants even after the 2015 crisis.

Differing from other Danish studies on immigration policy, we also looked at the frequency of all parliament speeches addressing immigration in 2009-2020. Also in this case, the growing importance given to immigration especially after the 2015 crisis is evident from the data. Moreover, we found that some parties (The Danish People's Party and The Red-Green Unity List) follow the same line in their election manifestos and in their contributions to the parliamentary debates, while the Social Liberal Party does not write much about immigration in its manifestos, while the party's politicians are more active in defending immigrants in the parliament.

After the qualitative analyses, we looked at the differences between the annotations of positive and negative immigration policies in the manifestos provided by the Comparative Manifesto Project and the scores of a lexicon-based sentiment analysis tool run on the lemmatised manifestos' immigration quasi-sentences. This work showed not only differences between the tool's annotation scores and the annotations by the Comparative Manifesto Project, but it also pointed out some of the communication strategies followed by the parties to promote their policy in favour or against immigration.

Topic modeling applied to the BOW and TF*IDF values of the noun lemmas extracted from the parliamentary speeches addressing the subject *Immigration* also provided interesting results. In fact, some of the topic groups returned by the LDA algorithm reflect themes that were debated not only in the parliament, but also in the media in the considered period. The interpretation of the topic modeling's results require human intervention. However, topic modeling could be easily run on parliamentary speeches from more countries and its results could be compared.

More sophisticated NLP methods could be applied on these data. However, it is important to stress that both data and tools that we used are freely available, and that they can support researchers from the humanities and social sciences in their analysis of political data of different type and size.

Finally, it must be noted that applying different strategies for analysing the Danish parliamentary speeches is particularly important, since the Danish parliament members must follow specific rules of conduit and language use when they debate in the Parliament. Therefore, it can be difficult to base the analysis of their political positions only on quantitative studies.

[18]Wearing burka has been forbidden in Denmark since 2018.

7. Bibliographical References

Alonso, S. and da Fonseca, S. C. (2012). Immigration, left and right. *Party Politics*, 18(6):865–884.

Baumgartner, F. R., Jones, B. D., and Wilkerson, J. (2011). Comparative Studies of Policy Dynamics. *Comparative Political Studies*, 44(8):947–972.

Blei, D. M. (2012). Probabilistic Topic Models. *Commun. ACM*, 55(4):77–84, April.

Burst, T., Krause, W., Lehmann, P., Lewandowski, J., Theres, M., Merz, N., Regel, S., and Zehnter, L. (2020). Manifesto Corpus, Version 2020-1.

Erjavec, T., Ogrodniczuk, M., Osenova, P., Ljubešić, N., Simov, K., Grigorova, V., Rudolf, M., Pančur, A., Kopp, M., Barkarson, S., Steingrímsson, S., van der Pol, H., Depoorter, G., de Does, J., Jongejan, B., Haltrup Hansen, D., Navarretta, C., Calzada Pérez, M., de Macedo, L. D., van Heusden, R., Marx, M., Çöltekin, Ç., Coole, M., Agnoloni, T., Frontini, F., Montemagni, S., Quochi, V., Venturi, G., Ruisi, M., Marchetti, C., Battistoni, R., Sebők, M., Ring, O., Darģis, R., Utka, A., Petkevičius, M., Briedienė, M., Krilavičius, T., Morkevičius, V., Bartolini, R., Cimino, A., Diwersy, S., Luxardo, G., and Rayson, P. (2021a). *Linguistically annotated multilingual comparable corpora of parliamentary debates ParlaMint.ana 2.1*. Slovenian language resource repository CLARIN.SI.

Erjavec, T., Ogrodniczuk, M., Osenova, P., Ljubešić, N., Simov, K., Grigorova, V., Rudolf, M., Pančur, A., Kopp, M., Barkarson, S., Steingrímsson, S., van der Pol, H., Depoorter, G., de Does, J., Jongejan, B., Haltrup Hansen, D., Navarretta, C., Calzada Pérez, M., de Macedo, L. D., van Heusden, R., Marx, M., Çöltekin, Ç., Coole, M., Agnoloni, T., Frontini, F., Montemagni, S., Quochi, V., Venturi, G., Ruisi, M., Marchetti, C., Battistoni, R., Sebők, M., Ring, O., Darģis, R., Utka, A., Petkevičius, M., Briedienė, M., Krilavičius, T., Morkevičius, V., Diwersy, S., Luxardo, G., and Rayson, P. (2021b). *Multilingual comparable corpora of parliamentary debates ParlaMint 2.1*. Slovenian language resource repository CLARIN.SI.

Erjavec, T., Ogrodniczuk, M., Osenova, P., Ljubešic, N., Simov, K., Pancur, A., Rudolf, M., Kopp, M., Barkarson, S., Steingrímsson, S., Çöltekin, Ç., de Does, J., Depuydt, K., Agnoloni, T., Venturi, G., Calzada Pérez, M., de Macedo, L., Navarretta, C., Luxardo, G., Coole, M., Rayson, P., Morkevicius, V., Krilavicius, T., Dargis, R., Ring, O., van Heusden, R., Marx, M., and Fiser, D. (2022). The ParlaMint corpora of parliamentary proceedings. *Language Resources and Evaluation*.

Gillis, N. and Vavasis, S. A. (2014). Fast and Robust Recursive Algorithms for Separable Nonnegative Matrix Factorization. *IEEE Transactions on Pattern Analysis and Machine Intelligence*, 36(4):698–714, April.

Grande, E., Schwarzbözl, T., and Fatke, M. (2019). Politicizing immigration in Western Europe. *Journal of European Public Policy*, 26(10):1444–1463.

Green-Pedersen, C. and Krogstrup, J. (2008). Immigration as a political issue in Denmark and Sweden. *European Journal of Political Research*, 47(5):610–634.

Greene, D. and Cross, J. P. (2017). Exploring the Political Agenda of the European Parliament Using a Dynamic Topic Modeling Approach. *Political Analysis*, 25(1):77–94.

Hagelund, A. (2021). After the refugee crisis: public discourse and policy change in Denmark, Norway and Sweden. *Comparative Migration Studies*, 8(1):17.

Hajlaoui, N., Kolovratnik, D., Väyrynen, J., Steinberger, R., and Varga, D. (2014). DCEP – Digital Corpus of the European Parliament. In *Proceedings of the Ninth International Conference on Language Resources and Evaluation (LREC'14)*, Reykjavik, Iceland. European Language Resources Association (ELRA).

Hansen, D., Navarretta, C., Offersgaard, L., and Wedekind, J. (2019). Towards the Automatic Classification of Speech Subjects in the Danish Parliament Corpus. In *CEUR Workshop Proceedings*, volume 2364, pages 166–174. CEUR workshop proceedings. https://cst.dk/DHN2019/DHN2019.html.

Jelodar, H., Wang, Y., Yuan, C., Feng, X., Jiang, X., Li, Y., and Zhao, L. (2019). Latent Dirichlet allocation (LDA) and topic modeling: models, applications, a survey. *Multimedia Tools and Applications*, 78(11):15169–15211.

Jongejan, B. (2016). Implementation of a Workflow Management System for Non-Expert Users. In *Proceedings of the Workshop on Language Technology Resources and Tools for Digital Humanities (LT4DH)*, pages 101–108, December.

Koehn, P. (2005). Europarl: A Parallel Corpus for Statistical Machine Translation. In *Conference Proceedings: the Tenth Machine Translation Summit*, pages 79–86, Phuket, Thailand. AAMT, AAMT.

Laver, M., Benoit, K., and Garry, J. (2003). Extracting Policy Positions from Political Texts Using Words as Data. *American Political Science Review*, 97(2):311–331.

Martin, F. and Johnson, M. (2015). More Efficient Topic Modelling Through a Noun Only Approach. In *Proceedings of the Australasian Language Technology Association Workshop 2015*, pages 111–115, Parramatta, Australia, December.

Natter, K., Czaika, M., and de Haas, H. (2020). Political party ideology and immigration policy reform: an empirical enquiry. *Political Research Exchange*, 2(1):10.

Navarretta, C. and Hansen, D. (2020). Identifying Parties in Manifestos and Parliament Speeches. In Darja Fiser, et al., editors, *Creating, Using and Linking of Parliamentary Corpora with Other Types of Politi-*

cal Discourse (ParlaCLARIN II), pages 51–57. European Language Resources Association.

Navarretta, C. and Hansen, D. H. (2022). The Subject Annotations of the Danish Parliament Corpus (2009-2017) - Evaluated with Automatic Multi-label Classification. In *Proceedings of LREC 2022*. ELRA.

Nielsen, F. Å. (2011). A new ANEW: evaluation of a word list for sentiment analysis in microblogs. In Matthew Rowe, et al., editors, *Proceedings of the ESWC2011 Workshop on Making Sense of Microposts: Big things come in small packages*, volume 718 of *CEUR Workshop Proceedings 93-98*. COEUR, May.

Petrocik, J. R. (1996). Issue Ownership in Presidential Elections, with a 1980 Case Study. *American Journal of Political Science*, 40(3):825–850.

Slapin, J. B. and Proksch, S.-O. (2008). A Scaling Model for Estimating Time-Series Party Positions from Texts. *American Journal of Political Science*, 52(3):705–722.

Zirn, C., Glavas, G., Nanni, F., Eichorst, J., and Stuckenschmidt, H. (2016). Classifying topics and detecting topic shifts in political manifestos. In *Proceedings of the International Conference on the Advances in Computational Analysis of Political Text (PolText 2016)*, pages 88–93. Dubrovnik, Croatia, July.

Zirn, C. (2014). Analyzing Positions and Topics in Political Discussions of the German Bundestag. In *ACL Student Research Workshop*, pages 26–33. ACL.

Proceedings of ParlaCLARIN III @ LREC2022 pages 81–91
Marseille, 20 June 2022

Parliamentary Discourse Research in Sociology: Literature Review

Jure Skubic*, Darja Fišer*♦
*Faculty of Arts, University of Ljubljana, Slovenia
♦Institute of Contemporary History, Ljubljana, Slovenia
*Aškerčeva cesta 2, 1000 Ljubljana, Slovenia
♦Privoz 11, 1000 Ljubljana, Slovenia
E-mail: jure.skubic@ff.uni-lj.si, darja.fiser@ff.uni-lj.si

Abstract

One of the major sociological research interests has always been the study of political discourse. This literature review gives an overview of the most prominent topics addressed and the most popular methods used by sociologists. We identify the commonalities and the differences of the approaches established in sociology with corpus-driven approaches in order to establish how parliamentary corpora and corpus-based approaches could be successfully integrated in sociological research. We also highlight how parliamentary corpora could be made even more useful for sociologists.

Keywords: parliamentary discourse, sociology, parliamentary corpora

1. Introduction

Parliamentary debates are an important source of sociologically relevant content since parliament is an institution responsible for shaping legislation that impacts people's everyday lives and is as such a source of power for members of parliament and other politicians (Bischof and Ilie, 2018). In addition, parliaments and parliamentary debates are crucial in creating political identities (Van Dijk, 2018) which too are of major interest and importance for sociological research.

This literature review has been conducted in the context of the ParlaMint II project (Erjavec et al., 2022) which compiles comparative corpora of parliamentary debates for multiple parliaments in Europe and aims to develop training materials and showcases in order to maximize their reuse in various disciplinary research communities that are interested in analyzing parliamentary debates. In this review, we focus primarily on the most prominent topics and research approaches in sociology. Its main aim is to identify the potential of better integration of corpus-based approaches and parliamentary corpora into sociological research.

The review consists of two parts. The first part is methodological and focuses on the description of research approaches which are most commonly used by sociologists when studying parliamentary debates. The second part presents the most prominent and sociologically relevant research topics of parliamentary debates and their approaches to data collection and analysis. We conclude the review with a discussion of the affordances and prerequisites for sociological research to benefit from the ParlaMint corpora and vice versa.

2. Literature Selection and Methods

Sociological research is frequently interdisciplinary since sociology as a discipline touches on various fields of social science, among others also on history, psychology, ecology, linguistics, and political science. It is mostly the interconnectedness with linguistics on the one hand and political science on the other that results in sociological interest in researching parliamentary debates and political speech. Sociology is also distinctive in its welcome of methodological diversity and its capacity to apply various methods to the study of social phenomena.

Sociology combines both, quantitative and qualitative research methods with the latter being especially popular because they work with non-numerical data and seek to interpret meaning from the data that help understand social life through the study of targeted population and places. This is highly important in sociological research because social and cultural contextual factors play a prominent role in analyzing parliamentary debates and political discourse.

One of the problems of qualitative analysis and the problem that sociology often faces is that researchers can influence data collection and analysis through subjective interpretation, leading them to make premature or unfunded conclusions. This exposes sociological research to subjectivism and bias and can impact and in extreme cases even change research outcomes. ParlaMint could help reduce the research bias by providing not only up-to-date, comprehensively, and transparently collected, and richly annotated corpora but also tutorials and showcases for sociologists that demonstrate the use of the corpora and its annotations in research.

2.1 Selection of Articles

This literature review presents an overview of the various qualitative, quantitative, and mixed methods approaches that sociologists use when researching political discourse. The reviewed articles were carefully selected among hundreds of sources which focus on parliamentary debates by considering some important research criteria. We identified the following scholarly search engines to look for the articles:

- Taylor and Francis Online (https://www.tandfonline.com),
- SAGE Journals (https://journals.sagepub.com),
- Semantic Scholar (https://www.semanticscholar.org), and
- Google Scholar (https://scholar.google.com).

We applied the following filters in order to identify the relevant articles:

- Publication period: 2012 – 2022,
- Discipline: Sociology and Social Science, and
- Article ranking: 'most relevant' and 'most cited'.

By using those filters, most prominent sociological journals were identified, such as Discourse and Society, European Journal of Cultural and Political Sociology, Journal of Ethnic and Migration Studies, and Gender and Society, although articles included in this review were also published elsewhere. All articles the title of which was considered potentially relevant were skimmed, especially the abstract, methodology and analysis sections, to confirm their relevance. It needs to be noted that due to language constraints, only articles in English have been chosen. This could be considered a limitation since we did not analyze the research in other languages which might show different results.

2.2 Overview of Methods and Topics

A total of 37 articles were determined as sociologically relevant and are listed in a Google spreadsheet.[1] We then thematically analyzed them and selected those which revolved around the most common topics. This resulted in 16 articles on 6 topics that were selected for a detailed analysis: Immigration and minorities (4 articles), Health and social care (3 articles), Victimization and criminalization (3 articles), Gender and discrimination (3 articles), Ideology, national identity, and political affiliation (2 papers), and Populism and addressing the public (1 paper).

The goal of sociological research of parliamentary discourse is to analyze political discourse and language, which results in specific methodological approaches. A total of 7 methodological approaches have been identified. Out of 16 articles, 10 employed a methodological framework of Discourse Studies (Discourse Analysis, Critical Discourse Analysis or Discourse Historical Approach), 4 employed Content Analysis and 2 a Mixed-methods approach, one combining content and keyword analysis and the other corpus-based and survey-assisted research. The fact that Discourse Studies was used altogether in over 60% (10) of the reviewed research means that this is the dominant methodological approach in sociological analyses of parliamentary discourse, closely followed by Content Analysis, another major research strand in sociology.

3. Research Methods

3.1 Discourse Studies (DS)

Discourse Studies refers to a field of research which includes various either qualitative or quantitative methods and different genres such as news reports or parliamentary debates (Van Dijk, 2018). In this review, we have identified three salient methods of Discourse Studies: Discourse Analysis (DA), Critical Discourse Analysis (CDA) and Discourse Historical Approach (DHA).

Discourse Analysis (DA) can be described as an interdisciplinary approach to the analysis of language in which speech, texts and conversations are analyzed (Konecki, 2017). It has emerged in the 1960s and is still one of the most widely used research methods in sociology, especially in cultural and political sociology, the focus of which is frequently the study of language, speech, and text.

Critical Discourse Analysis (CDA) has become one of the most visible branches of discourse analysis and examines the means by which political power is manifested or abused through discourse structures and practices (Dunmire, 2012). It is frequently applied to parliamentary communication with one of its major roles being to provide a critical context in which the debates occur.

Discourse Historical Approach (DHA) shares various common features with the CDA. The main distinctive feature of DHA is that it integrates the historical context and historical dimensions of discursive actions (Wodak, 2015).

Corpus-Assisted Discourse Studies (CADS) presents a useful link between sociological and linguistic research and is an invaluable research method for the study of political discourse and parliamentary data (Rubtcova et al. 2017). CADS methodological framework shows that the interconnection of sociological and corpus-based approaches can be mutually beneficial both in terms of ease to access the data as well as to obtain more reliable results. One of its major benefits is most definitely the elimination or at least reduction of the research bias. Because of the frequently qualitative nature of sociological studies, the sociological interpretation of data can quickly become too subjective which can result in biased research results.

---

[1] https://docs.google.com/spreadsheets/d/19xMBR-qHVZtQbYpgesgovFsiSfoMN1Q_pTAQCYvPxg8/edit#gid=1938758934

3.2 Content Analysis (CA)

Content Analysis (CA) focuses on the analysis of the society and social life by examining the content of the texts, images, and other media products. It is referred to as a research technique for making replicable and valid inferences from data to their contexts (Mihailescu, 2019). It is a common sociological method and employs a subjective interpretation of textual data "through the systematic classification process of coding and identifying themes or patterns" (Lilja, 2021).

The main difference between Content Analysis and Discourse Analysis (DA) is that the former focuses on the content, whereas the latter focuses on the language. We could therefore understand CA as a method for retrieving meaningful information from document and DA as focusing on the language that is used in a specific text and context.

Although content analysis was initially highly quantitative, the switch was made to qualitative content analysis where the focus fell more on the context of the textual understanding. Quantitative CA has again gained in popularity with the development of computational approaches to study larger amounts of texts and data more efficiently, to move from simple word counts to more advanced research of debates and discourse. It needs to be noted, however, that the majority of sociological data is still coded by researchers themselves and that the use of computational approaches is still underdeveloped.

3.3 Mixed Methods Approach

The mixed methods approach draws on the strengths of both qualitative and quantitative methods, which results in showing a more complete picture of the research problem (Shorten and Smith, 2017). One of its major benefits is its complementarity, which means that results produced by one of the methods can be elaborated and clarified with the findings from the other method (Molina-Azorin, 2016). In addition, it results in more in-depth findings, enhanced validity of the research, and limits research bias. In such a setting, researchers must develop a broader set of research skills and widen the repertoire of the methodologies used. Mixed methods requires a thorough integration and interconnection of the two methods where the results from each of them complement and further enforce one another.

4. Research Topics

Society constantly faces changes and challenges, and the role of politicians is to respond to them. This is why they constantly reflect on and respond to societal issues and challenges in parliamentary debates. This section gives an overview of the most prominent sociological research that look into societal issues as debated in parliament.

4.1 Immigration and Minorities

The topic of immigration, racism, and minorities is one of the most salient and most frequently discussed research topics in sociology.

4.1.1 Immigrant Rights

Research problem: Goenaga (2019) investigated immigrant voting rights in French and Swedish parliamentary debates. He examined how actors challenge and reinforce dominant ideas about the link between nationality and political rights. The aim of his research was to compare legislative debates that followed different paths towards democracy and show how different political cultures shape the structure of discursive conflicts around the political inclusion of foreigners in contemporary Western democracies.

Data collection: Goenaga analyzed legislative debates in France and Sweden between 1968 and 2017. The data consisted of 522 French and 149 Swedish statements from every debate in Swedish Riksdag and in the French Senate and National Assembly which focused on enfranchising non-citizen residents in both countries. Goenaga also used related statements made in debates on other topics that were identified through keyword searches. The statements were hand-coded according to different criteria and properties, such as the name, party, and sex of the speaker, as well as their position (for or against), whether they discriminated between non-citizens according to their country of origin, the frame and sub-frame speakers used to justify their positions and whether their argument referred to voting rights for local and national elections. The author also ensured that the categories were mutually exclusive and exhaustive across national contexts and actors by conducting a pilot analysis on media articles and grey literature on the same topic in France, the US and Sweden.

Research method: Goenaga used Discourse Analysis, intertwined with the research of social movements and the concept of framing theory. In sociology, this theory is predominantly used to analyze how people understand certain situations and activities. His analysis showed that the discursive strategies of the actors have consequences on the long run and that in both countries these discursive strategies are used differently but that certain similarities between strategies of right-wing and left-wing parties can be observed.

Discussion: Although the amount of analyzed data was quite extensive, Goenaga opted for manual collection of the data and hand coding. This enabled him to analyze the statements both comprehensibly and in depth and identify the main topics which were salient for his analysis.

4.1.2 Religious Rights

Research problem: Cheng (2015) researched the topic of banning the construction of minarets in Switzerland and studied the expressions of Islamophobia and racism in Swiss federal parliamentary debates on the popular initiative "Against the Construction of

Minarets" in March 2009. The debates focused on determining the validity of the said initiative and checking whether it breached any international laws. Cheng aimed to investigate whether political arguments for the ban of minarets were Islamophobic, Muslimophobic and/or racist. Her research revolved around the depiction and description of Muslims in Switzerland as well as the reasons for the implemented ban. She was mostly interested in political justifications of such decisions and the reasons behind it.

Data collection: Cheng obtained the relevant debates from the website of the Swiss parliament but gave no information about the size of the analyzed data or if it was manually coded in any way.

Research method: She relied on the methodological framework of Discourse Historical Approach (DHA) as introduced by Reisigl and Wodak (2017). She points out that DHA sees ideology as a vehicle for establishing and maintaining unequal power relations through discourse and that for the DHA, language is not powerful on its own but is rather made powerful by powerful people (Cheng, 2015).

Discussion: Cheng does not account for the processing and size of the analyzed data.

4.1.3 Media Influence on Political Discourse About Minorities

Research problem: Aydemir and Vliegenhart (2016) studied political discourse about minorities and focused on the question of how discursive opportunities shape representative patterns in the Netherlands and the UK. They studied to what extent media coverage on immigrant minorities can influence or shape parliamentary activities in the two countries.

Data collection: The dataset consisted of parliamentary questions posed by minority legislatures between 2002 and 2012. They were collected in a two-step procedure. First, all parliamentary questions were downloaded by manually entering the names of the relevant MPs. Then, only the documents which were specifically related to immigrant minorities were selected through a keyword search. The keywords were selected in a preliminary analysis of the most frequent words used in the discourse of immigration. This yielded 252 parliamentary questions for the Netherlands and 214 questions for the UK. The dataset for media analysis was collected through a keyword search for the same time period and with the same terms as before for three prominent and widely read newspapers from each country with different political ideologies. They only focused on the keywords in headlines and after the initial search, all the irrelevant articles were removed by manual inspection. This produced 731 media documents for the Dutch and 269 document for the UK media. After both datasets were collected, the authors manually coded them and searched for positive and negative tone on the minorities in both countries.

Research method: The authors performed Content Analysis on both datasets and used Regression Analysis which showed correlation between the two types of political discourse.

Discussion: The authors do not give a detailed description as to how the coding and content analyses were performed and do not publish the annotated dataset.

4.1.4 Immigration in the EU

Research problem: Gianfreda's (2019) paper on immigration in European Union is an illustrative example of the common difficulties that sociologists face when researching large amounts of data. She focused on how politicians position themselves when addressing the question of immigration in the EU.

Data collection: She analyzed parliamentary debates and mostly focused on low chambers' plenaries. Like many sociologists, she faced the problem of selecting the appropriate texts from a large amount of the available data. She relied on a list of search words which was compiled based on her deep knowledge of European integration and immigration. In addition, some manual work was needed to scan the relevant texts and exclude those with only passing reference to migration or European issues. Another challenge that needed to be overcome was the problem of retrieving debates from the parliamentary websites without having to manually select each. Gianfreda relied on Python-based script which helped her build a collection of speeches which were divided by political party and by politician; in that way she compiled her own corpus of machine-readable texts. Because of so many selected politicians, she needed to reduce their number to, on the one hand maintain a sufficiently large sample but on the other not be buried in too much data. She overcame it by selecting only the speeches made by key parliamentarians, e.g., those holding key roles within the political group, members of parliamentary commissions, etc.

Research method: She employed a mixed methods approach, combining qualitative content analysis and keyword analysis, for the analysis of party positioning on immigration discourse. The qualitative content analysis was performed using a manual qualitative coding software tool called MAXQDA[2] (VERBI GmbH, 1995), where texts were divided into "quasi-sentences" and then codified according to the previously set dimensions of the European Union. Quantitative keyword, analysis on the other hand, was conducted by using a tool of corpus linguistic called WMATRIX[3] (Rayson, 2008).

Discussion: Gianfreda pointed out numerous problems which social science researchers face when conducting their own research and showed that the use of computer software can help make their work much easier and

[2] https://www.maxqda.com

[3] https://ucrel.lancs.ac.uk/wmatrix/

much more efficient. In addition, a mixed methods approach "enables the researcher to reduce interpretation biases in the analysis of language through the use of software" (Gianfreda, 2019). With the methodology outlined above, Gianfreda shows that mixed methods are one of the most useful approaches when studying political discourse and that it offers interesting insights into not only how social science researchers should handle large amounts of data but also how they can minimize the interpretation bias and further improve the quality of their research.

4.2 Health and Social Care

Health and social care have always been high on the sociological agenda and a high volume of research focused on political representation and understanding of health and social care problems.

4.2.1 Reproduction Rights

Research problem: Eslen-Ziya (2021) conducted a study which focused on how population politics, reproduction rights, and fertility are addressed in Turkish parliamentary debates with the aim of stopping the decline in fertility and promote higher fertility rates.

Data collection: She analyzed parliamentary debates from 2008 until 2016 which were collected from an open-access database of the Turkish parliament. The preliminary document selection included a systematic investigation of data tracing by focusing on the 'three children' slogan introduced by Prime Minister Erdogan. This helped her determine the frequency of such debates. Once the preliminary selection of the text was completed, all the politicians' statements were merged in a simple plain text file upon which a keyword search was conducted to extract all the relevant paragraphs. Keywords such as 'three children', 'birth rate', 'abortion' and others were searched, and all the relevant paragraphs were then extracted for easier processing. The relevance of the debates was determined by applying an inductive research method which allowed her to see how the texts focused on the context of the population decline. After all the applied criteria and the selection, only 10 percent of the articles qualified for inclusion in further qualitative discursive analysis.

Research method: Eslen-Ziya employed a Discourse Analysis approach and focused her research on "normative, religious, and communicative dimensions of the population politics unfolding in Turkish parliament" (Eslen-Ziya, 2021).

Discussion: Eslen-Ziya's method included the analysis of parliamentary records, however, she fails to give an account of how her discursive analysis was performed and goes straight to the interpretation of results.

4.2.2 Mental Healthcare

Research problem: Joergensen and Praestegaard (2017) focused on the question of mental healthcare in Denmark. The aim of their study was to explore the issue of patient participation and how discourses about it are at play in official legal and political documents as well as patient recordings.

Data collection: They started by searching for legal and political documents published after 2009 that are relevant to patient participation within the Danish psychiatric context. Eight relevant documents were identified, two of which were focused on legislation about patient participation whereas the other six were guidelines which considered patient participation on a more operational level. In addition, the authors explored nurses' notes in patient records since they are the ones who actively deal with patients on everyday basis.

Research method: The authors employed a Critical Discourse Analysis as inspired by Fairclough (1995), which included the analysis of various textual documents. On the one hand, they analyzed political and legal documents and on the other they also focused on the nurses' notes in patient records about patient participation. The study related to the critical social-constructionist frame of understanding (Fuglsang, Bitsch Olsen, & Rasborg, 2013 in Joergensen and Praestegaard, 2017), in which the real world is understood as a series of social constructions and was designed as an exploratory critical documentary analysis. Their analysis was three-dimensional, focusing on basic text analysis, the analysis of the discourse practice and the analysis of the social practice. In the first part, the documents were read and analyzed word by word to grasp how patient participation is referred to. In the second part, the authors analyzed intertextual chains and coherence and connected the patient records with the findings of textual analysis. In the third part, the authors discussed the findings of textual analysis and discourse practices and examined how discourse practices influence social practices and therefore specify their nature.

Discussion: This research showed how incorporating various sources in the analysis ensures sociological broadness and yields more relevant and in-depth results than the analysis of only one source.

4.2.3 Housing Crisis

Research problem: White and Nandedkar (2019) analyzed the crisis of housing in New Zealand. This research introduces the problem of housing as one of the important social care topics and focuses on how politicians approach this problem in their political discourse and how the housing crisis is defined in different discourses.

Data collection: They conducted their research by analyzing the transcripts of the speeches, delivered in the New Zealand parliament. They limited their analysis to the terms of three consecutive governments, which attributed to the timespan between 2008 and 2017. They analyzed the discourse of the Labor Party and other smaller opposition parties. Their search terms were limited to 'housing supply' and 'housing affordability' and they identified 18 bills or 611 speeches from the actors which were then analyzed in detail. After that, another search was performed but was limited to the keyword 'crisis' which yielded additional 32 readings of 18 bills or 144 speeches. Once all the relevant texts were selected, the authors applied a manual coding technique which coded the data into two themes which were then qualitatively studied.

Research method: CDA was identified as particularly well suited for the study of discourse impact on the institutional and social organizations.

Discussion: The analysis is predominantly discursive with manually coded and selected texts. The authors note that this is the first such study in New Zealand and therefore consider the availability of the parliamentary documents especially valuable for such research.

4.3 Victimization and Criminalization

The topic of criminalization and victimization is relevant for sociological research and frequently observed in parliamentary debates.

4.3.1 Victimization

Research problem: Aronson (2021) investigated how individuals and groups can be positioned as victims by Swedish politicians and political discourse. He showed that the 'normal' majority has frequently been positioned as victims whereas the heterodox minorities were positioned as offenders.

Data collection: His analysis included eight longer political speeches as well as 56 addresses to the Swedish parliament. The speeches were uttered by leaders of all eight political parties which occupy seats in Swedish parliament and were gathered over the course of one year (from January 2019 to January 2020). The 56 political addresses were held in six parliamentary debates whereas eight additional political speeches were held during the 'democracy week' by party leaders. The official transcripts of the political debates were downloaded from the website of Swedish Riksdag whereas the transcripts of the eight speeches were gathered from the official website of 'democracy week'. It needs to be highlighted that all debates were conducted before the Covid-19 epidemic when the topics of criminality and migration were the most salient concerns of the Swedish parliament.

Research method: Discourse analysis was used to analyze the selected texts. All transcripts were closely read and reread by the author to become familiar with the data and temporary notes about patterns of interests were created. He mostly paid attention to and elaborated upon the patterns of consistency and those which were contrary to the main findings were given attention as the patterns of contradiction.

Discussion: The study lacks the description of not only how discourse analysis was performed but also the account of what was determined as crucial in the selected transcribed speeches and debates. This is yet another sociological research where data was gathered manually and downloaded directly from the respective websites.

4.3.2 LGBTQ+ Rights

Research problem: Redd and Russell's (2020) research is slightly different since it does not analyze parliamentary records but focuses on the study of the first apology for the criminalization of homosexuality to the LGBTQ+ community by the parliament in Victoria, Australia. To successfully develop the analysis, the authors outlined the conventional framework for understanding state responses and apologies to historic injustices within criminology. They were mostly interested in why the Victorian government was particularly concerned to seek forgiveness from the LGBTQ+ community and what was the basis for the apology.

Data collection: This analysis focuses on one particular parliamentary speech, namely the apology itself. It undertakes a line-by-line thematic coding of 25 pages of the apology.

Research method: The authors performed a Critical Discourse Analysis of the apology as well as analyzed and discussed the key topics that emerged from the discourse. These topics revolved around the inexplicable positioning of homophobia, the conjuring of post-homophobic society, the transformation of shame into state pride and subsuming the unhappy queer through the expectation of forgiveness. In the second part of their research, Redd and Russell applied a line-by-line thematic coding to the 25 pages of parliamentary documents with the help of NVivo software[4] (QSR International Pty Ltd., 2020), a qualitative data analysis tool which helps researchers organize and analyze qualitative data more efficiently and determine the main topics of a discourse analysis. The second analysis included the study of apologies made by the State Premier and the leader of the Labor party as well as 16 other politicians.

Discussion: This research is particularly interesting because it presents an analysis of a different but equally important type of political discourse. The utilization of the NVivo tool is also exemplary.

4.3.3 Drug Abuse

Research problem: Lilja (2021) explored how Russian parliamentary discourse discusses illegal drugs and their abuse.

Data collection: The research was based on a qualitative study of 177 speeches made in the lower house of the Russian parliament (State Duma) between 2014 and 2018. The data was collected by downloading all the relevant transcripts from the official website of the Russian parliament. Because of the large volume of the downloaded texts, the selection was further limited to only those speeches which explicitly discussed illegal drugs. The speeches which just mentioned the phrase 'illegal drugs' were

[4] https://www.qsrinternational.com/nvivo-qualitative-data-analysis-software/home

excluded. This yielded 177 speeches altogether which were included in the analysis. Although there are six political parties in the State Duma, only four were included in the analysis, which was the consequence of the aforementioned text selection criteria.

Research method: The author applied qualitative content analysis to analyze the speeches. The themes were defined and organized into a coding frame which distinguished between the extent of the problem, its causes, and solutions during a preliminary analysis of the data as well as based on the author's prior theoretical understanding of the studied topic. The coding frame was then used to annotate the dataset.

Discussion: Although such procedures are common in sociology, certain limitations can be observed. First, qualitative content analysis is subjective as it is based on the researcher's own knowledge of the topic and their belief about the saliency of certain themes. This can result in a biased preparation and coding of the material which can result in misleading or incomplete results.

5. Political Identities and Communication

Political identities as defined by Van Dijk (2004) are a type of social identities and as such constructed in different settings. Even though politicians can have different political affiliations and party memberships, they can share political identities. Similarly, a politician can display various political identities, however, there is usually one that prevails over others. Parliamentary discourse is therefore saturated with different political identities and the interaction between them results in a particular relationships not only between politicians but also between politicians and the public.

5.1 Gender Relations, Equality, and Discrimination

The relations between male and female politicians and gender discrimination and the differences between male and female language use in parliamentary discourse are relevant not only in sociology, but also in sociolinguistics, rhetoric, media, and other disciplines.

5.1.1 Surrogacy

Research problem: Eriksson (2021) researched discursive representation of gender equality policies and focused on how Nordic parliamentary debates talk about surrogacy.

Data collection: Her research material consisted of laws, bills, initiatives, and parliamentary proceedings between 2002 and 2018 with all documents publicly available on the official websites of both parliaments. Altogether 32 documents were included in the analysis. These documents were then manually coded and analyzed.

Research method: Eriksson's research combines the methodological framework of discourse analysis as well as rhetorical analysis and entails a combination of CDA, metaphor analysis and 'what's the problem' approach introduced by Bacchi and Eveline (2010). This is the only article in this review which employs the 'what's the problem' approach which focuses on analyzing the problem's discursive constitution in the policy or proposals as well as the underlying presuppositions and assumptions of the problem. Initial coding occurred in the preliminary analysis where Eriksson searched for keywords such as 'surrogacy' and 'equality' in order to get an overview of the important terms and discursive articulations. This enabled a deeper study of the connections between articulations as well as their usage. The second part of the research focused on the analysis of competing discourses by paying attention mostly to problem representations of altruistic and commercial surrogacy as well as domestic and cross-border surrogacy. Problem representation builds on the aforementioned approach and understanding of the discursive construction of social problems in policy documents. Eriksson also focused this part of her research on the analysis of metaphors and metonymy as rhetorical representation which conceal certain aspects and reinforce others.

Discussion: Methodologically speaking, this research is different from all the above-mentioned research and although Eriksson states differently, we could argue that she employed a mixed methods approach by combining three different but interconnected methodological approaches.

5.1.2 Gender Equality and Competitiveness

Research problem: Kylä-Laaso and Koskinen Sandberg (2020) analyzed the consequences of the Competitiveness Pact introduced by the Finnish government in order to increase the competitiveness of the Finnish economy by lowering labor costs. This pact mainly affected the feminized public sector which had clear gendered consequences and impacts. The authors studied affective institutional work and ordoliberal governance in the parliamentary discussion on these measures.

Data collection: Their research data consisted of Finnish parliament plenary sessions from 2015 to 2017 and included 27 different documents. These discussions were gathered from different stages of the process that lead up to the acceptance of Competitiveness Pact and were in downloaded from the official website of the Finnish parliament.

Research method: The authors utilized Critical Discourse Analysis, starting from the laws, and then moving on to the agreement over the pact. Those documents, in which the laws or the pact were central, provided the most information and were the most valuable. Various quotes were selected and analyzed based on how relevant the subject of the debate was.

Discussion: This research showed how CDA can be usefully applied when studying affects, gender equality and ordoliberal governance.

5.1.3 Gendered Language

Research problem: Bijeikiene and Utka (2006) focus on the linguistic features of gendered language in parliamentary discourse. They are interested in whether there exist gender-specific linguistic differences in political discourse and how the public sees and perceives such differences. In addition, they focus on examining what kind of language the general public considers gender-specific and whether this can be confirmed by a corpus linguistic study.

Data collection: The corpora consisted of stenographs from the Lithuanian parliament and the basic unit of study was the utterance. Almost 200 stenographs were randomly selected, one half for male and the other one for female politicians. No annotation other than the speaker's name was included.

Research method: The authors employed two methodological frameworks. The first one was sociolinguistic inquiry in which a questionnaire was prepared and distributed among university students to see how they perceive gender-specific language. The questionnaire consisted of two parts where the first part focused on respondents' opinion on existence of gender-specific language in political discourse, whereas the second part contained 11 short extracts from parliamentary talks and wanted to check if the respondents could determine whether the utterance was produced by a male or a female politician. The second method was corpus linguistics, where the answers of the first study were quantitatively checked in the two corpora of parliamentary debates.

Discussion: This research clearly show the importance of combining qualitative and quantitative methods and underlined the need for qualitative analysis results to be checked quantitatively to avoid possible research biases which could affect the final results of the research.

5.2 Ideology, National Identity, and Political Affiliation

The defining characteristics of parliamentary discourse are among others also its ideological nature, the influence it has on national identity and the construction of political identities according to the political affiliation.

5.2.1 Construction of the National Identity

Research problem: Riihimäki's (2019) studied the discursive construction of the national identity of the United Kingdom in the European Union.

Data collection: The timeframe of the analysis was between 1973 and 2015, from the year of UK becoming a member state until the year when a vote on an EU membership was promised. The data analyzed consisted of all the debates that occurred in House of Commons in that period and were all retrieved from the Hansard website. For debates between 1973 and 2004 the author used a local copy of Hansard corpus (which was prepared especially for her use) whereas for debates between 2004 and 2015 the data was collected from Commons Hansard archives and manually compiled into an unannotated corpus. Both corpora together comprised around 450 million words.

Research method: Riihimäki utilized Corpus-Linguistic methods to find relevant parts of text for a closer analysis using the CasualConc concordance[5] (Yasu, 2008). She searched for those excerpts in which the pronouns 'us' and 'we' were included and co-occurred with phrases 'European Union', 'European Community' or 'European Communities'. The relevant hits were then analyzed in two stages; firstly, the referents of the pronouns were manually identified and only those which referred to 'the UK' (meaning the country or British people) were included in the second stage of the study. In the second stage she read through the hits and searched for those instances in which character or actions of the United Kingdom in the EU were described. Those instances were then divided into identity categories. These identities were then further closely examined and analyzed by employing critical discourse analysis.

Discussion: Riihimäki shows that the methodological framework applied was particularly useful because pronoun use deserves a special attention inside CDA, especially in political rhetoric. Her approach also showed how important and useful corpus-linguistic methods can be in researching political discourse, mainly because they offer methodological approaches which help researchers gather data quickly and efficiently without employing too much manual work.

5.2.2 Negative People Representation

Research problem: Salim Nefes (2021) conducted a study which focused on how right-wing political discourse predicts a negative representation of certain groups of people, in this case Armenians, and how traditionalized values and a somewhat negative perception of people can be seen in the case of right-wing political discourse against immigrants and minorities.

Data collection: The study analyzed the mention of the word 'Armenian' in Turkish parliamentary debates and was conducted for parliamentary debates between 1983 and 2018. The unit of the analysis was a speech of the Turkish MP and the analysis happened in four methodological steps. The documents which contained the word 'Armenian' were selected and read. A coding scheme was developed which was then used for coding the data and calculating the intercoder reliability. The coders analyzed whether the general tone of the speech was negative. In the last step the data was quantitively analyzed.

Research method: The method employed was Content Analysis.

Discussion: Salim Nefes does not specify where the parliamentary texts were collected from and how the timeframe of the analyzed texts was chosen.

[5] https://sites.google.com/site/casualconc/

5.3 Populism and Addressing the Public

Political communication with the public and voters is a frequently researched sociological topic which has in recent years been extended to the study of populist political discourse on social media since they are becoming a frequently used communication channels through which politicians connect with the public.

5.3.1 Construction of (Extra)ordinariness

Research problem: Fetzer and Weizman (2018) analyzed how politicians, who are classified as 'extraordinary', use the quotations to refer to the general public (or the 'ordinary') and bring the public into the political arena.

Data collection: Fetzer and Weizman focused on the analysis of 20 sessions of PMQs and answers between David Cameron (then Prime Minister) and Jeremy Corbyn (then Leader of the Opposition) in 2015 and 2016. Transcripts of the debates were downloaded from the Hansard website whereas the comments, which were also analyzed, were gathered from commenter's section of the Channel 4 News as well as from YouTube. Quantitative analysis of the official transcripts focused on the question-response sequence between Cameron and Corbyn and in connection to that, 120 questions and responses were analyzed. Qualitative analysis, on the other hand, paid attention on the one hand to the question-response relationship between the two speakers as well as to a set of comments which explicitly referenced the "brought-in ordinariness" by Jeremy Corbyn. For qualitative analysis 2238 comments were downloaded and analyzed.

Research method: They base their research on Critical Discourse-Analytic perspective. Both quantitative and qualitative analyses are carried out in order to obtain best possible results.

Discussion: This research showed that although other data sources can be used together with parliamentary data, the latter present a basis for the analysis of parliamentary discourse and should be included in sociological research.

6. Conclusion

This review shows that sociological research of parliamentary discourse is based on real-world data gathered from parliamentary records and related official documents as well as mass and social media content. The data is nearly always collected hic and nunc with time-consuming, manual methods, which makes sociologists potentially a very important user group of the ParlaMint corpora. However, the review also shows that sociologists are predominantly interested in current events, which means that it is of crucial importance for the ParlaMint corpora to be updated on a regular basis. Given the prevalent methodological approaches, most scholars will wish to be able to examine the relevant debates in their entirety, which is why it is important that hits in ParlaMint contain links to the original parliamentary records or recordings.

Apart from the access and scope of the data included in ParlaMint, their encoding is equally important since as it is clearly shown in this review, sociology scholars have highly specific needs for the parts of parliamentary debates that are relevant for their study. For example, some researchers will wish to focus only on the MP's questions to the government, so it would be very useful if they were explicitly marked in the ParlaMint corpora. More importantly, since most sociological research is focused on a specific concept, a major struggle in the research community is to define the relevant query terms, which are most commonly defined on a highly intuitive basis or in a highly reductionist way. It would therefore be a major added value to the entire research area if the ParlaMint corpora contained semantic annotations, indicating the subject of discussion.

The review clearly shows that sociologists collect, code, and analyze data by themselves instead of relying on existing corpora. One of the tasks of ParlaMint is therefore to show to sociologists that the data relevant for their research is already collected and processed and to show them how such data can be used in sociological research. It needs to be noted, though, that sociologists will often need to add additional annotations as well as combine parliamentary data with other data sources, so it would be very helpful to ensure smooth export and import options from the concordancer to an annotation software.

In terms of approaches to data analysis, this review indicates the need for technical support for more systematic, transparent, and replicable quantitative and qualitative analyses, which makes corpus-based approaches ideally suited for sociological research of parliamentary discourse. It is therefore of paramount importance that rich and user-friendly documentation on how the ParlaMint data was collected, processed, and annotated is made available, along with quick user manuals, tutorials and showcases that demonstrate the use of ParlaMint corpora and features of the concordancers.

This review also shows that sociological research of political discourse are frequently limited to a national level and only occasionally research it comparatively or transnationally. This underlines the potential and the added value of the ParlaMint corpora which enables researchers to access comparably sampled, uniformly coded and annotated corpora of 17 European parliaments with further corpora being added in the second phase of the project. Another reason for the lack of pan-European analyses of parliamentary debates is also the language barrier to access the parliamentary transcripts released in the national languages. This is why machine translations of the transcripts which are planned in ParlaMint would enable more cross-lingual research of parliamentary political discourse.

7. Acknowledgements

The work described in this paper was funded by the Slovenian Research Agency research programme P6-0436: *Digital Humanities: resources, tools, and methods* (2022-2027), and the DARIAH-SI research infrastructure. The work presented in this paper is supported by the Social Sciences & Humanities Open Cloud (SSHOC) project (https://www.sshopencloud.eu/) as well as ParlaMint project (https://www.clarin.eu/parlamint).

8. References

Aronson, Olov. (2021). Victimhood in Swedish political discourse". *Discourse and Society,* 32(3): 292 - 306.

Aydemir, Nermin and Vliegenthart, Rens. (2018). Public discourse on minorities: how discursive opportunities shape representative patterns in the Netherlands and the UK. *National Papers,* 46(2): 237-251.

Bijeikiene, Vilma and Utka, Andrius. (2006) Gender-Specific features in Lithuanian parliamentary Discourse: An interdisciplinary sociolinguistic and corpus-based study. *SKY Journal of Linguistics,* 19: 63 – 99.

Bischof, Karin and Ilie, Cornelia. (2018). Democracy and discriminatory strategies in parliamentary discourse. *Journal of Language and Politics*, 17(5): 585-593

Cheng E, Jennifer. (2015). Islamophobia, Muslimophobia or racism? Parliamentary discourses on Islam and Muslims in debates on the minaret ban on Switzerland. *Discourse and Society,* 26(5): 562 – 586.

Dunmire, Patricia L. (2012) Political discourse analysis: Exploring the language of Politics and the Politics of language. *Language and Linguistics Compass,* 6: 735-751.

Eslen-Ziya, Hande. (2021) Discursive Construction of Population Politics: Parliamentary Debates on Declining Fertility Rates in Turkey. *Årgang,* 45(2-3): 127-140.

Eranti, Veikko, Blokker, Paul and Vieten M., Ulrike (2020). The many flavours of politics. *European Journal of Cultural and Political Sociology.* 7(4): 405-408.

Eriksson, Lise. (2021). Outsourcing problems or regulating altruism? Parliamentary debates on domestic and cross-border surrogacy in Finland and Norway. *European Journal of Women's Studies,* 29(1): 1-16.

Erjavec, T., Ogrodniczuk, M., Osenova, P. et al. (2022). The ParlaMint corpora of parliamentary proceedings. *Lang Resources & Evaluation.*

Fetzer Anita and Weizman, Elda. (2018). 'What I would say to John and everyone like John is...': The construction of ordinariness through quotations in mediated political discourse. *Discourse and Society,* 29(5): 495-513.

Gianfreda, Stella. (2019). Using a Mixed-Method Approach to Examine Party Positioning on Immigration and the European Union in Parliamentary Proceedings. *SAGE Research Methods Cases Part 2.*

Goenaga, Austin. (2019). Defending popular sovereignity: discursive conflict in French and Swedish parliamentary debates on immigrant voting rights (1968-2017). *Citizenship Studies,* 23(8): 870-891.

Joergensen, Kim and Praestegaard, Jeanette. (2017). Patient participation as discursive practice—A critical discourse analysis of Danish mental healthcare. *Nursing Inquiry* 25(2): 1-11.

Konecki, Krzysztof. (2017). Qualitative Sociology. In K.O. Korgen (Ed.) *The Cambridge Handbook of Sociology. Core Areas in Sociology and the Development of the Discipline*, Vol. 1. Cambridge: Cambridge University Press, pp. 143-152.

Kylä-Laaso, Miikaeli and Koskinen Sandberg, Paula. (2020). Affective Institutional Work and Ordoliberal Governance: Gender Equality in Parliamentary Debates on the Competitiveness Pact in Finland. *NORA - Nordic Journal of Feminist and Gender Research*, 28(2): 86-98.

Lilja, My. (2021). Russian Political Discourse on Illegal Drugs: A Thematic Analysis of Parliamentary Debates. *Substance Use and Misuse,* 56(6): 1010-1017.

Mihailescu, Mimi. (2019). Content analysis: a digital method. The University of Warwick.

Molina-Azorin, Jose. (2016). Mixed methods research: An opportunity to improve our studies and our research skills. *European Journal of Management and Business Economics:* 25(2): 37-38.

Redd, Curtis and Russel K., Emma. (2020). It all started here and it all ends here too: Homosexual criminalization and the queer politics of apology. *Criminology and Criminal Justice,* 20(5): 590-603.

Reisigl, Martin and Wodak, Ruth. (2017). The Discourse-Historical Approach (DHA). In J. Flowerdew and J.E. Richardson (Eds.) *The Routledge Handbook of Critical Discourse.* Routledge Handbooks Online, pp. 87-118.

Riihimäki, Jenni. (2019). At the heart and in the margins: Discursive construction of British national identity in relation to the EU in British parliamentary debates from 1973 to 2015. *Discourse and Society,* 30(4): 412-431.

Rubtcova, Mariia, Vasilieva, Elena, Pavenkov, Vladimir and Pavenkov, Oleg. 2017. Corpus-based conceptualization in sociology: possibilities and limits. *Espacio Abierto,* 26(2): 187-199

Salim Nefes, Türkay. (2021). Perceived group threats and right-wing political party membership as driving forces of negative descriptions in Turkish Parliamentary debates (1983-2018). *Journal of Ethnic and Migration Studies*: 1-15.

Shorten, Allison and Smith, Joanna. (2017). Mixed methods research: expanding the evidence base. *Evidence-based nursing*, 20: 74-75.

Van Dijk, Teun A. (2004). Text and context of parliamentary debates. Universitat Pompeu Fabra, Bracelona, Spain

Van Dijk, Teun A. (2018). Discourse and Migration. In R. Zapata-Barrero and E. Yalaz (Eds.) *Qualitative Research in European Migration Studies*. Springer Open, pp. 227-247.

White, Iain and Nandedkar, Gauri. (2019). The housing crisis as an ideological artefact: Analysing how political discourse defines, diagnoses and responds. *Housing Studies*, 36(2): 213-234.

Wodak, Ruth. (2015). Critical Discourse Analysis, Discourse-Historical Approach. *The International Encyclopedia of Language and Social Interaction*: 1-14

Proceedings of ParlaCLARIN III @ LREC2022 pages 92–100
Marseille, 20 June 2022

FrameASt: A Framework for Second-level Agenda Setting in Parliamentary Debates through the Lens of Comparative Agenda Topics

Christopher Klamm, Ines Rehbein, Simone Paolo Ponzetto
Data and Web Science Group
Mannheim University, Germany
{klamm, rehbein, ponzetto}@uni-mannheim.de

Abstract

This paper presents a framework for studying second-level political agenda setting in parliamentary debates, based on the selection of policy topics used by political actors to discuss a specific issue on the parliamentary agenda. For example, the COVID-19 pandemic as an agenda item can be contextualised as a health issue or as a civil rights issue, as a matter of macroeconomics or can be discussed in the context of social welfare. Our framework allows us to observe differences regarding *how* different parties discuss the *same* agenda item by emphasizing different topical aspects of the item. We apply and evaluate our framework on data from the German Bundestag and discuss the merits and limitations of our approach. In addition, we present a new annotated data set of parliamentary debates, following the coding schema of policy topics developed in the Comparative Agendas Project (CAP), and release models for topic classification in parliamentary debates.

Keywords: framing, agenda setting, comparative agendas project

1. Introduction

In recent years, the concept of *framing* (Bateson, 1955; Goffman, 1974; Tversky and Kahnemann, 1984) has received more and more attention in the social sciences, focussing mostly on the analysis of media communication and its impact on politics (Entman, 1993; Scheufele, 1999; Boydstun, 2013). The importance of *framing* lies in its power to shape the way in which we perceive, organize and interpret the world around us. Studies on framing have identified different types of framing effects, such as *entity framing* (Entman, 1993), i.e., the selection and highlighting of some aspects of a perceived reality, in order "to promote problem definition, causal interpretation, moral evaluation, and/or treatment recommendation for the item described." (Entman, 1993, p.52). Another related framing type is *agenda setting* (Iyengar and Kinder, 1987; McCombs and Reynolds, 2002, etc.), looking at how the media influences which topics succeed in gaining public attention or, for *political* agenda setting, which topics receive attention in politics (for example, by succeeding in being put on the agenda in parliament). In short, agenda setting is "more concerned with which issues are emphasized, i.e., *what* is covered, than *how* such issues are reported and discussed" (Weaver, 2007, p.142). An extension of the concept is *second-level agenda setting* or *attribute agenda setting* which –in contrast to first-level agenda setting– does not primarily consider which issues are salient in the discourse but which attributes of the issue are highlighted and how they are presented. Thus, second-level agenda setting is closely related to framing, as pointed out by Weaver (2007).

In our work, we consider both aspects, (i) *what* issues are being covered in parliamentary debates and (ii) *how* they are being discussed by different political actors and parties. We investigate this by looking at parliamentary

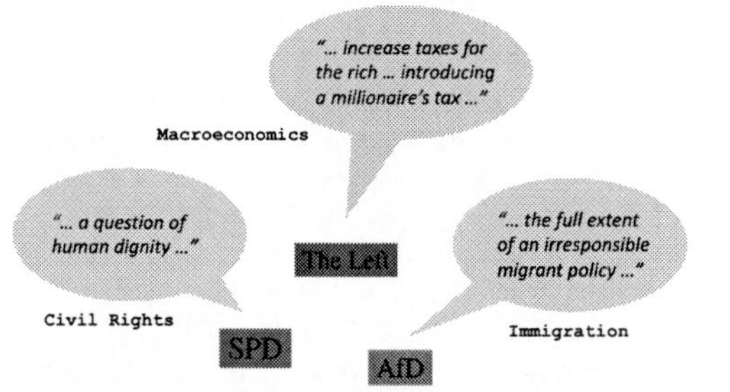

Figure 1: Example for second-level agenda setting in parliamentary debates from the German Bundestag where speakers from different parties highlight different aspects (Civil Rights, Macroeconomics, Immigration) of the same agenda item (Immigration).

speeches held by members of *different* political parties, but on the *same* agenda item. This setting allows us to control for topic while, at the same time, observe crucial differences in *how* parties discuss a particular topic.

For illustration, consider a parliamentary debate on the policy topic of Immigration and, more specifically, on benefits for asylum seekers. All contributions to this agenda item are expected to address the topic under discussion but might do so by emphasizing different aspects related to this issue (Figure 1).[1] One party might blame the government for their allegedly irresponsible immigration policy, another party might focus on civil rights aspects while yet another party might discuss the topic from a macroeconomic perspective by proposing a millionaire's tax. As a result, this setting provides

[1] All three excerpts are taken from a debate in the German Bundestag on 14/03/2019, Session 86, agenda item "Zusatzpunkt 6".

us with an ideal testbed that allows us to analyse and compare how parties frame the discussion of the *same* topic in different ways.

This paper proposes **FrameASt**, a **Frame**work for Second-level **A**genda **S**et**t**ing in Parliamentary Debates. We conceptualise framing as described above and operationalise it by looking at the differences in the selection of agenda policy topics by different political actors, based on the Comparative Agendas Project (CAP) framework (Bevan, 2019) (Section 2). To identify the different CAP topics in the debates, we develop supervised CAP topic classifiers, as described in Section 3. We evaluate our classifiers on a data set of interpellations annotated within the Comparative Agendas Project and present a new data set for German parliamentary debates, annotated with major and minor CAP topics. In Section 5 we discuss applications and potential limitations of our framework before we conclude and outline avenues for future work.

2. Related Work

We first review related work on topic classification (§2.1) and framing in parliamentary debates (§2.2) and then introduce the Comparative Agendas Project (Bevan, 2019) (§2.3).

2.1. Topic Classification for Political Text

Previous work on topic classification for political text has looked at both, unsupervised and supervised approaches. Herzog et al. (2018) predict Comparative Agenda topics for debates from the UK House of Commons, using an unsupervised topic modelling approach with transfer topic labelling. Similar in spirit is the work of Brand et al. (2021) who also use the CAP codebook to detect policy agendas, however, their approach is based on Heterogeneous Information Networks (HIN) and node embeddings for identifying policy fields in German parliamentary debates. Kreutz and Daelemans (2021) is an example for a semi-supervised approach based on CAP policy agendas. Their method makes use of an automatically generated lexicon, based on graph propagation.

Many supervised approaches have been using data from the Manifesto Project database[2]. Zirn et al. (2016) predict coarse topics on the sentence level for electoral manifestos for English (Zirn et al., 2016) and (Glavaš et al., 2017) predict topics in a cross-lingual setting (Glavaš et al., 2017). Verberne et al. (2014) also work with political manifestos but predict a set of over 200 fine-grained topics on the level of semantically coherent text segments. Subramanian et al. (2018) apply deep neural networks for manifesto policy classification where they first predict the labels, based on a hierarchical multitask model, and then use probabilistic soft logic to refine them.

More recent work explores transformer-based transfer learning (Vaswani et al., 2017) for topic classification. Abercrombie et al. (2019) present a corpus of UK parliamentary debates, annotated with policy preference codes (i.e., the domain of a policy issue and the stance towards this issue) from the Manifestos Project and develop models for the automatic prediction of those topics. Koh et al. (2021) use transformers to predict labels for English political manifestos on the sentence level.

In our work, we compare a simple feature-based bag-of-words SVM classifier to transformer-based BERT models (Devlin et al., 2019), fine-tuned for the prediction of CAP topics on the level of semantically coherent segments.

2.2. Framing in Parliamentary Debates

While most work on framing has studied how the selection and presentation of topics in the mass media shapes public opinion, far fewer studies have looked at agenda setting and framing in political communication.

Naderi and Hirst (2016) study framing strategies in Canadian parliamentary debates, focussing on the recognition of a set of predefined frames on the topic of same-sex marriage. Their work can be described as entity framing in the sense of Entman (1993).

Umney and Lloyd (2018) take an original approach to framing from the perspective of design studies and investigate how political actors make use of precedents to reframe the political discourse in parliamentary debates. Otjes (2019) points out the lack of agenda setting studies in the context of parliamentary settings, due to the fact that this process usually takes place behind closed doors and thus the data needed for empirical studies is not available. An exception is the Dutch parliament, the *Tweede Kamer*, where the decision of what to put on the agenda is made in public. This allows Otjes to study how parties from the government and opposition act to promote their "own" issues[3] and, at the same time, fight other parties' attempts to do the same. The relevance of this practice has been pointed out by Otjes (2019, p.731).

> "If a party is able to set the tone in parliament, they may be able to set the themes for the election campaign."

We follow previous work (Otjes, 2019; Green-Pedersen and Mortensen, 2010) and look at agenda setting in parliament from an *issue ownership* (or *issue competition*) perspective (Walgrave et al., 2015), based on the assumption that parties have a strong preference for promoting policy issues that are associated with them and where voters assume that they are competent to deal with this issue. In contrast to Otjes (2019), we are not able to study the selection of agenda items in parliament, due to the lack of data. However, what we can investigate is *how* the different agenda items are discussed

[2]https://manifesto-project.wzb.eu/

[3]For a definition of *issue ownership*, see, e.g., Walgrave et al. (2015; Stubager (2018).

1	Macroeconomics	*6*	Education	*12*	Law and Crime	*17*	Technology
2	Civil Rights	*7*	Environment	*13*	Social Welfare	*18*	Foreign Trade
3	Health	*8*	Energy	*14*	Housing	*19*	International Affairs
4	Agriculture	*9*	Immigration	*15*	Domestic Commerce	*20*	Governmental Operations
5	Labor	*10*	Transportation	*16*	Defense	*21*	Public Lands
						23	Culture

Table 1: The 21 major agenda policy topics in the CAP schema (agendas 11 and 22 have been removed by the CAP project when revising and unifying the annotations from multiple participating projects).

by the different parties. As put by Otjes (2019), "Political competition focuses on selective emphasis of issues rather than direct confrontation on those issues". This *selective emphasis* is the focus of our framework, and we propose to study it by comparing the *differences* in the selection of policy topics by the different parties in debates of the *same* agenda item.

2.3. The Comparative Agendas Project

The main goal of the initial Comparative Agendas Project was to track agenda setting in the news, i.e., how much attention is being directed towards an issue. In order to achieve this, Baumgartner and Jones (1993) used distant reading techniques by looking at the headlines and abstracts of over 22,000 media articles, to identify the key topics covered in the news. This early work triggered many follow-up studies on identifying and tracking topical issues in different types of political text and for many countries (for an overview, see (Baumgartner et al., 2019)). A major contribution of project is that they make their data available to the research community, which enabled comparative studies of public policy on a large scale.

The unified schema of the CAP data (Bevan, 2019) focusses on topical issues, intentionally ignoring the framing of those issues (i.e., aspects such as positive or negative stance or ideological position). The reason behind not encoding those aspects in the CAP schema is by no means a lack of interest but rather due to the contextual sensitivity of framing that requires not only a lot of thought during coding but also in-depth knowledge of the issue at hand. This would make the large-scale annotation of text infeasible. Despite this, the CAP topics (see Table 1) provide a valuable basis for framing analysis, as we hope to show in our work.

3. CAP Topic Classification

We now present different classifiers trained to predict the 21 major CAP policy labels that we later use in our analysis. We model the identification of the policy topics as a segment-level classification task. Our first model is a feature-based SVM classifier that we compare to a transfer learning approach based on transformers (Devlin et al., 2019).

3.1. Text Segmentation

To segment the speeches into semantically coherent texts, we apply the unsupervised text segmentation algorithm of Glavaš et al. (2016) which creates a semantic relatedness graph of the input text, based on the similarity of word embeddings for words in the text. To obtain semantically coherent text segments, a graph-based segmentation algorithm then tries to find maximal cliques in the relatedness graph.

3.2. Topic Classification

We adapt the graph segmentation model to German[4] and apply it to the speeches in our corpus. We use a relatedness threshold of 0.1 and a minimal segment size of 1. The first parameter is used in the construction of the relatedness graph while the second parameter defines the minimal segment size, where 1 specifies a minimum number of one sentence per segment. The parameters have an impact on the number of segments produced by the model and have been chosen so that the segment size is reasonably large while allowing the model to split up larger, semantically unrelated text passages. During segmentation, the 25,311 speeches have been split up into 37,553 segments which are the input to our topic classifiers.

SVM Topic Classifier We train an SVM topic classifier on the Parliamentary Question Database from the CAP project[5], a data set with more than 10,000 major and minor interpellations posed by parliamentarians (mostly from the opposition parties) to the government (Breunig and Schnatterer, 2019). The data set ranges over the 8th to the 15th legislative periods (1976–2005). Each interpellation has been assigned a major and a minor CAP topic.

We first applied some standard preprocessing and clean-up steps to the data where we also removed meta-information, such as listings of politicians' names and header/footer information. We removed stopwords and punctuation and extracted a) a tokenised and b) a lemmatised version of the data.[6] After preprocessing and clean-up, the interpellations have an average length of 388 tokens. The length range varies from 17 to 7,253 tokens per interpellation, with a standard deviation of 429 tokens.

We then trained feature-based text classification models on the preprocessed data, based on bag-of-words (BOW)

[4]The original model has been developed for English.

[5]The annotations are available from `https://www.comparativeagendas.net/datasets_codebooks`.

[6]For lemmatisation, we used the spaCy library: `https://spacy.io` with the `de_core_news_sm` model.

id	Topic	SVM	BERT	ParlBERT	support
19	International	77.4	78.7	**80.0**	1,126
16	Defense	84.0	**85.0**	**85.0**	1,099
20	Government	66.1	69.6	**71.3**	989
2	Civil Rights	**79.3**	78.8	76.5	978
7	Environment	76.3	76.3	**76.6**	845
10	Transportation	83.8	**87.7**	86.0	800
12	Law & Crime	66.3	65.7	**67.1**	492
8	Energy	76,2	76.0	**78.6**	424
3	Health	76.8	**82.3**	78.2	418
15	Domestic Com.	57.1	**66.6**	64.4	382
9	Immigration	74.8	80.3	**81.0**	376
5	Labor	67.9	**70.0**	69.1	344
1	Macroeconom.	61.5	61.1	**62.8**	339
4	Agriculture	77.9	**78.7**	76.3	292
13	Social Welfare	**55.1**	54,1	49,2	253
17	Technology	58.7	**67.8**	63.0	252
6	Education	64.0	67.6	**71.6**	183
14	Housing	73.0	78.5	**79.6**	178
18	Foreign Trade	51.0	58.1	**61,5**	139
23	Culture	**68.8**	64.2	54.6	69
21	Public Lands	32.4	42.4	**45.4**	55
	total f1-micro	73.7	76,8	76.5	10,033

Table 2: Results (micro F1) for different classifiers (SVM, GermanBERT (BERT) and GermanParlaBERTarian (ParlBERT)) for CAP topics. Support shows the number of training instances for each class.

features with and without tf-idf weighing. We experimented with different classification algorithms from the scikit-learn library[7], where the linear SVM achieved best results. Hyperparameters have been determined in a 5-fold cross-validation setup (20k features, w/o tf-idf on lemmatised unigrams). Other parameters have been set to *penalty: l2, loss: squared hinge, C: 1.0, max_iter: 1,000.*[8]

Our best SVM classifier achieves a micro F1 over all 21 agenda topics of 73.7% on the in-domain interpellation data (Table 2). Results for the individual classes range from 32.4 to 84.0, with higher scores for the more frequent labels, as is common for supervised machine learning models. The 10 policy topics with the highest F1 scores are Defense (84%), Transportation (84%), Civil Rights (79%), Agriculture (78%), Health (77%), International Affairs (77%), Energy (76%), Environment (76%), Immigration (75%) and Housing (73%).

GermanParlaBERTarian (ParlBERT) To obtain topic predictions, we first adopted an existing GermanBERT [9] language model with adaptive pre-training on German parliamentary debates from the DeuParl corpus (Walter et al., 2021). This domain adaptation step is a form of transfer learning, with the goal of adapting a model trained on a *source domain*, for example Wikipedia, to a *target domain*, such as parlamentary debates (Ruder, 2019).

The data we used to perform this adaptation includes sentences from different decades and legislative terms, spanning a time period from 1867-2020, with a broad range of speakers from all political parties in Germany. We used unsupervised masked language modelling for two epochs with a learning rate of $5e-5$ and a batch size of 16 on more than 8 million sentences with a minimum sequence length of 250. Then we fine-tuned the model on the CAP interpellation data for topic prediction. We trained the model for 5 epochs, with a learning rate of $5e-5$ and a batch size of 16. All experiments were averaged across ten runs with different splits. The splits as well as the models will be made publicly available.

Table 2 shows the performance of GermanBERT without domain adaption (f1-micro 76.8%) and ParlBERT with domain adaption (f1-micro 76.5%). Unlike the positive effects of domain adaptation reported for other NLP tasks (Beltagy et al., 2019; Lee et al., 2020), we did not see any substantial improvements but observed results in the same range as for GermanBERT with task-specific fine-tuning. However, compared to GermanBERT, ParlBERT seems to yield higher results on low-frequency topics.

While the BERT-based models generally outperform the SVM classifier, for some topics the SVM achieves higher results (e.g., Civil Rights, Energy, Social Welfare, Culture). This indicates that the performance is highly topic-dependent. Overall, GermanBERT and ParlBERT show a promising performance for CAP topic classification while, at the same time, the differences in results across topics illustrate the computational challenges for topics with small sample sizes and the overall need for more research in the area of few-shot learning.

4. Data and Annotation

The data we use in our work are parliamentary debates from the German Bundestag (mostly) from the 19th legislative period (Oct 24, 2017 to Nov 18, 2021). Our corpus includes over 14 mio. tokens from speeches held by 759 different speakers (Table 3).[10] [11]

4.1. Sampling

From this corpus, we selected a sample of speeches for manual annotation. Our objective was to create a gold standard controlled for topic, with roughly the same amount of text for each party. To obtain our goal, we sampled the data as follows.

First, we identified agenda items from the Bundestag debates that covered different policy topics in the CAP

[7] https://scikit-learn.org

[8] We also experimented with a larger number of (unigram and ngram) features and with other algorithms from the scikit-learn library but obtained best results for the linear SVM with unigram features.

[9] https://huggingface.co/bert-base-german-cased with HuggingFace (Wolf et al., 2020)

[10] The abbreviations in Table 3 refer to the *Christian Democratic Union* in Germany and *Christian Social Union* in Bavaria CDU/CSU; the *Social Democratic Party* SPD; the *Alternative for Germany* AfD; the *Free Democratic Party* FDP; the *Greens* The Greens and *The Left* The Left.

[11] We removed 84 speeches for which the given speaker information was not sufficient to unambiguously identify the party affiliation (e.g., *Roth* could refer to Michael Roth (SPD) or to Claudia Roth (Greens).

party	# speeches	# tokens	# spk
CDU/CSU	7,635	4,862,654	259
SPD	5,321	3,158,315	167
AfD	3,465	1,844,707	95
FDP	3,067	1,593,108	89
The Greens	2,866	1,522,305	70
The Left	2,671	1,394,089	72
cross-bencher	200	86,170	7
total	25,225	14,461,348	759

Table 3: Some statistics for our corpus of Bundestag debates (token counts excluding punctuation). *Cross-bencher* refers to members of the parliament not affiliated with any political party.

schema. The identification of agenda items was based on the supervised SVM classifier described in Section 3. We used the model to predict major CAP policies for all speeches in our data and then assigned the majority label to the agenda item, to determine the *main topic* for this item. For illustation, let us assume that we have an agenda item i on some topic t and we have all the parliamentary debate contributions by politicians from different parties on this particular agenda item. Let us also assume that we have 10 debate contributions for this agenda item and that our classifier predicted the major CAP policies "Immigration" for 6 of the 10 speeches and "Civil Rights" and "Social Welfare" for the remaining four speeches (see Table 4 below). Then the majority label for this agenda item, i.e., its *main topic*, would be "Immigration".

Agenda item i with 10 speeches										
Speech:	1	2	3	4	5	6	7	8	9	10
Topic:	I	I	C	I	S	C	I	I	C	I
Majority label for i: I (Immigration)										

Table 4: Example for determining the majority topic for an agenda item i with 10 speeches. *Topic* refers to the CAP topic predicted by the SVM. I, C and S stand for **I**mmigration, **C**ivil Rights and **S**ocial Welfare.

Based on the majority labels for agenda items, we identified relevant agendas for each major CAP policy label from which we then selected and manually validated one agenda item for manual annotation, based on the following criteria: (a) we select agenda items that include speeches by members from each of the 6 parties and (b) we select agenda items where at least 60% of the predictions made by the classifier agree on a topic (which is what we call the *main topic* of the agenda item). However, we do not select items where all or nearly all (i.e., 80% or more) of the predictions agree on the topic, as we want to avoid creating an unrealistically "easy" validation set.

Following this procedure, we extracted a validation set

party	# speeches	# tokens	# spk
CDU/CSU	57	37,636	47
SPD	45	26,124	37
AfD	25	14,514	22
FDP	22	12,466	19
The Greens	25	13,574	18
The Left	22	12,295	19
cross-bencher	1	284	1
total	197	116,893	163

Table 5: Some statistics for our manually annotated test set (token counts excluding punctuation).

for manual annotation with more than 100,000 tokens and with 7 to 14 speeches per agenda item (see Table 5). The advantage of our sampling procedure is that it allows us to compare speeches by political actors from different parties on exactly the same topic (i.e., agenda item) and to investigate which aspects of this agenda item have been emphasized by each party.

4.2. Annotation

The CAP coding schema includes 21 major topics and more than 200 fine-grained subtopics. We follow the CAP schema and annotate major and minor topics in our data set, to be used for an in-domain evaluation of our classifiers.

Annotation Process The annotators are two NLP researchers with experience in linguistic annotation but have not worked with the CAP schema before.[12] They were presented with the speeches, one at a time, and were instructed to first read through the whole text of the speech. Then they segmented each speech into semantically coherent text segments, based on the policy topics discussed in the text, and assigned one major and minor CAP topic label to each text segment. The annotators were instructed to introduce new segment boundaries only if they noticed a change in topic.

For annotation, we split our data into three batches. The first batch included one speech only for each major CAP label, to familiarize the annotators with the relevant topics for this agenda item. The second batch was considered as a training round where each speech was annotated independently by each of the annotators. The third batch has been annotated after the completion of the training round and reflects the quality of the annotatons. After each round of annotation, all disagreements have been resolved in discussion.

Inter-Annotator Agreement We now report results for inter-annotator agreement (IAA) for the 21 major CAP topics for the second (training round) and third batch of labelled debates in our new dataset. We collect the set of all CAP labels that have been assigned to a specific speech and compare the sets of labels assigned by the two annotators. As our data includes multiple

[12]The first two authors of the paper.

labels per speech, we cannot compute Cohen's kappa or related measures. Instead, we report the Jaccard similarity between the two sets of assigned labels for each speech.

Given two sets of labels, A and B, we compute the Jaccard similarity coefficient for each speech in our data as shown below (Equation 1).[13]

$$J(A, B) = \frac{|A \cap B|}{|A \cup B|} \quad (1)$$

The average over the Jaccard similarity coefficients for all speeches in the second batch (training round) is 0.59, for the third batch the score increases to 0.74.

Challenges for Annotation Both annotators found the task challenging, due to the scarse guidelines in the codebook which only presented the annotators with minimal descriptions of each CAP policy topic but did not include a more theoretical discussion on how to distinguish between related and overlapping topics. Other challenges for annotation were posed by the identification of the exact segment boundaries. Here the two annotators often identified a change in topic but did not agree on the exact point of segmentation (i.e., topic change).

4.3. Topic Classification on Parliamentary Debates from the German Bundestag

We now evaluate our topic classifiers on the newly created data set from the German Bundestag. After the manual annotation step had been completed, we mapped the annotated major and minor CAP topic labels onto the automatically created text segments (see Section 3.1), to create a new data set of parliamentary debates with major and minor CAP topic labels on the segment level. This procedure can result in more than one gold label per segment in cases where the human annotators decided on a topic change for segments that have not been split by the text segmentation algorithm. As our classifier can only predict one label per segment, we decided on a lenient evaluation strategy that does not punish the classifier for non-optimal segmentation decisions. Our procedure is as follows: For each text segment, we count the predicted label as a true positive (TP) if it is included in the set of manually assigned labels for this segment, and as a false positive (FP) otherwise. We then report the accuracy for each topic and micro F1 over all topic classes.

Table 6 reports results for the three classifiers on the segments from our new dataset of parliamentary debates from the Bundestag, annotated for CAP topics. As expected, results are a bit lower than for the in-domain interpellation data. This might reflect an out-of-domain effect for the debates. It is also conceivable that our interpretation of the CAP guidelines was slightly different than the one of the original annotators. Another possible explanation for the lower results is the automatic segmentation process which might not always yield optimal results.

Overall, we observe a similar trend as for the interpellations data (Table 2), with lower results for the less frequent classes (such as Culture, Foreign Trade, Technology, Social Welfare). A bit surprising is the decrease in results for some of the more frequent classes (Government Operations, Environment, Transportation). Taking a look at the data, we notice that for the "Environment" class, only 4 out of 10 instances in the ParlaBERT results have been predicted correctly. Four of the incorrect predictions have been annotated as "Energy" in the gold data set while the remaining two cases were labelled as "Agriculture". For "Transportation", on the other hand, 12 of the 14 incorrect predictions have been annotated as "Energy" by the human coders and another one as "Environment". This reflects the close thematic interconnection of the three topics, Energy, Transport and Environment, in recent parliamentary debates which poses a challenge for CAP topic classification.

id	Topic	SVM	BERT	ParlBERT
19	International	28.1	86.7	75.0
16	Defense	42.9	**100.0**	85.7
20	Government Operations	34.3	33.3	**44.8**
2	Civil Rights	63.0	90.0	**94.7**
7	Environment	38.5	28.6	**40.0**
10	Transportation	43.8	**58.3**	33.3
12	Law and Crime	61.5	83.3	**90.0**
8	Energy	90.9	**100.0**	**100.0**
3	Health	**100.0**	**100.0**	90.0
15	Domestic Commerce	**88.9**	58.8	70.6
9	Immigration	**100.0**	**100.0**	92.9
5	Labor	72.2	95.0	**95.2**
1	Macroeconomics	**100.0**	90.0	**100.0**
4	Agriculture	**100.0**	**100.0**	94.4
13	Social Welfare	60.0	**71.4**	40.0
17	Technology	60.0	**66.7**	50.0
6	Education	**57.1**	25.0	0
14	Housing	**100.0**	**100.0**	**100.0**
18	Foreign Trade	0	0	0
23	Culture	0	0	0
21	Public Lands	n/a	n/a	n/a
	total f1-micro	58.3	68.7	**70.2**
	(true positives)	(147/252)	(173/252)	(177/252)

Table 6: Results (micro F1) for the CAP topic classification models (SVM, (German)BERT and ParlBERT) on the newly annotated data set of parliamentary debates (252 segments).

5. Potential Applications and Limitations

We now summarise the main components of our framework and discuss potential applications as well as limitations of our work.

Figure 2 illustrates the different components of our pipeline. Given **(1)** a set of parliamentary speeches, we **(2)** predict CAP topics for all speeches in our parliamentary data, using our supervised topic classifier. Next, we group all speeches that belong to the *same*

[13]The Jaccard similarity for two identical sets is 1.0. A comparison of two sets where the second set is a subset half the size of the first set (e.g., $s_1 = [1, 2, 3, 4]$ and $s_2 = [1, 4]$) would yield a Jaccard similarity of 0.5.

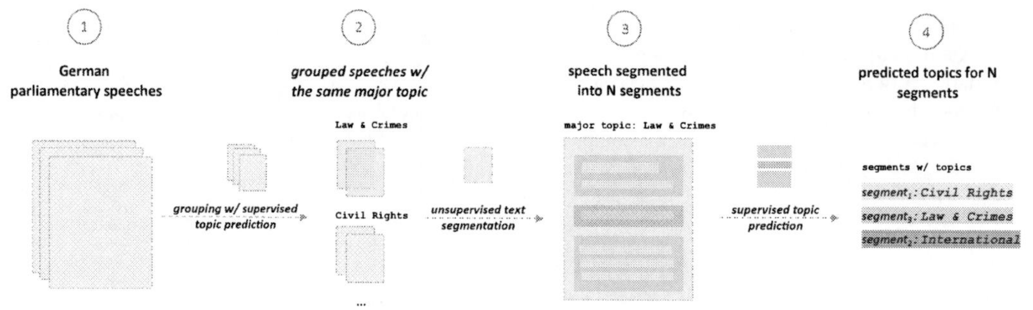

Figure 2: Overview of our framework illustrating the workflow for a given **(1) set of parliamentary speeches (2) grouped along shared topics** and **(3) applied segmentation** with **(4) supervised topic prediction** for all identified segments.

agenda item and determine the dominant topic for this set of speeches, based on the majority label predicted by our CAP topic classifier. We only include topics with a prediction accuracy of at least 75% (Defense (85%), Transportation (88%), Civil Rights (79%), Agriculture (79%), Health (82%), International Affairs (79%), Energy (76%), Environment (76%), Immigration (80%) and Housing (78%)). We then use **(3)** the unsupervised text segmentation model of Glavaš et al. (2016) and split the speeches into semantically coherent text segments. In the next step, **(4)** we use our topic classifier to predict CAP topics for each *speech segment*, which results in a set of semantically coherent, topic-annotated speech segments for each agenda item.

Our framework provides us with the means for comparing *how* different parties discuss the same *main topic* (or dominant topic, based on the majority predictions of the CAP topic classifier) of an agenda item, i.e., *which topics* are emphasized by each party in the plenary debates. In addition, it allows us to track the salience of specific topics over time. We plan to use our methodology to study the emergence of new topics over a longer period of time (e.g., climate change) and whether and how they have been adopted by political actors in the parliamentary setting.

Figure 3 shows a prototypical use case of our framework. It illustrates the distribution of CAP topics (e.g., Defense, Transportation, International Affairs, etc.) that have been used by the different German parties (SPD, CDU/CSU, AfD, The Left, The Greens and the FDP) when discussing *the same* main topic. For example, for the debates of all agenda items that have been predicted a certain majority topic, *which other topics have been used by members of the different parties in debates of this particular main topic*?

Overall, we can observe that the normalized distribution of topics across all parties follows a slightly different pattern. We can identify topics that seem to be more associated with certain parties. For instance, the CAP topic "Civil Rights" is more often emphasized in debate contributions by the Left, the Greens, and

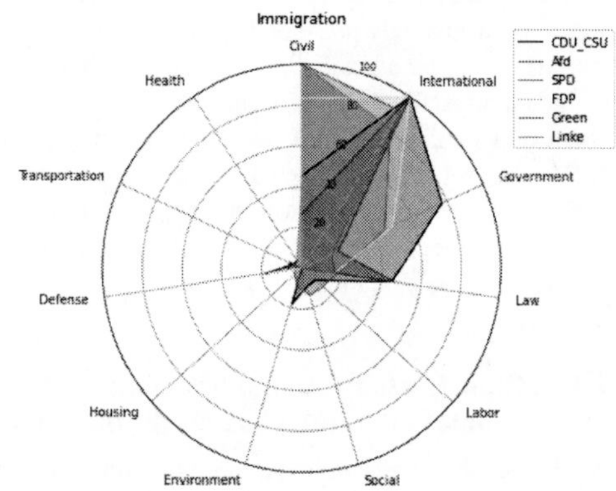

Figure 3: Normalized distribution of the associated topics per party AfD, SPD, CDU/CSU, The Left, FDP and The Greens in Germany regarding the major topic Immigration.

the SPD. In contrast, the AfD shows a below-average use of the "Civil Rights" topic in their speeches when talking about immigration, putting a stronger focus on "Law and Crime". In comparison, the CDU/CSU seems to associate the topic more often with aspects related to "Government Operations". This examaple should give the reader a first idea of possible applications and research questions that could be studied with our framework for second-level agenda setting in parliamentary debates.

There are also limitations to our work. In particular, our framework only allows us to investigate *which policy issues* have been emphasized in the debates, but not the stance of a particular party towards this issue. For example, two parties might emphasize the same policy issue but might still persue diametrically opposed interests. One straightforward way to address this issue is the extension of our framework with topic-based (or issue-based) stance detection. We plan to persue this avenue in future work.

6. Conclusion

In the paper, we introduced a framework for the analysis of plenary debates, with a focus on second-level agenda setting. Our framework allows us to observe differences in how political parties discuss the same policy issues by highlighting different thematic aspects of the issue. We have applied our framework to data from the German Bundestag and contribute a new annotated dataset of parliamentary debates. Our annotation experiment shows the challenges for topic annotation in political debates and the computational challenges for topic classification for datasets with unbalanced and small sample sizes. We hope that our new corpus will serve as a way to better understand the variety of topic aspects associated with an agenda item in political debates.[14]

7. Acknowledgements

This work was supported in part by the SFB 884 on the Political Economy of Reforms at the University of Mannheim (projects B6 and C4), funded by the German Research Foundation (DFG), and by the Ministry of Science, Research and the Arts Baden Württemberg (MWK).

8. Bibliographical References

Abercrombie, G., Nanni, F., Batista-Navarro, R., and Ponzetto, S. P. (2019). Policy preference detection in parliamentary debate motions. In *Proceedings of the 23rd Conference on Computational Natural Language Learning (CoNLL)*, pages 249–259, Hong Kong, China, November. Association for Computational Linguistics.

Bateson, G. (1955). A theory of play and fantasy. *Psychiatric Research Reports*, 2:39–51.

Baumgartner, F. R. and Jones, B. D. (1993). *Agendas and instability in American politics*. Chicago: University of Chicago Press.

Baumgartner, F. R., Breunig, C., and Grossman, E. (2019). *Comparative Policy Agendas: Theory, Tools, Data*. Oxford: Oxford University Press.

Beltagy, I., Lo, K., and Cohan, A. (2019). SciBERT: A pretrained language model for scientific text. In *Proceedings of the 2019 Conference on Empirical Methods in Natural Language Processing and the 9th International Joint Conference on Natural Language Processing (EMNLP-IJCNLP)*, pages 3615–3620, Hong Kong, China, November. Association for Computational Linguistics.

Bevan, S. (2019). Gone fishing: The creation of the Comparative Agendas Project master codebook. In Frank R. Baumgartner, et al., editors, *Comparative Policy Agendas: Theory, Tools, Data*. Oxford: Oxford University Press.

Boydstun, A. E. (2013). *Making the news: Politics, the media, and agenda setting*. Chicago: U. of Chicago Press.

[14]The dataset and topic classifiers are available for download: https://github.com/chkla/FrameASt.

Brand, A., Schünemann, W. J., König, T., and Preböck, T. (2021). Detecting policy fields in German parliamentary materials with heterogeneous information networks and node embeddings. In *The 1st Workshop of Computational Linguistics for Political Text Analysis (CPSS)*.

Breunig, C. and Schnatterer, T. (2019). Policy agendas in Germany. In Frank R. Baumgartner, et al., editors, *Comparative Agendas Project: Theory, Tools, Data*. Oxford: Oxford University Press.

Devlin, J., Chang, M., Lee, K., and Toutanova, K. (2019). BERT: pre-training of deep bidirectional transformers for language understanding. In Jill Burstein, et al., editors, *Proceedings of the 2019 Conference of the North American Chapter of the Association for Computational Linguistics: Human Language Technologies, NAACL-HLT 2019, Minneapolis, MN, USA, June 2-7, 2019, Volume 1 (Long and Short Papers)*, pages 4171–4186. Association for Computational Linguistics.

Entman, R. M. (1993). Framing: Toward clarification of a fractured paradigm. *Journal of Communication*, 43:51–58.

Glavaš, G., Nanni, F., and Ponzetto, S. P. (2016). Unsupervised text segmentation using semantic relatedness graphs. In *Proceedings of the Fifth Joint Conference on Lexical and Computational Semantics*, pages 125–130, Berlin, Germany, August. Association for Computational Linguistics.

Glavaš, G., Nanni, F., and Ponzetto, S. P. (2017). Crosslingual classification of topics in political texts. In *Proceedings of the Second Workshop on NLP and Computational Social Science*, pages 42–46, Vancouver, Canada, August. Association for Computational Linguistics.

Goffman, E. (1974). *Frame analysis*. New York: Free Press.

Green-Pedersen, C. and Mortensen, P. B. (2010). Who sets the agenda and who responds to in the Danish parliament? A new model of issue competition and agenda-setting. *European Journal of Political Research*, 49(2):257–281.

Herzog, A., John, P., and Mikhaylov, S. J. (2018). Transfer topic labeling with domain-specific knowledge base: An analysis of UK house of commons speeches 1935-2014. *CoRR*, abs/1806.00793.

Iyengar, S. and Kinder, D. R. (1987). *News that matters: Television and American opinion*. Chicago: University of Chicago Press.

Koh, A., Boey, D. K. S., and Béchara, H. (2021). Predicting policy domains from party manifestos with bert and convolutional neural networks. In *The 1st Workshop of Computational Linguistics for Political Text Analysis (CPSS)*.

Kreutz, T. and Daelemans, W. (2021). A semi-supervised approach to classifying political agenda issues. In *The 1st Workshop of Computational Linguistics for Political Text Analysis (CPSS)*.

Lee, J., Yoon, W., Kim, S., Kim, D., Kim, S., So, C. H., and Kang, J. (2020). BioBERT: a pre-trained biomedical language representation model for biomedical text mining. *Bioinformatics*, 36(4):1234–1240.

McCombs, M. and Reynolds, A. (2002). News influence on our pictures of the world. In J. Bryant et al., editors, *Media Effects: Advances in Theory and Research*, pages 1–18. Mahwah: LEA.

Naderi, N. and Hirst, G. (2016). Argumentation mining in parliamentary discourse. In Matteo Baldoni, et al., editors, *Principles and Practice of Multi-Agent Systems*, pages 16–25, Cham. Springer International Publishing.

Otjes, S. (2019). No politics in the agenda-setting meeting: plenary agenda setting in the Netherlands. *West European Politics*, 42(4):728–754.

Ruder, S. (2019). *Neural Transfer Learning for Natural Language Processing*. Ph.D. thesis, National University of Ireland, Galway.

Scheufele, D. A. (1999). Framing as a theory of media effects. *Journal of Communication*, 49(1):103–122.

Stubager, R. (2018). What is issue ownership and how should we measure it? *Political Behaviour*, 40:345–370.

Subramanian, S., Cohn, T., and Baldwin, T. (2018). Hierarchical structured model for fine-to-coarse manifesto text analysis. In *Proceedings of the 2018 Conference of the North American Chapter of the Association for Computational Linguistics: Human Language Technologies, Volume 1 (Long Papers)*, pages 1964–1974, New Orleans, Louisiana, June. Association for Computational Linguistics.

Tversky, A. and Kahnemann, D. (1984). Choices, values, and frames. *American Psychologist*, 39(4):341–350.

Umney, D. and Lloyd, P. (2018). Designing frames: The use of precedents in parliamentary debate. *Design Studies*, 54:201–218.

Vaswani, A., Shazeer, N., Parmar, N., Uszkoreit, J., Jones, L., Gomez, A. N., Kaiser, Ł., and Polosukhin, I. (2017). Attention is all you need. In *Advances in Neural Information Processing Systems*, pages 5998–6008.

Verberne, S., Dhondt, E., van den Bosch, A., and Marx, M. (2014). Automatic thematic classification of election manifestos. *Information Processing & Management*, 50(4):554–567.

Walgrave, S., Tresch, A., and Lefevere, J. (2015). The conceptualisation and measurement of issue ownership. *West European Politics*, 38(4):778–796.

Walter, T., Kirschner, C., Eger, S., Glavas, G., Lauscher, A., and Ponzetto, S. P. (2021). Diachronic analysis of German parliamentary proceedings: Ideological shifts through the lens of political biases. In J. Stephen Downie, et al., editors, *ACM/IEEE Joint Conference on Digital Libraries, JCDL 2021, Champaign, IL, USA, September 27-30, 2021*, pages 51–60. IEEE.

Weaver, D. H. (2007). Thoughts on agenda setting, framing, and priming. *Journal of Communication*, 57(1):142–147.

Wolf, T., Debut, L., Sanh, V., Chaumond, J., Delangue, C., Moi, A., Cistac, P., Rault, T., Louf, R., Funtowicz, M., Davison, J., Shleifer, S., von Platen, P., Ma, C., Jernite, Y., Plu, J., Xu, C., Le Scao, T., Gugger, S., Drame, M., Lhoest, Q., and Rush, A. (2020). Transformers: State-of-the-art natural language processing. In *Proceedings of the 2020 Conference on Empirical Methods in Natural Language Processing: System Demonstrations*, pages 38–45, Online, October. Association for Computational Linguistics.

Zirn, C., Glavaš, G., Nanni, F., Eichorts, J., , and Stuckenschmidt, H. (2016). Classifying topics and detecting topic shifts in political manifestos. In *The International Conference on the Advances in Computational Analysis of Political Text*.

Proceedings of ParlaCLARIN III @ LREC2022 pages 101–106
Marseille, 20 June 2022

Comparing Formulaic Language in Human and Machine Translation: Insight from a Parliamentary Corpus

Yves Bestgen
Laboratoire d'analyse statistique des textes
Université catholique de Louvain
Place Cardinal Mercier, 10 1348 Louvain-la-Neuve, Belgium
yves.bestgen@uclouvain.be

Abstract

A recent study has shown that, compared to human translations, neural machine translations contain more strongly-associated formulaic sequences made of relatively high-frequency words, but far less strongly-associated formulaic sequences made of relatively rare words. These results were obtained on the basis of translations of quality newspaper articles in which human translations can be thought to be not very literal. The present study attempts to replicate this research using a parliamentary corpus. The results confirm the observations on the news corpus, but the differences are less strong. They suggest that the use of text genres that usually result in more literal translations, such as parliamentary corpora, might be preferable when comparing human and machine translations.

Keywords: neural machine translation, human translation, parliamentary corpus, multiword unit

1. Introduction

Due to the success of neural machine translation systems, more and more research is being conducted to compare their translations to human translations. Most of these studies take a global view of quality (Popel et al., 2020; Läubli et al., 2018; Wu et al., 2016), but others focus on much more specific dimensions that could be further improved, such as lexical diversity and textual cohesion (De Clercq et al., 2021; Vanmassenhove et al., 2019).

In a recent study, Bestgen (2021) analyzed the frequency of use of a specific category of formulaic sequences, the "habitually occurring lexical combinations" (Laufer and Waldman, 2011), which are statistically typical of the language because they are observed "with markedly high frequency, relative to the component words" (Baldwin and Kim, 2010). To identify them, he used the CollGram technique which relies on two lexical association indices: mutual information (MI) and t-score, calculated on the basis of the frequencies in a reference corpus (Bernardini, 2007; Bestgen and Granger, 2014; Durrant and Schmitt, 2009). A discussion of two automatic procedures that at least partially implement this technique is given in Bestgen (2019). He showed that neural machine translations contain more strongly-associated formulaic sequences made of relatively high-frequency words, identified by the t-score, such as *you know*, *out of* or *more than*, but far less strongly-associated formulaic sequences made of relatively rare words, identified by the MI, such as *self-fulfilling prophecy*, *sparsely populated* or *sunnier climes*.

These observations can be linked with a series of studies that have shown similar differences in foreign language learning (Bestgen and Granger, 2014; Durrant and Schmitt, 2009) and which have proposed to interpret them in the framework of the usage-based model of language learning which "hold that a major determining force in the acquisition of formulas is the frequency of occurrence and co-occurrence of linguistic forms in the input" (Durrant and Schmitt, 2009). It is obviously tempting to use the same explanation for differences in translation, as neural models also seem to be affected by frequency of use (Koehn and Knowles, 2017; Li et al., 2020).

A competing explanation is however possible. All the texts analyzed in Bestgen (2021) were quality newspaper articles written in French and published in *Le Monde diplomatique*, and then translated in English for one of its international editions. However, as Ponomarenko (2019) pointed out following Bielsa and Bassnett (2009), "Translation of news implies a higher degree of re-writing and re-telling than in any other type of translation" (p.40) and "International news, however, tends to prefer domestication of information instead of translation accuracy, which also has its particular reasons" (p.35). As it is important in this kind of texts that the translated version is as relevant and interesting as possible for the target readers, often from another culture, lexical and syntactic modifications, deletions and additions are frequent. All these modifications make the translation of this kind of texts less literal than the one expected from a machine translation system and thus risk to affect the differences in the use of formulaic sequences.

In this context, parliamentary corpora are a perfectly justified point of comparison. Translation accuracy is the main objective. For example, the criteria that European parliamentary debates translations must meet include: "the delivered target text is complete (no omissions nor additions are permitted)" and "the target text is a faithful, accurate and consistent translation of the

News corpus

Original French

Au-delà du logiciel libre. Le temps des biens communs. Jusqu'où ira le droit de propriété?
Pour tout ce qui peut être représenté par de l'information, son extension semble ne devoir connaître aucune limite.

Human translation

The internet and common goods. Own or share? Is there any limit to property?
Current developments might suggest not, as property rights are steadily extended.

Machine translation (DeepL)

Beyond Free Software. The time of the commons. How far will property rights go?
For everything that can be represented by information, its extension seems to know no limits.

Parliamentary corpus

Original French

Nous savons que la Commission va bientôt réformer la politique commune de la pêche.
Cette proposition de règlement du Conseil est la première d' une série qui permettra d' élaborer cette réforme.

Human translation

We know that the Commission is going to reform the common fisheries policy shortly.
This proposal for a Council Regulation is the first in a series which will make it possible to draw up this reform.

Machine translation (DeepL)

We know that the Commission will soon reform the Common Fisheries Policy.
This proposal for a Council Regulation is the first of a series that will allow this reform to be developed.

Figure 1: Human and machine translation of a French excerpt from each of the two corpora.

source text" (Sosoni, 2011).

Figure 1 illustrates this difference in translation between these two types of texts. It shows a brief extract from each corpus in its original and translated versions. The excerpt from the news corpus shows the different translation strategies used by the human and the machine, with the human version showing several reformulations affecting both the lexicon and the syntax and the deletion of one constituent in the last sentence. Such differences are not present in the extract from the parliamentary corpus.

The objective of the present study is to determine whether machine translations of parliamentary texts differ from human translations in the use of phraseology, in order to confirm or refute the findings from the news corpus. The three following hypotheses are tested: compared to human translations, machine translations will contain more strongly-associated collocations made of high-frequency words, less strongly-associated formulaic sequences made of rare words and thus a larger ratio between these two indices. An positive conclusion, in addition to confirming the links between machine translation and foreign language learning, will suggest a way to make machine translations more similar to human translations, especially since the fully automatic nature of the analysis facilitates its large-scale use.

2. Method

2.1. Parliamentary Corpus

The material for this study is taken from the Europarl corpus v7 (Koehn, 2005) (Philipp Koehn, 2012) available at `https://www.statmt.org/europarl`. In order to have parallel texts of which the original is in French and the translation in English, information rarely directly provided in the Europarl corpus because it was not developed for this purpose (Cartoni and Meyer, 2012; Islam and Mehler, 2012), I employed the preprocessed version, freely available at `https://zenodo.org/record/1066474#.WnnEM3wiHcs`, obtained by means of the EuroparlExtract toolkit (Ustaszewski, 2019) (Ustaszewski, Michael, 2017).

Two hundred texts of 3,500 to 4,500 characters, for a total of 120,000 words, were randomly selected among all texts written in French and translated into English. These thresholds were set in order to have texts long enough for collocation analysis, but not exceeding the 5,000-character limit imposed by the automatic translators used so that the document could be translated in a single operation.

Between February 14 and 16, 2022, three neural machine translation systems were used to translate these texts into English: the online version of *DeepL* (`https://deepl.com/translator`) and *Google Translate* (`https://translate.google.com`) and the *Office 365* version of *Microsoft Translator*.

2.2. Procedure

All contiguous word pairs (bigrams) were extracted from the CLAWS7 tokenized version (Rayson, 1991) of each translated text. Bigrams, not including a proper noun, that could be found in the British National Corpus (BNC, `https://www.natcorp.ox.ac.uk`), were assigned an MI and a t-score on the basis of the frequencies in this reference corpus. Bigrams with $MI \geq 5$ or with $t \geq 6$ were deemed to be highly collocational (Bestgen, 2018; Durrant and Schmitt, 2009). On this basis, three GollGram indices were calculated for each translated text: the percentage of highly collocational bigrams for MI, the same percentage for the t-

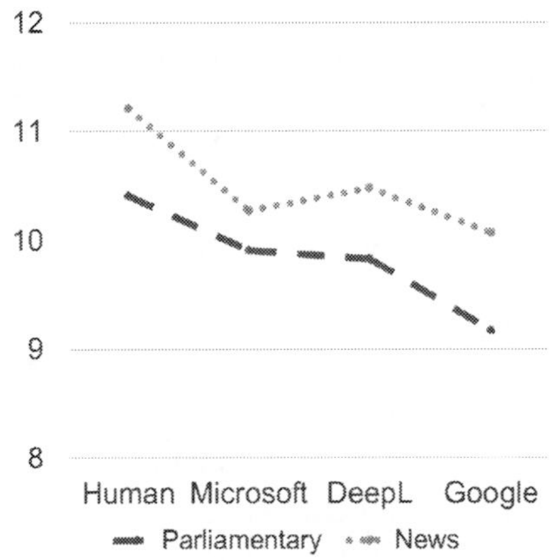

Figure 2: Mean percentages of highly collocational bigrams for MI.

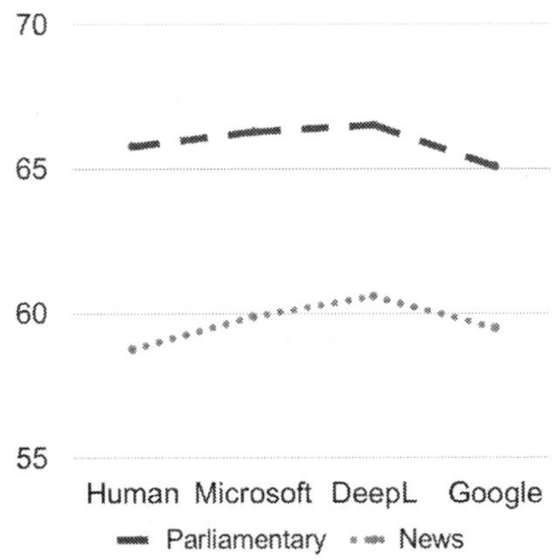

Figure 3: Mean percentages of highly collocational bigrams for t-score.

score and the ratio between these two percentages (%t-score / %MI).

This procedure is in all points identical to the one used in the analysis of the news corpus (Bestgen, 2021). The only difference is that the machine translations of the news corpus were undertaken in March-April 2021. According to Porte (2013) terminology, the present study is thus an *approximate* replication that "might help us generalize, for example, the findings from the original study to a new population, setting, or modality" (p.11).

3. Results

3.1. Parliamentary Corpus

The mean percentages of highly collocational bigrams for the MI and t-score and the mean ratio for the four translation type of the two genres of text are shown in Figures 2 to 4. The differences observed on the parliamentary corpus are very similar to those obtained with the news corpus. This section is focused on the anal-

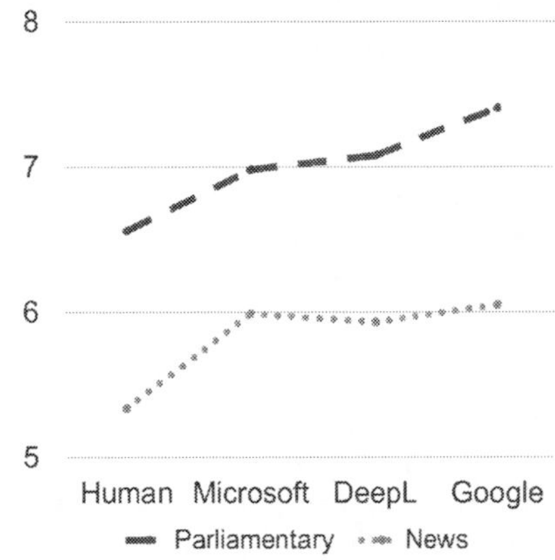

Figure 4: Mean ratio between t-score and MI.

	MI	Micro.	DeepL	Google
		MI		
Human	Di	-0.50	-0.59	-1.24
	d	0.38	0.44	0.89
	p	0.67	0.69	0.81
Micro.	Di		-0.09	-0.74
	d		0.11	0.67
	p		0.55	0.76
DeepL	Di			-0.65
	d			0.61
	p			0.71
		t-score		
Human	Di	0.51	0.76	-0.69
	d	0.15	0.31	0.26
	p	0.60	0.60	0.63
Micro.	Di		0.25	-1.20
	s		0.09	0.45
	p		0.55	0.80
DeepL	Di			-1.44
	d			0.72
	p			0.76
		Ratio		
Human	Di	0.42	0.52	0.84
	d	0.39	0.50	0.77
	p	0.69	0.70	0.81
Micro.	Di		0.10	0.42
	d		0.14	0.47
	p		0.56	0.71
DeepL	Di			0.31
	d			0.37
	p			0.66

Table 1: Differences (column translator minus row translator) and effect sizes for the two indices and the ratio in the four translation types. Di = Difference, d = Cohen's d, p = proportion of texts in which the mean effect is observed.

ysis of the Parliamentary corpus while the comparison with the news corpus is presented in the next section.

Table 1 presents the differences between the mean scores for every pairs of translators for the parliamentary corpus. The Student's t-test for non-independent measures was used to determine whether these mean differences were statistically significant. Due to the large number of tests performed (18), the Bonferroni procedure was used to compensate for the inflated Type I error rates, with the threshold for an alpha of 0.05 (two-tailed) set at 0.0027 (two-tailed). These tests indicate that all differences are significant, except for those between *Microsoft Translator* and *DeepL* for the three indices and the difference for the t-score between the human and *Microsoft* translations.

Table 1 also gives two effect sizes. Cohen's d informs about the size of the difference between the means as a function of its variability. It is usual to consider that a d of 0.20 indicates a small effect size, a d of 0.50 a medium effect and a d of 0.80 a large effect (Cohen, 1988). The second effect size is the proportion of texts for which the difference between the two translations has the same sign as the mean difference. The maximum value of 1.0 means that texts produced by a translator always have larger scores than those translated by the other translator while the minimum value of 0.50 indicates no difference for this measure between the two translators.

As these results show, the three hypotheses about the differences between human and machine translations are all confirmed by statistically significant differences, except for the difference in t-score between human and Microsoft translations, which is nevertheless in the right direction.

In these analyses, Cohen's d for MI and for the ratio are often medium and sometimes even large and the differences are present in a large proportion of texts. For the t-score on the other hand, all effect sizes are small. This could be explained by the fact that the collocations highlighted by this lexical association measure are mostly very frequent in the language and thus more easily learned by automatic systems (Koehn and Knowles, 2017; Li et al., 2020).

The comparison of the texts translated by *Microsoft Translator* and by *DeepL* does not show, as indicated above, any statistically significant difference and the effect sizes are very small. The outputs of *Google Translate* on the other hand contain fewer highly collocational bigrams for MI and for t-score than these two other machine translators, potentially suggesting less efficiency of this translator for collocation processing.

3.2. Comparison between the Two Genres

As shown in Figures 2 to 4, all the observed trends are very similar in the two corpora, indicating that the two genres of text lead to the same conclusions. However, there is a strong contrast in the mean values. The MI scores are lower in the parliamentary corpus while the t-scores are higher. This is the case for both human and machine translations. This observation is most probably explained by a difference between the text genres, a difference that should already be present in the original French texts.

The comparison of the effect sizes between the two types of translation (Table 2 in Bestgen (2021)) clearly indicates that the differences are much stronger in the news corpus. This observation is consistent with the hypothesis of a greater literalness of the human translations in the parliamentary corpus.

4. Conclusion

The analyses carried out on the parliamentary corpus have made it possible to replicate the conclusions obtained with a news corpus. The observed trends are very similar, but the differences are less strong in the parliamentary corpus. This observation seems to confirm the usefulness of the parliamentary genre for the comparison of human and machine translation. Indeed, one can think that the less literal nature of the translations in news (Ponomarenko, 2019; Sosoni, 2011) favors the identification of differences between the two types of translations. The differences observed in the parliamentary corpus thus seem to be more directly related to the translators effectiveness rather than to other factors.

Among the directions for future research, there is certainly the analysis of translations from English to French, but also between other languages. Here again, the Europarl corpus, as well as parliamentary debates in multilingual countries, allows for a great deal of experimentation. A potential difficulty is that the approach used requires a reference corpus in the target language. This problem does not seem too serious since it has been shown that freely available Wacky corpora (Baroni et al., 2009) can be used without altering the results of the CollGram technique (Bestgen, 2016). Confirming these results in other languages, but also in other genres of texts, would allow to take advantage of them to try to improve machine translation systems. A unanswered question is whether identical results would be obtained on the basis of a genre-specific reference corpus, which is very easy to obtain for European parliamentary debates. This corpus would be composed of documents originally produced in English. It would also be interesting to use other approaches to phraseology, especially more qualitative ones, to confirm the conclusions. Finally, the difference in mean values between the two text genres justifies an analysis of the original texts with the same technique.

5. Acknowledgements

The author is a Research Associate of the Fonds de la Recherche Scientifique (F.R.S-FNRS).

6. Bibliographical References

Baldwin, T. and Kim, S. N. (2010). Multiword expressions. In Nitin Indurkhya et al., editors, *Handbook of*

Natural Language Processing, pages 267–292. CRC Press.

Baroni, M., Bernardini, S., Ferraresi, A., and Zanchetta, E. (2009). The WaCky wide web: A collection of very large linguistically processed web-crawled corpora. *Language Resources and Evaluation*, 43:209–226.

Bernardini, S. (2007). Collocations in translated language. combining parallel, comparable and reference corpora. In *Proceedings of the Corpus Linguistics Conference*, pages 1–16. Lancaster University.

Bestgen, Y. and Granger, S. (2014). Quantifying the development of phraseological competence in L2 English writing: An automated approach. *Journal of Second Language Writing*, 26:28–41.

Bestgen, Y. (2016). Evaluation automatique de textes. Validation interne et externe d'indices phraséologiques pour l'évaluation automatique de textes rédigés en anglais langue étrangère. *Traitement automatique des langues*, 57(3):91–115.

Bestgen, Y. (2018). Normalisation en traduction : analyse automatique des collocations dans des corpus. *Des mots aux actes*, 7:459–469.

Bestgen, Y. (2019). Evaluation de textes en anglais langue ètrangère et séries phraséologiques : comparaison de deux procédures automatiques librement accessibles. *Revue française de linguistique appliquée*, 24:81–94.

Bestgen, Y. (2021). Using CollGram to compare formulaic language in human and machine translation. In *Proceedings of the Translation and Interpreting Technology Online Conference*, pages 174–180, Held Online, July. INCOMA Ltd.

Bielsa, E. and Bassnett, S. (2009). *Translation in Global News*. Routledge.

Cartoni, B. and Meyer, T. (2012). Extracting directional and comparable corpora from a multilingual corpus for translation studies. In *Proceedings of the Eighth International Conference on Language Resources and Evaluation (LREC'12)*, pages 2132–2137, Istanbul, Turkey, May. European Language Resources Association (ELRA).

Cohen, J. (1988). *Statistical power analysis for the behavioral sciences*. Erlbaum.

De Clercq, O., De Sutter, G., Loock, R., Cappelle, B., and Plevoets, K. (2021). Uncovering Machine Translationese Using Corpus Analysis Techniques to Distinguish between Original and Machine-Translated French. *Translation Quarterly*, 101:21–45.

Durrant, P. and Schmitt, N. (2009). To what extent do native and non-native writers make use of collocations? *International Review of Applied Linguistics in Language Teaching*, 47:157–177.

Islam, Z. and Mehler, A. (2012). Customization of the Europarl corpus for translation studies. In Nicoletta Calzolari, et al., editors, *Proceedings of the Eighth International Conference on Language Resources and Evaluation, LREC 2012, Istanbul, Turkey, May 23-25, 2012*, pages 2505–2510. European Language Resources Association (ELRA).

Koehn, P. and Knowles, R. (2017). Six challenges for neural machine translation.

Koehn, P. (2005). Europarl: A Parallel Corpus for Statistical Machine Translation. In *Conference Proceedings: the tenth Machine Translation Summit*, pages 79–86, Phuket, Thailand. AAMT, AAMT.

Läubli, S., Sennrich, R., and Volk, M. (2018). Has machine translation achieved human parity? a case for document-level evaluation. In *Proceedings of the 2018 Conference on Empirical Methods in Natural Language Processing*, pages 4791–4796, Brussels, Belgium, October-November. Association for Computational Linguistics.

Laufer, B. and Waldman, T. (2011). Verb-noun collocations in second language writing: A corpus analysis of learners' English. *Language Learning*, 61:647–672.

Li, M., Roller, S., Kulikov, I., Welleck, S., Boureau, Y.-L., Cho, K., and Weston, J. (2020). Don't say that! making inconsistent dialogue unlikely with unlikelihood training. In *Proceedings of the 58th Annual Meeting of the Association for Computational Linguistics*, pages 4715–4728. Association for Computational Linguistics.

Ponomarenko, L. (2019). *Translating identities in multilingual news*. Ph.D. thesis, Universitat Autonoma de Barcelona.

Popel, M., Tomkova, M., Tomek, J., Kaiser, L., Uszkoreit, J., Bojar, O., and Zabokrtsky, Z. (2020). Transforming machine translation: A deep learning system reaches news translation quality comparable to human professionals. *Nature Communications*, 11:1–15.

Porte, G. (2013). Who needs replication? *CALICO Journal*, 30:10–15.

Rayson, P. (1991). *Matrix: A statistical method and software tool for linguistic analysis through corpus comparison*. Ph.D. thesis, Lancaster University.

Sosoni, V. (2011). Training translators to work for the EU institutions: luxury or necessity? *The Journal of Specialised Translation*, 16:77–108.

Ustaszewski, M. (2019). Optimising the Europarl corpus for translation studies with the Europarl Extract toolkit. *Perspectives*, 27:107–123.

Vanmassenhove, E., Shterionov, D., and Way, A. (2019). Lost in translation: Loss and decay of linguistic richness in machine translation. In *Proceedings of Machine Translation Summit XVII: Research Track*, pages 222–232, Dublin, Ireland, August. European Association for Machine Translation.

Wu, Y., Schuster, M., Chen, Z., Le, Q. V., Norouzi, M., Macherey, W., Krikun, M., Cao, Y., Gao, Q., Macherey, K., Klingner, J., Shah, A., Johnson, M., Liu, X., Łukasz Kaiser, Gouws, S., Kato, Y., Kudo, T., Kazawa, H., Stevens, K., Kurian, G., Patil, N.,

Wang, W., Young, C., Smith, J., Riesa, J., Rudnick, A., Vinyals, O., Corrado, G., Hughes, M., and Dean, J. (2016). Google's neural machine translation system: Bridging the gap between human and machine translation.

7. Language Resource References

Philipp Koehn. (2012). *European Parliament Proceedings Parallel Corpus 1996-2011.* available at https://www.statmt.org/europarl/.

Ustaszewski, Michael. (2017). *EuroparlExtract - Directional Parallel Corpora Extracted from the European Parliament Proceedings Parallel Corpus.* Zenodo, available at https://doi.org/10.5281/zenodo.1066474.

Proceedings of ParlaCLARIN III @ LREC2022 pages 107–110
Marseille, 20 June 2022

Adding the Basque Parliament Corpus to ParlaMint Project

Jon Alkorta, Mikel Iruskieta
HiTZ Basque Center for Language Technologies - Ixa, University of the Basque Country (UPV/EHU)
jon.alkorta@ehu.eus, mikel.iruskieta@ehu.eus

Abstract

The aim of this work is to describe the collection created with transcript of the Basque parliamentary speeches. This corpus follows the constraints of the ParlaMint project. The Basque ParlaMint corpus consists of two versions: the first version stands for what was said in the Basque Parliament, that is, the original bilingual corpus in Basque and in Spanish to analyse what and how it was said, while the second is only in Basque with the original and translated passages to promote studies on the content of the parliament speeches.

Keywords: corpus, Basque, bilingualism, parliament

1. Introduction

There are three parliaments in the Basque Country and Navarre:

i) The Parliament of Navarre sited in Iruñea/Pamplona is the Navarre autonomous unicameral parliament.

ii) The Parliament of Navarre and Béarn is sited in Pau.

iii) The Basque Parliament is sited in Vitoria-Gasteiz (headquarters) and in Gernika (the symbolic town of Basque laws).

Elected Basque representatives have a representation in these three parliaments and with the aim to build a parliamentary data in Basque language, we decided to choose one of them where we think that Basque language is used most: the Basque Parliament (*Eusko Legebiltzarra*, in Basque).

The Basque Parliament is composed of seventy-five deputies elected from these three provinces: Araba, Biscay and Gipuzkoa and each province has twenty-five deputies. And the spokespersons from all the parties with a significant representation can speak Basque. This is the composition of the chamber after the last elections, held on September 26, 2016 and July 12, 2020 and the distribution of seats:

- Partido Nacionalista Vasco (EAJ-PNV): 28 deputies (37.36% votes) / 31 deputies (39.12% votes): Basque christian-democratic and conservative-liberal party.
- Euskal Herria Bildu (EH Bildu): 18 deputies (21.13% votes) / 21 deputies (27.84% votes): Basque left-wing political coalition.
- Partido Socialista de Euskadi-Euskadiko Ezkerra (PSE-EE / PSOE): 9 deputies (11.86% votes) / 10 deputies (13.64% votes). Spanish social-democratic political party.
- Podemos-Izquierda Unida (Podemos-IU): 11 deputies (14.76% votes) / 6 deputies (8.03% votes): Spanish left-wing electoral coalition.
- Partido Popular (PP) + Ciudadanos (Cs): 9 deputies (10.11% votes) of PP and 0 deputies (2.02% votes) of Ciudadanos / 6 deputies (6.75% votes): Spanish conservative and Christian-democratic political party.
- Vox (Vox): 0 deputy (0.07% votes) / 1 deputy (1.96% votes): Spanish right-wing conservative nationalist political party.

The Basque Government is composed through an agreement between EAJ-PNV and PSE-EE/PSOE, the two political parties that are in the government of the parliament from its creation in 1979 (with an exception where PSE-EE/PSOE governed with PP).

The official languages of this parliament are Basque and Castilian-Spanish and the speech transcripts are produced in two ways *i*) original transcript: as they were said (Basque and/or Spanish), and *ii*) reflected translation transcript: in another text column, Basque is translated to Spanish and Spanish is translated to Basque.

The chair of the Basque Parliament accepted to add the transcriptions to the ParlaMint: Towards Comparable Parliamentary Corpora project (CLARIN-ERIC) (Erjavec et al., 2021).

The aim of this paper is to describe the two versions of the Basque parliamentary corpus: the Basque version (with original and translated excerpts) and the original bilingual version (as it was stated in the parliament). We decide to compile two versions to promote research in Basque (a low resourced language) and offer NLP (Natural Language Processing) based tools for search. On the other hand, we build the original corpus to analyse language in use.

Other corpora compilations are possible, for example, we could create the Spanish corpus or a parallel Basque-Spanish translation corpus, in order to offer data for machine translation studies, but this is out of our scope, and we leave this and other works for the future.

2. Related Works

Basque Parliament texts have been used on many occasions for the study of NLP. Mainly, two areas of study are distinguished: i) studies related to voice processing and ii) those related to text processing.

As long as the Basque Parliament offers the transcript, video, and audio of the sessions, the data has been exploited in some speech processing tasks (Bordel et al., 2011; Etchegoyhen et al., 2021; Pérez et al., 2012).

Bordel et al. (2011) present an automatic video subtitling system to subtitle the video recordings of the Plenary Sessions. Authors aligned the audio in Basque and Spanish, searching the minimum edit distance once they converted them to phonetic streams.

Etchegoyhen et al. (2021) present Mintzai-ST, the first publicly available corpus for speech translation in the pair Basque-Spanish. This is a Basque-Spanish parallel corpus compiled with both speech and text data. The corpus collects Session Diaries from 2011 to 2018. In total, the corpus consists of 370 videos (1,146.18 hours) and 217 PDF documents (Session Diaries and 18,625,252 words). The translations are bidirectional (Basque-Spanish and Spanish-Basque) and the corpus could be employed for research purposes.

Pérez et al. (2012) present Euskoparl, a parallel corpus in Spanish and Basque with both text and speech data. This corpus is aligned at sentence level and divided in train and test datasets. The train dataset consists of 741,780 pairs of sentences (22,668,478 words in Spanish and 18,161,805 words in Basque). The test dataset consists of 30,000 pairs of sentences (915,528 words in Spanish and 733,900 words in Basque).

Our work follows the ParlaMint project (Erjavec et al., 2022). The aim of this work is to build European parliamentary data into comparable, interpretable and highly communicative resource. During the first stage of the project (July 2020 – May 2021) corpora from 17 languages and parliaments were complied, analysed and made available (on GitHub) for research powered by CLARIN-ERIC. To mention some of the languages that participated in the first stage, we should mention Danish (Jongejan et al., 2021), Czech (Kopp et al., 2021) and Polish (Ogrodniczuk, 2018) among others.

In the second stage, more languages will be added to this project and, for example, the texts from the Basque parliament. Moreover, CLARIN-ERIC is promoting the use of parliamentary data in the university curricula (Fišer and de Maiti, 2020).

3. Methodology

3.1. Criteria

The aim of this work is to describe the creation of a bilingual Basque Parliament corpus for studies that aim to analyze what was said and how, and also the creation of an entirely Basque corpus. The Basque corpus will be very useful for the community to analyse the content of the Basque Parliament using Basque NLP tools. To do so, we use the excerpts of the original corpus that are in Basque, as well as the translated passages into Basque by the chamber.

3.2. Resources and Steps

To create the corpus, we follow the ParlaMint criteria, to include the Basque Parliament corpus in the project (`https://github.com/clarin-eric/ParlaMint`) which is labelled with ES-PV (Basque Country).

These are the steps in the corpus creation:

- Permission. Obtain permission from the parliament.
- Convert documents from DOC to TEI-XML format.
- Convert documents from TEI-XML to TEI-ParlaMintXML format.
- Check and validate TEI-XML.
- Metadata file. Describe the Basque Parliament, political parties and parliamentarians at the metadata file.
- Add morphosyntactic information with UDPipe analyser.

3.3. Development

i) **Collect the parliamentary data.**
The secretary of the senior lawyer send the transcripts from the Basque Parliament (and their translations, where possible), to include a corpus of Basque in the project ParlaMint. The request (2021/1887) was granted on March 21, 2021. The texts obtained are from the speeches between February, 2015 and February, 2021.

ii) **Create the original version.**
The parliamentary data is divided into several files, and each file corresponds to one parliamentary act. Sometimes, in a day, there is more than one parliamentary act.

In each DOC file, there are two columns. The left column contains the original speech, while the right column translated the original speech to the other official language. The original corpus contains only the text in the left column and we create TEI-XML format document using this text.

iii) **Create the Basque version.**
In this case, we choose the passages written in Basque from the left column (original text) and from the right column (translated text), by means of a script. The script first calculates how likely the paragraphs are to be in Basque or Spanish.

Next, the script takes the paragraphs most likely to be written in Basque from the left column or from the right column, if Spanish text was detected on the left column. After this, using the only text in Basque, we have created another TEI-XML document file of each parliamentary act.

iv) **Metadata file.**
Finally, we have created the metadata file that is valid for both versions of the corpus. The root file is in Basque, Spanish and English and contains information on: the title, the size, the date of creation of the corpus, as well as political parties, parliamentarians, sessions and positions of the Basque Parliament.

4. Corpus Description

	Basque corpus	Bilingual corpus
Basque	7.37	1.98
Spanish		7.35
Unidentified		0.05
Total	**7.37**	**9.38**

Table 1: Estimation of size of the corpus in words (in millions)

Table 1 shows the characteristics of both versions. The version in Basque has 7,37 million words. In contrast, in the bilingual version, 7.35 million words are in Spanish (%78.4), while 1.98 million words are in Basque (%21.39). Finally, 50 thousand words have not been identified[1] (%0.12). The Basque Parliament corpus is available on GitHub.

4.1. The Metadata File

The metadata file contains information on all aspects related to the parliamentary speeches, which is: the title, authors, project to which it belongs, the size of the corpus, licence, the taxonomy of the participants, organizations, and acts related to parliamentary speeches. Likewise, the data on the legislative periods (3 in total) and a governing body (the Basque Government) are detailed.
Secondly, the political parties are listed (8 in total): EAJ/PNV, EH Bildu, PSE-EE, Elkarrekin Podemos, Ezker Anitza, PP(+Cs), Vox and UPyD. The date on which the political parties were created, their acronym and their Wikipedia web page are also specified in the entry of each political party.
In the third place, parliamentarians are listed. In total, there are 176 parliamentarians. In each entry of the parliamentarian, the following information is detailed: name and two surnames, date and place of birth, gender, their political party affiliation, and their Wikipedia web page (if available).

[1]The unidentified words can be words in other languages, or Basque or Spanish words from short sentences that have been assigned the same probability of being in Spanish or Basque by the script.

Finally, the list of files containing parliamentary sessions is enumerated. Each file corresponds to a parliamentary session.

4.2. Basque and Original Versions

All files in the bilingual version have the same structure. At the beginning, there is a metadata section about the file. Then there is the body of the file. There, each paragraph is segmented. The Basque version maintains the same structure.

5. Hypothesis and Discussion

The characteristics of the corpus may be adequate to analyse some factors related to language and society.

5.1. Sociolinguistic Study

Diglossic situation (if there is a language considered to be of low variety usage and another used for high variety usage) between Basque and Spanish could be analysed.
The amount of words in Spanish and Basque in the corpus already shows that Spanish is used more in the Basque Parliament (which is considered as a high-level institution), which already reflects the diglossic situation in the Basque Parliament.
However, a more exhaustive analysis of this phenomenon can be done using NLP tools. Some interesting research questions arise for future work:

- Which language do parliamentarians speak when they have to say something important?
    - We hypothesize that parliamentarians change their language according to the importance of what they have to say.

      In other words, in our opinion, parliamentarians mainly use Basque when they greet or say something irrelevant, and they use Spanish when they have to say something important or when they have to address the other parliamentarians.

- Do parliamentarians use one language to express objective or narrative facts and another language to express subjectivity or their point of view?
    - We believe that parliamentarians use Basque when they have to say something objective or factual. However, parliamentarians use Spanish to express their opinion or address other parliamentarians. This is also related to the diglossic situation, since it would show that for parliamentarians, Basque is not useful to express opinions.

In relation to our hypotheses, Gagnon (2006) studied the sociolinguistic situation in the Parliament of Canada with a similar approach.

5.2. Other Possible Studies

The Basque corpus could be useful to answer the following question: Are translated paragraphs in Basque more complex or simpler if we compare with those original language forms in Basque?
The version in Basque may be suitable for the task called "text complexity". That is, taking into account some parameters, we can analyse if the translated texts differ a lot from the original texts in terms of complexity.
It can be assumed that the translated paragraphs are more complex, since they are texts created a posteriori. The syntactic structure can be more complex and the lexicon can be less repetitive, taking into account the characteristics of oral language.
Liu and Afzaal (2021) and Ausloos (2012) studied similar hypothesis with original and translated texts in English.

6. Conclusion and Future Work

In conclusion, we present the transcript and corrected written corpus of the speeches of the Basque Parliament. The corpus consists of two versions. One version is entirely in Basque and it is based on the original and translated texts. The second version is based on original texts and is bilingual, although most of the texts in Spanish. The two versions follow the format established in the ParlaMint project. For this reason, both versions are in XML format.
In this situation, the future works that we propose are the following works:

- To follow the ParlaMint document format since this corpus is in the xml format, but not in the TEI-ParlaMintXML format.
- To tag the paragraphs in both versions. We would like to tag paragraph indicating if the paragraphs are in Basque or Spanish (in the original and bilingual version) or if the paragraphs are original or translations (in the Basque version) in order to have more data for the different studies.
- To carry out the linguistic processing following the guidelines of the ParlaMint project. That is, we would add morphosyntactic information using Universal Dependencies framework and NER in both versions.
- Finally, we would like to study some hypotheses that we have raised in Section 5.

7. Acknowledgements

We would like to thank Kike Fernández (HiTZ Center-EHU/UPV) for his technical help in this work, INTELE network (Ministerio Ciencia, Innovación y Universidades de España RED2018-102797-E), and the ParlaMint project (CLARIN-ERIC) for the financial support.

8. Bibliographical References

Ausloos, M. (2012). Measuring complexity with multifractals in texts translation effects. *Chaos, Solitons & Fractals*, 45(11):1349–1357.

Bordel, G., Nieto, S., Penagarikano, M., Rodriguez-Fuentes, L. J., and Varona, A. (2011). Automatic subtitling of the basque parliament plenary sessions videos. In *Twelfth Annual Conference of the International Speech Communication Association*.

Erjavec, T., Ogrodniczuk, M., Osenova, P., Pančur, A., Ljubešič, N., Agnoloni, T., Barkarson, S., Pérez, M. C., Çöltekin, Ç., Coole, M., et al. (2021). Parlamint: comparable corpora of european parliamentary data. In *Proceedings of CLARIN annual conference 2021, 27-29 September, 2021, virtual edition*, pages 20–25. Utrecht University.

Erjavec, T., Ogrodniczuk, M., Osenova, P., Ljubešić, N., Simov, K., Pančur, A., Rudolf, M., Kopp, M., Barkarson, S., Steingrímsson, S., et al. (2022). The parlamint corpora of parliamentary proceedings. *Language resources and evaluation*, pages 1–34.

Etchegoyhen, T., Arzelus, H., Ugarte, H. G., Alvarez, A., González-Docasal, A., and Fernandez, E. B. (2021). Mintzai-ST: Corpus and baselines for Basque-Spanish speech translation. *Proc. IberSPEECH 2021*, pages 190–194.

Fišer, D. and de Maiti, K. P. (2020). Voices of the parliament. *Modern Languages Open*.

Gagnon, C. (2006). Language plurality as power struggle, or:: Translating politics in canada. *Target. International Journal of Translation Studies*, 18(1):69–90.

Jongejan, B., Hansen, D. H., and Navarretta, C. (2021). Enhancing CLARIN-DK resources while building the Danish ParlaMint corpus. In *CLARIN Annual Conference 2021*, page 73.

Kopp, M., Stankov, V., Kruza, J. O., Straňák, P., and Bojar, O. (2021). ParCzech 3.0: A large Czech speech corpus with rich metadata. In *International Conference on Text, Speech, and Dialogue*, pages 293–304. Springer.

Liu, K. and Afzaal, M. (2021). Syntactic complexity in translated and non-translated texts: A corpus-based study of simplification. *Plos One*, 16(6):e0253454.

Ogrodniczuk, M. (2018). Polish parliamentary corpus. In *Proceedings of the LREC 2018 workshop ParlaCLARIN: creating and using parliamentary corpora*, pages 15–19.

Pérez, A., Alcaide, J. M., and Torres, M.-I. (2012). EuskoParl: a speech and text Spanish-Basque parallel corpus. In *Thirteenth Annual Conference of the International Speech Communication Association*.

Proceedings of ParlaCLARIN III @ LREC2022 pages 111–116
Marseille, 20 June 2022

ParlaSpeech-HR – a Freely Available ASR Dataset for Croatian Bootstrapped from the ParlaMint Corpus

Nikola Ljubešić[1,2], Danijel Koržinek[3], Peter Rupnik[1], Ivo-Pavao Jazbec
[1]Jožef Stefan Institute, Slovenia
[2] Faculty of Computer and Information Science, University of Ljubljana, Slovenia
[3] Polish-Japanese Academy of Information Technology, Poland
nikola.ljubesic@ijs.si, danijel@pja.edu.pl, peter.rupnik@ijs.si, ipjazbec@gmail.com

Abstract

This paper presents our bootstrapping efforts of producing the first large freely available Croatian automatic speech recognition (ASR) dataset, 1,816 hours in size, obtained from parliamentary transcripts and recordings from the ParlaMint corpus. The bootstrapping approach to the dataset building relies on a commercial ASR system for initial data alignment, and building a multilingual-transformer-based ASR system from the initial data for full data alignment. Experiments on the resulting dataset show that the difference between the spoken content and the parliamentary transcripts is present in ∼4-5% of words, which is also the word error rate of our best-performing ASR system. Interestingly, fine-tuning transformer models on either normalized or original data does not show a difference in performance. Models pre-trained on a subset of raw speech data consisting of Slavic languages only show to perform better than those pre-trained on a wider set of languages. With our public release of data, models and code, we are paving the way forward for the preparation of the multi-modal corpus of Croatian parliamentary proceedings, as well as for the development of similar free datasets, models and corpora for other under-resourced languages.

Keywords: parliamentary data, automatic speech recognition, free language resources, Croatian language

1. Introduction

In recent years we have witnessed huge advances in speech technology, primarily by applying the self-supervision paradigm over raw speech data. (Baevski et al., 2020) The new paradigm allows for good ASR systems to be built only with a few tens of hours of speech segments and corresponding transcripts. (Babu et al., 2021)

For Croatian, or any other closely-related language from the HBS macro-language group, including also Bosnian, Montenegrin and Serbian, there are, sadly, no freely available ASR datasets or systems. There has been work on ASR for the HBS macro-language (Martinčić-Ipšić et al., 2008; Popović et al., 2015; Nouza et al., 2016), but none resulted in an open dataset or system, stalling the development of speech technologies for these languages significantly.[1]

Parliamentary proceedings are a very well known source of speech data with already available transcripts (Mansikkaniemi et al., 2017; Helgadóttir et al., 2017; Kirkedal et al., 2020; Solberg and Ortiz, 2022) due to a significant number of countries making the transcripts and recordings freely available under a public license.

For exploiting resources consisting of speech recordings and their transcripts, the transcripts have to be aligned to the speech recordings, which is often a technical challenge due to the amount of data available and no or only high-level alignment between the two modalities. There exists a well established methodology in performing such alignment by using an existing ASR system to automatically transcribe the speech recordings, to align the automatic transcripts from the ASR system with the previously available human transcripts, obtaining thereby alignments between speech recordings and human transcripts. (Katsamanis et al., 2011; Marasek et al., 2014; Panayotov et al., 2015)

This work describes the bootstrapping approach to building the first freely available ASR dataset for Croatian from the parliamentary proceedings available through the ParlaMint corpus (Erjavec et al., 2022). Given the lack of any datasets or models for Croatian and related languages prior to the start of our efforts, the described approach consists of two phases - aligning a smaller amount of data through a commercial ASR system, and then training an in-house ASR system for the alignment of all available data. With this approach the costs of the construction process are kept at their bare minimum.

The main contributions of this paper are the following: we share the first freely available ASR dataset for Croatian, and a methodology for building ASR datasets for other under-resourced languages from parliamentary data. We present our insights into the quality of parliamentary transcripts that are known to deviate from the speech recordings. We investigate the necessity of performing data normalization prior to training state-of-the-art ASR models from parliamentary data. Finally, we map the path forward in creating a multimodal cor-

[1]During our work on ParlaSpeech, the VoxPopuli dataset (Wang et al., 2021) was released, containing parliamentary debates from the European parliament, including also Croatian with 42 hours of transcribed speech. The transcription has, however, significant issues with one half of the text missing non-ascii characters.

pus of Croatian parliamentary proceedings, and call out the parliamentary data community to join the ParlaSpeech initiative in building ASR datasets and multimodal corpora for other under-resourced languages.

2. Dataset Construction

The dataset presented in this paper was constructed in a bootstrapping manner, first constructing a 72-hours corpus by exploiting the commercial Google Speech-To-Text (STT) system[2], then training an in-house ASR system on that corpus, and finally applying that ASR system over all available recordings of the Croatian parliamentary proceedings from the ParlaMint corpus (Erjavec et al., 2021; Erjavec et al., 2022).

The textual source of the data is the Croatian portion of the ParlaMint corpus, containing the proceedings of the Croatian parliament in its 9th term (2016-2020), 20.65 million words in size. The human transcripts were normalized via a rule-based normalization method[3] inspired by (Ebden and Sproat, 2015), primarily focused on expanding numerals, acronyms and abbreviations.

The audio modality of the parliamentary proceedings was collected from the official YouTube channel of the Croatian Parliament[4] where all video recordings of the parliamentary debates are available. The recordings were downloaded with the youtube-dl tool[5] and encoded as wav in 16Khz, 16-bit, single channel.

The total length of the downloaded 755 audio recordings is 2821 hours, with an average length of 3.7 hours. The maximum length of a video is 6.76 hours. After applying Voice Activity Detection (VAD) (Silero, 2021) over the recordings, the length of pure speech recordings identified is 2,419.19 hours.

2.1. Initial Data Alignment via the Commercial ASR System

Given that no openly available training data or ASR system existed before the activities we describe in this paper, in the first iteration of our efforts, we had to rely on commercially available ASR systems. We chose to use the Google STT system due to the fact that it supports the Croatian language, and that it was supported in the code base used for this initial alignment, based on simple forced alignment(Plüss et al., 2020), which assumes that both data modalities come in the same, monotonic order. This required some rough manual alignment to be performed first, making sure that each identified subsection of audio and transcripts is in monotonic order. Given that we have in the meantime developed an alignment method which does not require monotonic data ordering, described in Section 2.3, this manual step will not be needed in the future application of our bootstrapping approach. Using the speech-to-text Google ASR system proved to fit into the 300 hours of Google Cloud usage that comes for free, so no fees were paid to Google.

From all the (audio, human transcript, automatic transcript) triplets generated in the process, 96 hours in length, we decided to keep those where the Levenshtein distance between the two transcripts, normalized by the average length of these transcripts, is equal or lower than 0.2. Loosely speaking, this means that only those segments were kept where the two transcripts are not different more than 20% on the character level. We identified this threshold to be useful via manual inspection. The resulting initial ASR training dataset was 72 hours in size.

2.2. Full Data Alignment via the In-House ASR System

With the initial ASR training dataset, consisting of 72 hours of speech recordings and normalized human transcript, we trained our in-house ASR system that would allow us to automatically transcribe, and then align, all the data available from the ParlaMint corpus and the Croatian parliament's recordings collection. Our chosen ASR technology was the recently released transformer-based multilingual XLS-R model (Babu et al., 2021), which showed to provide very good transcription results already with limited amount of training data. XLS-R is a multilingual model that was pre-trained also on Croatian raw speech data.

We split the available data into a 66-hours training portion and 3-hour development and testing portions, running the fine-tuning procedure for 8 epochs. The preliminary evaluation results of the fine-tuned model over the initial training dataset are 13.68% of word error rate (WER) and 4.56% of character error rate (CER). This ASR system was used to transcribe the whole collection of audio recordings of 2,419.19 hours. With this we were able to drop our small collection of 72 hours of transcribed data and focus solely to producing the new collection, which also included most, if not all, of the initially aligned data.

Once the whole collection of audio recordings was successfully transcribed, we moved to the non-trivial problem of aligning human transcriptions available in the ParlaMint corpus and the automatic transcriptions obtained from our initial ASR system.

This alignment was hard in particular because of a different ordering of utterances in the recordings and in the official transcripts that are part of the ParlaMint corpus. It was due to the attempt by the transcribers to achieve logical (thematic) grouping instead of chronological ordering in the transcripts. Because of that, the explanation of the bill, reports of the parliamentary bodies dealing with the bill, discussions by the parliamentary groups representatives, and MPs themselves,

[2] `https://cloud.google.com/speech-to-text/`

[3] `https://github.com/danijel3/TextNormalize`

[4] `https://www.youtube.com/c/InternetTVHrvatskogasabora`

[5] `https://github.com/ytdl-org/youtube-dl/`

were followed by possible voting on amendments, and voting on the bill itself, although they may have taken place over the span of several days or weeks.

The process of obtaining the best utterance-level alignment of the whole corpus involved several steps. The desired output was supposed to contain short utterance segments (no longer than 20 seconds) with matching transcripts. The transcripts are matched on the audio level, so the pronunciation of all the words is naturally assumed, but due to imperfections of the simple rule-based normalization system, a match with the original, unnormalized transcript was also required. Furthermore, not all audio was transcribed in the original text and those fragments that were transcribed could contain simplifications, abstractions, deletions (e.g. due to substandard or unintelligible speech) or simply errors. It was decided that in this initial step, not all the data need be included and the rest can be completed once a better ASR system is developed, or by performing manual verification.

After obtaining the automatic transcription using our in-house system described above, the next step was to match the VAD derived segments to the human transcript without knowing their location or order within the larger transcript. The technical details of the procedure are described in section 2.3.

Once the match between the audio and human transcripts was acquired, there were still many errors that mostly occur on the boundaries of segments - especially if those boundaries are internal to continuous speech (i.e. not neighboring silence). To mitigate this further, the segments were joined together to longer portions of speech (up to 20 minutes long) and this was then aligned using the standard Viterbi forced alignment by our alternate WFST ASR system. This gave us word-level alignment of the whole corpus, from which the desired 20 second segments were easily extracted.

Following the above procedure, we managed to process around 82% of the input data which gave us a total of 1,976.97 hours of aligned speech with matching 14M words of human transcription.

2.3. Matching ASR Output to Long Text Corpora

This section provides a description of an engineering problem and what is undoubtedly just one of many possible solutions for it, but was optimal for our case. Ultimately, the problem can be described as matching a sequence of short text segments to a large corpus. There are sub-sequences of the shorter texts that occur in the same order in the large corpus, but all those matches have a level of discrepancy due to both errors in the ASR output as well as within the human transcripts.

To begin with, the whole text (both short and long) was converted to integer sequences where each word is represented by a single number instead of character strings - this improves both space and time complexity of the rest of the process. To start things off, we need to perform global lookup of the beginning of each sub-sequence within the long text. We do this by looking at all the locations of the first word within the first segment of the sub-sequence and choosing the position that has the smallest word-level Levenshtein edit distance. If no match is found or the match is not unique, we repeat the same process with the next word or segment and simply offset the result.

Once we identify the start of the sub-sequence, we heuristically match the rest of the segments by iterating forward until the match falls below a certain threshold. Then we start by repeating the global lookup procedure again and treat the rest of the segments as a new subsequence. If this also fails, we simply exit the procedure and discard the rest of the file.

The code of our approach will be released at the time of the final version of this manuscript.

3. Dataset Description and Availability

The full data alignment procedure resulted in 1,976.97 hours of speech recordings and their respective human and automatic transcripts. We applied the same filtering criterion via the normalized Levenshtein distance between human and automatic transcripts as with our initial dataset, discarding all the alignments where more than ~20% of the transcripts differ. Applying this filter removed 146.58 hours, and thus we have obtained our final dataset presented in this paper, consisting of 1,816.34 hours of spoken data and their transcription.

We decided to brand the resulting dataset under the name ParlaSpeech-HR, encoding thereby our efforts as a continuation of the ParlaMint project, as well as the hope that many ParlaMint corpora will become ParlaSpeech datasets in the near future. This is especially crucial for a number of low-resource languages where parliamentary data are quite likely the single best source of a significant amount of spoken data and human transcripts.

The ParlaSpeech-HR corpus consists of 403,925 entries, each of which consists of the following attributes: (1) a path to the wave file, which also represents the ID of the entry, (2) the name of the original YouTube file, (3) the start (in milliseconds) of the entry in the original recording, (4) the end (in milliseconds) of the entry in the original recording, (5) a list of words from the human transcript, (6) local time offsets for each word in the human transcript, (7) a list of words from the normalized human transcript, (8) local time offsets for each word in the normalized human transcript, and (9) manually corrected normalized words, available for 484 entries only, used in an analysis in Section 4, (10) speaker information, if the segment was produced by only one speaker. Out of all 403,925 entries, only 22,076 entries have multiple speakers present, where we omitted the speaker information for simplicity. Each speaker description consists of the following information: (1) name, (2) gender, (3) year of birth, (4) party affiliation, (5) party status (ruling coali-

tion or opposition).
Overall there are 310 speakers present in the dataset, the most prominent one having 21,761 instances, the least frequent one having only two. Out of the 310 speakers, 234 are men, while 76 are women. There are 317,882 instances spoken by men, and 63,967 instances spoken by women.
To be able to use the dataset for benchmarking purposes, the dataset was further divided in a training, a development and a test portion, with three goals in mind: (1) having as many diverse speakers in the test portion, (2) having a gender balance in the test portion, and (3) not wasting unique speaker information on the development set. Having these three goals in mind, we decided to proceed as follows. Development data consist of 500 segments coming from the 5 most frequent speakers (four men and one woman), while test data consist of 513 segments that come from 3 male (258 segments) and 3 female speakers (255 segments). There are no segments coming from the 6 test speakers in the two remaining subsets. Given that there are 22,076 instances without speaker information, and therefore not being assigned to any of the three subsets, the training subset consists of the remaining 380,836 instances. The assignment of each of the instances into the three subsets (train, dev, test) is encoded as the last piece of information in the description of each instance. Segment-level statistics from the final dataset are presented in Table 1. We make the dataset freely available under the CC-BY-SA license via the CLARIN.SI repository.[6]

4. Correspondence of the Manual Transcripts and the Audio Recordings

Given that parliamentary transcripts are regularly a standardised approximation of what was actually said, we performed a short analysis of those differences by manually correcting 484 segments consisting of 2.16 hours of speech.
Comparing the automatically normalized segments with their manually corrected counterparts, we obtain a WER metric value of 4.69% and a CER metric of 2.64%, pointing towards the conclusion that there was a rather low level of interventions necessary in the transcripts, but also that a ceiling for any automatic evaluation lies at these two measurements. Manual interventions are present in 290 segments, i.e., 59.9% of all analysed segments, showing that this low noise is still rather distributed across all segments.
Manually inspecting a subset of the differences showed the issues to be mostly due to inconsistency in the work of transcribers (primarily regarding the compliance to the standard or elimination of fillers), typos introduced by transcribers, and in less frequent cases, issues with automatic normalization (either wrongly normalized phenomena or unnormalized phenomena).

[6]`http://hdl.handle.net/11356/1494`

It is important to remember that we filtered out 7% of all segments in which the automatic and manual transcriptions were in significant disagreement, and some of those segments probably also consisted of examples where the transcripts differed more significantly from what was actually uttered.

5. Experiments with the ParlaSpeech-HR Dataset

5.1. Training Initial Baseline Systems

Our initial systems were trained on the initial ASR dataset, containing 66 hours of speech, using either the Kaldi toolkit (Povey et al., 2011), or the HuggingFace library (Wolf et al., 2019). They Kaldi systems served two purposes: as a baseline to monitor progress of our transformer-based systems and as a fast alternative to perform speech-to-text alignment. Table 2 shows several results obtained using different models.
The first experiment used models pre-trained on a different, commercial dataset (McAuliffe et al., 2017), that was later fine-tuned on our training set in the second experiment. The next two experiments used the TDNN and chain model architectures commonly used in Kaldi (Povey et al., 2016). The final baseline system is the initial XLS-R-based model. The results show a significant improvement when the baseline model is further trained on our data, as well as the superior performance of transformer-based models.

5.2. Training ASR Systems on Normalized or Original Text

The two entries in the middle part of Table 2 compare XLS-R when trained on original and normalized transcripts, respectively. Given the significant capacity of transformer models, our hypothesis was that we could train future models on original data without need for noisy normalization of training data and de-normalization of automatically transcribed text. To reiterate, normalization was primarily focused on expanding numerical values in digital format and frequent acronyms and abbreviations.
In these experiments 110 hours were used for training.We trained the XLS-R transformer model for 8 epochs. The results in Table 2 show that there is barely any difference in the quality of the two outputs. Given that the normalized phenomena are not highly frequent, we performed a short focused analysis of the ASR output trained on the original text. The transformer model showed to be highly effective both on generating numerals in the digit form, as well on acronyms and abbreviations that occurred in the test dataset.

5.3. Comparing XLS-R and Slavic Models

Given the quick developments on the front of speech transformer models, during the finalisation of this paper, a new model pre-trained only on the Slavic por-

	sum	min	max	mean	median
spoken (seconds)	6,538,823	8	20	16.2	19.1
original (# of words)	14,533,541	1	82	35.7	38
normalized (# of words)	14,679,339	1	84	36.1	38

Table 1: Segment-level statistics calculated over the 403,925 segments available in the ParlaSpeech-HR dataset. Information is given on the spoken mode, and the original human and transcripts, and the automatically normalized transcripts.

System	WER	CER
GMM/WFST baseline	66.92%	50.43%
GMM/WFST adapted	30.54%	12.60%
TDNN/WFST	22.51%	9.78%
TDNN/WFST chain	16.38%	6.91%
XLS-R-66-initial	13.94%	5.42%
XLS-R-110-original	10.57%	3.23%
XLS-R-110-normalized	10.15%	3.04%
XLS-R-300	7.61%	2.34%
Slavic-300	6.79%	2.22%
Slavic-300+lm	4.30%	1.88%

Table 2: Output of various ASR systems. The first group of experiments was performed on the initial 66 hours of training data, the second on 110 hours, and the third on 300 hours.

tion of the VoxPopuli dataset has emerged,[7] which had been pre-trained on 89.9 thousand hours of raw speech. In this, last set of experiments, we compare the XLS-R model to the Slavic model, investigating whether a model pre-trained on a narrower set of languages, but no new data, would perform better. We fine-tune each of the models on 300 hours of training data. The experiments are performed on the original data, so no normalization of the transcripts was performed.

The results presented in the first two rows of the third section of Table 2 show that the Slavic model seems to be slightly better than XLS-R, with a relative error reduction of 11% on WER and a 5% error reduction on CER.

Given that the HuggingFace transformers library recently included support for adding language models to the ASR process, we perform a final experiment with adding to the Slavic model a 5-gram language model, trained on the whole ParlaMint corpus. The performance of the model further improves to 4.3% of word-error-rate and 1.88% of character-error-rate. While these results might sound very strong, the relatedness of the training, the testing, and the language model data has to be taken into account, and further experiments are needed on more diverse data.

We release the three models described in this section in the HuggingFace model repository.[8]

6. Conclusion

With the development of the ParlaSpeech-HR dataset we believe to have put the Croatian language on the map of the hastily developing language technologies. During our experiments we have shown that (1) automatic alignment of non-monotonic speech and human transcripts is very much possible, (2) there is significant difference in the spoken content and the human transcripts of parliamentary proceedings (around 5% of words are affected), (3) transformer models significantly outperform Kaldi-based models, (4) for transformer models it is not important for the data to be normalized as these have enough capacity to learn to produce digits and frequent abbreviations, (5) models pre-trained on a more limited set of related languages seem to perform better than general multilingual models, and (6) even in the case of data where the training and the testing domains are similar, a language model can still improve the output of transformer models.

We will continue our efforts by (1) producing the multimodal corpus of Croatian parliamentary proceedings, (2) performing speaker profiling experiments, and (3) applying the presented bootstrapping methodology to other under-resourced languages in dire need of similar datasets. We have high hopes that the ParlaSpeech methodology is a great opportunity for other under-resourced languages to obtain cheap, high-quality ASR datasets. Along these hopes, we make our code available at `https://github.com/clarinsi/parlaspeech`.

Acknowledgements

This work has received funding from the European Union's Connecting Europe Facility 2014-2020 - CEF Telecom, under Grant Agreement No. INEA/CEF/ICT/A2020/2278341. This communication reflects only the author's view. The Agency is not responsible for any use that may be made of the information it contains.

This work was also funded by the CLARIN ERIC project "ParlaMint", the Slovenian-Flemish bilateral basic research project "Linguistic landscape of hate speech on social media" (N06-0099 and FWO-G070619N) and the research programme "Language resources and technologies for Slovene" (P6-0411).

[7] `https://huggingface.co/facebook/wav2vec2-large-slavic-voxpopuli-v2`

[8] `https://huggingface.co/classla/wav2vec2-xls-r-parlaspeech-hr`
`https://huggingface.co/classla/wav2vec2-large-slavic-parlaspeech-hr`
`https://huggingface.co/classla/wav2vec2-large-slavic-parlaspeech-hr-lm`

7. Bibliographical References

Babu, A., Wang, C., Tjandra, A., Lakhotia, K., Xu, Q., Goyal, N., Singh, K., von Platen, P., Saraf, Y., Pino, J., et al. (2021). XLS-R: Self-supervised cross-lingual speech representation learning at scale. *arXiv preprint arXiv:2111.09296.*

Baevski, A., Zhou, H., Mohamed, A., and Auli, M. (2020). wav2vec 2.0: A framework for self-supervised learning of speech representations. *arXiv preprint arXiv:2006.11477.*

Ebden, P. and Sproat, R. (2015). The Kestrel TTS text normalization system. *Natural Language Engineering*, 21(3):333–353.

Erjavec, T., Ogrodniczuk, M., Osenova, P., Ljubešić, N., Simov, K., Grigorova, V., Rudolf, M., Pančur, A., Kopp, M., Barkarson, S., Steingrímsson, S., van der Pol, H., Depoorter, G., de Does, J., Jongejan, B., Haltrup Hansen, D., Navarretta, C., Calzada Pérez, M., de Macedo, L. D., van Heusden, R., Marx, M., Çöltekin, Ç., Coole, M., Agnoloni, T., Frontini, F., Montemagni, S., Quochi, V., Venturi, G., Ruisi, M., Marchetti, C., Battistoni, R., Sebők, M., Ring, O., Darģis, R., Utka, A., Petkevičius, M., Briedienė, M., Krilavičius, T., Morkevičius, V., Diwersy, S., Luxardo, G., and Rayson, P. (2021). Multilingual comparable corpora of parliamentary debates ParlaMint 2.1. Slovenian language resource repository CLARIN.SI.

Erjavec, T., Ogrodniczuk, M., Osenova, P., Ljubešić, N., Simov, K., Pančur, A., Rudolf, M., Kopp, M., Barkarson, S., Steingrímsson, S., et al. (2022). The ParlaMint corpora of parliamentary proceedings. *Language resources and evaluation*, pages 1–34.

Helgadóttir, I. R., Kjaran, R., Nikulásdóttir, A. B., and Gudhnason, J. (2017). Building an ASR Corpus Using Althingi's Parliamentary Speeches. In *INTERSPEECH*, pages 2163–2167.

Katsamanis, A., Black, M., Georgiou, P. G., Goldstein, L., and Narayanan, S. (2011). SailAlign: Robust long speech-text alignment. In *Proc. of workshop on new tools and methods for very-large scale phonetics research.*

Kirkedal, A., Stepanović, M., and Plank, B. (2020). FT speech: Danish parliament speech corpus. In *Interspeech 2020*. ISCA, oct.

Mansikkaniemi, A., Smit, P., Kurimo, M., et al. (2017). Automatic Construction of the Finnish Parliament Speech Corpus. In *INTERSPEECH*, volume 8, pages 3762–3766.

Marasek, K., Koržinek, D., and Brocki, Ł. (2014). System for automatic transcription of sessions of the Polish senate. *Archives of Acoustics*, 39(4):501–509.

Martinčić-Ipšić, S., Ribarić, S., and Ipšić, I. (2008). Acoustic modelling for Croatian speech recognition and synthesis. *Informatica*, 19(2):227–254.

McAuliffe, M., Socolof, M., Mihuc, S., Wagner, M., and Sonderegger, M. (2017). Montreal Forced Aligner: Trainable Text-Speech Alignment Using Kaldi. In *Interspeech*, volume 2017, pages 498–502.

Nouza, J., Safarik, R., and Cerva, P. (2016). ASR for South Slavic Languages Developed in Almost Automated Way. In *INTERSPEECH*, pages 3868–3872.

Panayotov, V., Chen, G., Povey, D., and Khudanpur, S. (2015). Librispeech: an asr corpus based on public domain audio books. In *2015 IEEE international conference on acoustics, speech and signal processing (ICASSP)*, pages 5206–5210. IEEE.

Plüss, M., Neukom, L., Scheller, C., and Vogel, M. (2020). Swiss Parliaments Corpus, an Automatically Aligned Swiss German Speech to Standard German text corpus.

Popović, B., Ostrogonac, S., Pakoci, E., Jakovljević, N., and Delić, V. (2015). Deep neural network based continuous speech recognition for Serbian using the Kaldi toolkit. In *International Conference on Speech and Computer*, pages 186–192. Springer.

Povey, D., Ghoshal, A., Boulianne, G., Burget, L., Glembek, O., Goel, N., Hannemann, M., Motlicek, P., Qian, Y., Schwarz, P., et al. (2011). The Kaldi speech recognition toolkit. In *IEEE 2011 workshop on automatic speech recognition and understanding*, number CONF. IEEE Signal Processing Society.

Povey, D., Peddinti, V., Galvez, D., Ghahremani, P., Manohar, V., Na, X., Wang, Y., and Khudanpur, S. (2016). Purely sequence-trained neural networks for ASR based on lattice-free MMI. In *Interspeech*, pages 2751–2755.

Silero. (2021). Silero VAD: pre-trained enterprise-grade Voice Activity Detector (VAD), Number Detector and Language Classifier. `https://github.com/snakers4/silero-vad`.

Solberg, P. E. and Ortiz, P. (2022). The Norwegian Parliamentary Speech Corpus. *CoRR*, abs/2201.10881.

Wang, C., Riviere, M., Lee, A., Wu, A., Talnikar, C., Haziza, D., Williamson, M., Pino, J., and Dupoux, E. (2021). VoxPopuli: A large-scale multilingual speech corpus for representation learning, semi-supervised learning and interpretation. In *Proceedings of the 59th Annual Meeting of the Association for Computational Linguistics and the 11th International Joint Conference on Natural Language Processing (Volume 1: Long Papers)*, pages 993–1003, Online, August. Association for Computational Linguistics.

Wolf, T., Debut, L., Sanh, V., Chaumond, J., Delangue, C., Moi, A., Cistac, P., Rault, T., Louf, R., Funtowicz, M., et al. (2019). Huggingface's transformers: State-of-the-art natural language processing. *arXiv preprint arXiv:1910.03771.*

Proceedings of ParlaCLARIN III @ LREC2022 pages 117–124
Marseille, 20 June 2022

Making Italian Parliamentary Records Machine-Actionable: The Construction of the ParlaMint-IT Corpus

**Tommaso Agnoloni[1], Roberto Bartolini[2], Francesca Frontini[2], Carlo Marchetti[3]
Simonetta Montemagni[2], Valeria Quochi[2], Manuela Ruisi[3], Giulia Venturi[2]**
[1]CNR-IGSG, Firenze Italy; [2]CNR-ILC, Pisa Italy; [3]Senato della Repubblica, Roma Italy
[1]tommaso.agnoloni@igsg.cnr.it, [2]name.surname@ilc.cnr.it, [3]name.surname@senato.it

Abstract

This paper describes the process of acquisition, cleaning, interpretation, coding and linguistic annotation of a collection of parliamentary debates from the Senate of the Italian Republic covering the COVID-19 pandemic emergency period and a former period for reference and comparison according to the CLARIN ParlaMint prescriptions. The corpus contains 1199 sessions and 79,373 speeches for a total of about 31 million words, and was encoded according to the ParlaCLARIN TEI XML format. It includes extensive metadata about the speakers, sessions, political parties and parliamentary groups. As required by the ParlaMint initiative, the corpus was also linguistically annotated for sentences, tokens, POS tags, lemmas and dependency syntax according to the universal dependencies guidelines. Named entity annotation and classification is also included. All linguistic annotation was performed automatically using state-of-the-art NLP technology with no manual revision. The Italian dataset is freely available as part of the larger ParlaMint 2.1 corpus deposited and archived in CLARIN repository together with all other national corpora. It is also available for direct analysis and inspection via various CLARIN services and has already been used both for research and educational purposes.

Keywords: parliamentary debates, CLARIN ParlaMint, corpus creation, corpus annotation

1. Introduction

Parliamentary data is an interesting source of data for various types of investigations and analyses, in addition to the obvious applications in political studies. Due to their richness and uniqueness, parliamentary records have in fact been a fundamental resource for several research questions in different disciplines of the humanities and social sciences for the last half century (see Fišer and Lenardič (2018) for a brief overview of the different fields of studies). With the recent push towards open data and open participation, it becomes increasingly important to release actionable data sets of parliamentary debates and records in order to support empirical research and development of integrated analytical tools. Projects have recently flourished in many countries and for many languages on the construction of corpora of parliamentary debates as language resources to be used in language- and content-based web applications in order to support political discourse studies. An overview of existing projects in this sense can be found by consulting the dedicated CLARIN Resource Family of Parliamentary Corpora[1]. One of the most widely used is the Hansard Corpus, providing historical and contemporary data for the British Parliament[2].

Building on this landscaping work, the CLARIN infrastructure has decided to fund the ParlaMint project for fostering the creation of a harmonised, comparable multilingual corpus of parliamentary data in order to boost the field of comparative studies and the uptake of digital language technologies into political social sciences and cultural studies.

In this work we describe the steps taken and the challenges faced for the construction of the Italian section of the ParlaMint corpus, following the common guidelines and approach defined by the ParlaMint community. The Italian corpus is therefore constructed so as to be interoperable with all other ParlaMint corpora and is therefore comparable with the growing collection of national data sets.

The paper is structured as follows: in section 2 we first provide the background of our work. Sections 3 and 4 describe the steps that led to the creation of the corpus from the original data obtained from the Senate and its conversion and structuring according to the ParlaMint format. Section 5 describes the automatic linguistic annotation of the texts of the debates and discusses related issues, while section 6 reports on the conversion tool developed to transform the CoNLL-U annotations into the required ParlaMint.ana format. Finally, section 7 concludes by summarising the main difficulties encountered with an indication of the potential improvements for future works; furthermore, a brief mention is made to some of the current applications of the corpus.

2. Background and Context

The Italian Parliament is a perfect bicameral system and consists of the Senate (www.senato.it) and the Chamber of Deputies (www.camera.it). The two chambers are autonomous and independent also as regards technical, administrative and organisational aspects.

The Senate is organised into parliamentary groups according to the political party each senator belongs to; a

[1]`https://www.clarin.eu/resource-families/parliamentary-corpora`

[2]`https://www.clarin.ac.uk/hansard-corpus`

mixed group is foreseen for those senators whose formations do not reach at least 10 members and for senators not enrolled in any component. Senators representing linguistic minorities are allowed to form a Group composed of at least five members. Senators-for-life, in the autonomy of their legitimacy, may not become part of any Group[3].

The CLARIN ParlaMint project is a recent initiative, financially supported by CLARIN ERIC, that aims at the creation of a machine-actionable multilingual set of corpora of parliamentary debates, i.e. which can be directly analysed by online tools and technology for dealing with language-based content, esp. in the fields of political social sciences and cultural studies. Started as a small pilot project for 4 languages and parliaments, the project now comprises 17 languages and is in the process of expanding[4]. Given its initial focus on emergencies, the corpora focus on the COVID-19 pandemic period and include data from a previous period to be used as a reference; details for the Italian corpus will be given in section 3 below; for common issues on the multilingual corpus see Erjavec et al. (2022). An important achievement of the project was the definition of a common TEI format[5] which follows the ParlaCLARIN recommendations (Erjavec and Pančur, 2019)[6] but further constrains the schema for ensuring full comparability of the corpora across languages. All language datasets come in two variants: the ParlaMint TEI corpora (Erjavec et al., 2021a), which contain fully marked-up text of the transcribed speeches, and the linguistically annotated corpora (Erjavec et al., 2021b), which add linguistic annotation to the marked-up version of the texts.

3. Construction of the ParlaMint-IT Corpus

This section describes the creation of the Italian ParlaMint TEI corpus, that is the XML version containing the marked-up transcriptions, which constitute the core part of the work.

The very first and fundamental step in the creation of the Italian corpus of parliamentary debates is the acquisition, cleaning and structuring of the stenographic verbatim records of the required parliamentary sittings. As a consequence of the total independence of the two Italian parliament chambers, the processes for the production, digitisation and publication of the stenographic transcriptions of the sessions of the Chamber of Deputies and of the Senate are different and still not interoperable. For time constraints and practical reasons, in this work we deal with data from the Senate only. The covered time-span ranges from March 15 2013 (i.e. the beginning of 17th legislative term) to November 18 2020 (i.e. the date of the last data retrieval, corresponding to the current 18th legislative term). The whole corpus consists of 1199 files, one for each plenary session.

The COVID-19 sub-corpus contains sessions starting from November 1 2019 (as conventionally agreed for all ParlaMint corpora) and contains 115 sessions/files; the reference sub-corpus instead contains 1084 sessions/files, covering the preceding period. The source documents containing the transcriptions were made available in bulk by the Information Technology Service of the Senate. The same documents can however also be retrieved directly from the Senate website[7], so that the whole process should be reproducible. Although, starting from 2018, the transcripts of the plenary sessions of the Senate are also published in the Akoma Ntoso format (Palmirani and Vitali, 2011)[8], in order to uniformly cover transcripts from all the required time spans (thus including years before 2018), the HTML format was chosen as the source format for the whole corpus. Moreover, the HTML files contain additional annotations (for speeches, speakers, etc.), expressed by means of proprietary XML tags "embedded" into the HTML encoding; particularly useful is the original segmentation into utterances (tag <INTERVENTO>) and speaker annotation (tag <ORATORE>), which had to be ported to the TEI ParlaMint encoding.

Before the actual TEI encoding could start, the original HTML corpus was therefore pre-processed with the goal of extracting all the "embedded" XML annotation and discarding (almost) every HTML annotation. This produced an intermediate XML corpus which retained only paragraphs, <p>, and italic formatting, <i> HTML tags, as they represent textual segments and (potentially) parenthetical expressions. A small fraction of the intermediate files (62/1199) required manual correction in order to force XML well-formedness for their subsequent DOM (Document Object Model) parsing.

At this stage, only the transcripts of the speeches are kept from the original HTML corpus for the subsequent ParlaMint encoding (tag <RESSTEN> , i.e. *Resoconto Stenografico* 'verbatim report'). Annexed documents for the session, if any, are discarded in the current release, as these are not in focus within the project. Plenary verbatim records in fact usually are attached with annexes such as the texts of control and policy-setting documents. In particular, the texts of the motions, questions and interpellations spoken during the plenary are published in Annex B when they are submitted to the House, whereas resolutions and other documents introduced during the discussion are published in Annex A

[3] https://www.senato.it/en/

[4] https://www.clarin.eu/content/parlamint-towards-comparable-parliamentary-corpora

[5] https://github.com/clarin-eric/ParlaMint/blob/main/README.md

[6] https://clarin-eric.github.io/Parla-CLARIN/

[7] https://www.senato.it/Leg17/3809?testo_generico=911

[8] www.akomantoso.org

of the report of the sitting.

ParlaMint additionally requires that corpora have extensive metadata (speaker name, gender, party affiliation, MP or guest status) and that each speech is marked with its speakers and their role(s) (chair, regular speaker, etc.).

In our case, metadata about the members of the Senate and the political groups were obtained from the open data portal `http://dati.senato.it`, and stored into structured metadata tables, as described in section 4 below. The main purpose of the Senate data portal is to make available, in open and freely reusable formats, most of the data already published on the institutional website of the Senate; this in order to ensure greater transparency on the work of the institution and to encourage the concrete participation of citizens in decision-making processes. In particular, the data referring to the composition of the Senate, to the bills, and to the activity of the senators (presentation of documents and bills, interventions and electronic voting) are openly published starting from the XIII legislature, and are updated on a daily basis. The project is coordinated with a similar initiative by the Chamber of Deputies (`http://dati.camera.it`).

4. Data Encoding in the ParlaMint TEI Format

The corpus of speeches was encoded in the ParlaMint format by developing a specific transformer that reads the input documents and data, transforms them into the required target structure and writes the ParlaMint-XML output. The input of this transformer consists in the aforementioned intermediate XML corpus and structured metadata tables (in comma separated values format). The reading, transformation and writing is implemented by means of Java XML DOM manipulation[9].

The expected output, as specified by the ParlaMint documentation, consists of a corpus root file, and a set of XML documents with the transcriptions of the plenary sessions, one session per file. The corpus root file must contain the general corpus header providing all corpus-level metadata (such as edition, funding, contributors, etc.) and includes the list of files that encode the actual transcriptions of the parliamentary sittings. It must also include all controlled vocabulary terms encoded in the form of taxonomies, i.e. metadata about speakers, political groups, parties, government in charge; these are referred to in the actual transcription files via the appropriately created term ids.

For the encoding of the corpus root file, the required metadata about speakers and political groups were mostly automatically obtained by querying the Senate Data portal `dati.senato.it` where data is represented in RDF according to the Ontologia Senato della Repubblica ontology (OSR)[10] and exposed both through a SPARQL endpoint and via up-to date structured open data for the most common predefined queries[11]. In particular, we collected the list of senators and the composition of parliamentary groups with all the changes that have occurred during the legislature.

For speakers who are not members of the Senate (mostly members of the government in charge who might either be members of the Chamber of Deputies or not members of the Parliament at all) manual insertion of their metadata was necessary and done by accessing their personal pages from the Senate website.

For all speakers we were thus able to populate data about: gender, date and place of birth (reconciled with persistent URIs from the GeoNames dataset[12]), affiliation to political groups over time, and link to the personal web page on the institutional website. Metadata about governments in charge over time, role of speakers in governments, coalition of political groups supporting or opposing the governments, also required manual encoding using institutional web pages as sources.

The collected data was then appropriately transformed in the target structures required by the ParlaMint Schema. Consistent interlinking of speakers with speeches was guaranteed thanks to the use of the same identifiers in all the source data and documents, appropriately transformed following the ParlaMint naming conventions for identifiers (*i.e.* human readable ids).

The rest of the corpus root is composed and structured by hard-coding in the Java source code the desired output for the different XML elements. The encoding of the document corpus of transcriptions was accomplished by parsing into a DOM the intermediate XML documents, traversing the documents and applying the appropriate transformations from the source elements to the target elements. Text not belonging to speeches was mapped onto `<note>` elements. Whenever possible, the type of the note is assigned via the `@type` attribute, with the following possible values: "role", "speaker", "time", "summary", "voting". Incident annotations are detected among the italics `<i>` HTML annotation in the source files, based on a heuristic applied to the content of the tagged text (i.e. a list of keywords triggering incident text). In a similar way, the type of parenthetical clauses (kinesic, vocal, parenthesis and their type attribute) are annotated based on a heuristic analysis of their textual content. For example, if the text originally marked in italics contains words like *brusio* 'buzz', *commenti* 'comments', *ilarità* 'hilarity', *proteste* 'complaints' or *richiami* 'admonitions', then a `<vocal>` tag with type "noise", "speaking", "laughter" or "shouting" is used for the annotation of that portion of text. Particular attention is paid to the removal

[9] `https://github.com/atomm/ResAulaSenato2ParlaMintTEI`

[10] `http://dati.senato.it/osr/`; for a graphic visualisation see also `https://dati.senato.it/DatiSenato/browse/19?testo_generico=15`

[11] `https://dati.senato.it/DatiSenato/browse/scarica_i_dati`

[12] `http://www.geonames.org/`

of those HTML tags that are useless for the purpose of a TEI encoding (e.g. <i> tags not denoting parenthetical expressions or <a> HTML links) without breaking the resulting text segments with carriage returns or useless punctuation, which would result in a noisy input to the subsequent linguistic analysis pipeline. The speakers' identifiers, available in the source documents, were mapped to the identifiers used in the corpus root and kept consistent.

5. Automatic Linguistic Annotation

The automatic linguistic annotation of the corpus has been articulated in two stages. The first one includes the following levels of analysis: sentence splitting, tokenisation, part-of-speech tagging, lemmatisation and dependency parsing. Annotation was performed by the STANZA neural pipeline[13] which is reported to achieve state-of-the-art or competitive performance for different languages (Qi et al., 2020). The choice was motivated by the fact that the pipeline uses the annotation formalism devised in the Universal Dependency (UD) initiative (Nivre, 2015), which was a project requirement for guaranteeing interoperability and comparability with all other ParlaMint corpora. Among the different Italian available models, we used the *italian-isdt-ud-2.5* model, trained on the Italian Stanford Dependency Treebank, which represents the biggest UD Treebank for Italian covering different textual genres (Bosco et al., 2013).

The second stage consisted in the automatic Named Entity Recognition (NER). Since the STANZA package did not include a NER model for the Italian language at the time we performed the annotation, and NER annotation was a mandatory requirement, it was carried out by running, on the same raw data, the ItaliaNLP NER module (Dell'Orletta et al., 2014) [14], which assigns three standard named entity tags – i.e. Person, Organisation, Location – and achieves state-of-the-art performance.

Both tools output the annotated texts in CoNLL format, but follow different tokenisation approaches: STANZA tokenises according to UD principles, namely subtokenises agglutinated forms such as complex prepositions (e.g. *della* 'of+the.fem' becomes `di la` 'of the.fem') or verbs with enclitic pronouns (e.g. *farlo* 'to-do+it' becomes `fare lo`), while the *ItaliaNLP NER* does not (*della* and *farlo* are considered simple tokens). The outputs of the linguistic and Named Entity annotation therefore had to be post-processed for re-alignment in order to produce a unified annotation.

For this last step, a number of alignment rules were defined specifically devoted to handling mismatches. This step turned out to be cyclic, as conversion errors revealed exceptional cases of misalignment that needed to be tackled with new heuristics.

Even though both the linguistic annotation pipeline and the NER module used here achieve state-of-the-art performance for Italian, it is well known that Machine Learning algorithms suffer from a drop of accuracy when tested on domains outside of the data on which they were trained (Gildea, 2001). Speech transcriptions of parliamentary debates represent a language variety which differs from the written language testified in the used training corpora: we can thus look at them as Out-of-Domain texts for which the results of the automatic linguistic annotation need to be carefully assessed.

For this reason, we felt that the impact of the linguistic peculiarities of the language variety of the corpus on the performance of automatic linguistic and NE annotation, both from a quantitative and qualitative perspective, needed to be investigated. With this goal in mind, we started manually revising the automatic annotation of speech transcriptions of parliamentary debates: the result of this process, still ongoing at the time of writing, will be used as an evaluation benchmark. Preliminary results achieved so far show that language-specific features of the debates from the COVID pandemic period negatively affect the performance of automatic annotation, more than features from the debates of the earlier period. We hypothesise that this follows from the fact that the earlier debates belong to a specific variety of language use, which Nencioni (1976) identifies as 'spoken-written', i.e. a variety characterised by an hybrid nature featuring a co-occurrence of traits typical of both written and spoken language. Thus, they are linguistically more similar to the written texts which the linguistic annotation tools were trained on. In addition, they contain several normative references (e.g. *article 5 of law n. 184, paragraph 2, states [...]*) that make the transcriptions more similar to a written legal text. On the contrary, the debates of the COVID-19 period are mostly characterised by traits specific to the spontaneous speech (such as rethorical questions in interrogative forms to convey illocutionary force to an assertion, e.g. *is it ever possibile [...]*, interruptions), since the debates deal with issues that are more emotionally engaging given the historical period, such as the prison riot which happened in March 2020 calling for better anti-COVID measures.

6. Data Encoding in the TEI ParlaMint *.ana* Format

The unified CoNLL-U format obtained with the post-processing described above had finally to be back-converted to the ParlaMint TEI *.ana* format, i.e. the final format for the encoding of linguistic annotation. For this task a converter was developed in C++[15] which takes in input both the original ParlaMint-IT.xml cor-

[13] https://stanfordnlp.github.io/stanza/index.HTML

[14] http://www.italianlp.it/demo/t2k-text-to-knowledge/

[15] https://github.com/cnr-ilc/conllu2Parlamint_TEI

pus and the unified CoNLL-U dataset and outputs a valid ParlaMint-IT.*ana* corpus.

Similarly to the main corpus version, the expected output of the linguistic annotation consists in a corpus root file and a number of XML files encoded according to the *ParlaMint.ana* format. Each file represents one parliamentary session and contains the linguistically annotated transcriptions of all the speeches occurring in that session. The root.*ana* file instead adds two taxonomies to the corresponding root file of the not annotated base corpus: i.e. a taxonomy for Named Entities and a taxonomy for the syntactic dependency relations, which explicitly define the tags and categories used in the annotation files.

The ParlaMint format encodes the basic linguistic annotation in-line, according to the TEI Lightweight Linguistic Annotation guidelines (Bański et al., 2018) and therefore encodes sentences (<s>), word tokens (<w>), punctuation symbols (<pc>) as XML elements, while the rest of the basic linguistic information is encoded in the form of attributes of <w>. All the original morpho-syntactic information is concatenated into the @msd attribute[16]. Agglutinated forms that are treated as multi-token forms in UD are represented as nested words <w>[17].

Named Entities are represented in a similar way, with the outer element being <name>. Syntactic dependencies are represented instead by a <linkGrp> element under <s> which groups all dependency relations as <link>. Each link must specify the relation type, and refer to head and dependent tokens. The relation type itself is a pointer to the categories defined in the previously mentioned <taxonomy> in the root file.

The non-annotated input corpus is structurally divided into folders by years, from 2013 to 2020; each folder/year contains all the sessions of that year in TEI XML format. Each session contains sections, motions, information on the speakers and their roles, all encoded with the appropriate tag; the text of the speeches is divided into small narratives, i.e. segments, encoded with the <seg> tag (as described in section 3 above). Each segment may contain several utterances/sentences, and was automatically annotated linguistically as described in section 5 above. Each session therefore contains a variable number of segments each of which has a unique identifier.

The input unified CoNLL-U dataset has a parallel structure: each session has associated a folder of linguistically analysed files, in CoNLL-U tabular format, which correspond exactly to the number of segments <seg> the session contains. The names of the files maintain the semantics of the sessions: i.e. the files corresponding to the session YYY.xml of a certain year, which contains N segments, correspond to N CoNLL-U files contained in the YYY folder and are identified by the file names YYY.seg1.udner, YYY.seg2.udener, ...YYY.segN.udner. The content of the CoNLL-U file consists of a list of linguistically annotated word forms, one for each line, corresponding to the tokenisation of the text; a blank line separates the sentences[18].

In this format, in the case of multi-token items the numeric identifier can be a range; for Italian this occurs very frequently in the representation of agglutinated forms such as complex prepositions and enclitic particles attached to verbs as in the example below:

```
5      .........
6-7 dei _ _ _ _ _ _ _
start_char=178|end\char=181
6 di di ADP E _ 8 case _ _
7 i il DET RD  Definite=def|Gender=Masc|
Number=Plur|PronType=Art 8 det _ _
8      ..........
```

The production of the linguistically annotated TEI Corpus takes place through a Manager that moves within the CoNLL-U dataset structure described above by applying a conversion code from the CoNLL-U format to the ParlaMint TEI XML. The Manager handles one year (folder) at the time and takes as input the list of XML files that compose each year of parliamentary sessions. Each file, which represents a session, is parsed and the text contained in each <seg> is replaced by the result of the actual CoNLL-U to XML converter which parses the corresponding *.udner* file and produces an XML sub-tree with <seg> as the parent node. In this way there is a one-to-one correspondence between the starting (non-annotated) files and the linguistically annotated ones.

The heart of the production process of the linguistically annotated parliamentary corpus is represented by the transformation of the CoNLL-U files (representing linguistically annotated segments) into the corresponding segment of the XML file. All annotation contained in the CoNLL-U files was therefore converted to the TEI ParlaMint linguistic annotation common format[19] according to the following conversion algorithm:

1. First, a <seg> node is generated which replaces

[16]For details and examples see https://clarin-eric.github.io/parla-clarin/#sec-linguistic

[17]Although this creates mixed content and thus may not be the ideal representation, we adhered to the project specification. The interested reader might want to follow the discussion that led to this decision here https://github.com/clarin-eric/ParlaMint/issues/61

[18]For practical purposes, the fields of the CoNLL-U data structure are stored in an variable *entry* and are the well known *id, form, lemma, upos, xpos, feats, head, deprel*, plus an additional field for encoding *named entities*. For details on Universal Dependencies see also https://universaldependencies.org/format.HTML

[19]More details can be found at https://clarin-eric.github.io/parla-clarin/#sec-linguistic

the homologous node of the input XML file. This node has an @xml:id attribute obtained by concatenating the name of the file with the year, and the session and segment indices.

2. The CoNLL-U (*.udner*) file is parsed one line at a time and every time an empty line is encountered a new sentence <s> is generated as a child node of the current <seg>. The node <s> also receives an @xml:id attribute generated by concatenating a progressive numeric index (a sentence counter) to the father's id. All sentence nodes then will always be children of the current segment node.

3. For each input line a word <w> or a punctuation node <pc> is generated as an ordered child of the current node[20]. The *entry.form* value is stored as the content of <w>[21] while the attributes of the node are populated as follows:

   - @xml:id: by concatenating the id of the parent node with the value of *entry.id*;
   - @lemma: with the *entry.lemma* value;
   - @pos: with the *entry.upos* value;
   - @msd: by concatenating the value of *entry.xpos* and *entry.feat*;

4. At the end of each sentence, a child <linkGrp> node of the current sentence is also generated and will have as many <link> child nodes as there are functional relations in the sentence. The <link> node has the following attributes:

   - @ana: is the entry value *deprel*;
   - @target: contains references to the xml:id of both the head and the dependent;

In addition to being required, this conversion step was also useful for identifying errors in the alignment of the outputs of the linguistic and Named Entity annotations described in section 5 above, and entered the cyclic revision process that led to the final clean version.

7. Conclusions and Future Work

In this paper we have described in detail the far from trivial process that produced the Italian section of the ParlaMint corpora (Erjavec et al., 2021a), and we have learnt that: 1) the most onerous part of the work is the structuring of the base parliamentary debates corpus which involved cleaning, transformation and interpretation via heuristics of the transcripts in their original, non-standard and loosely structured format; 2) because of the differences in tokenisation, annotating linguistic features and NEs with different tools generated a substantial processing overhead for performing a good re-alignment. The experience of using different tools for linguistic annotation and NER thus proved too time-consuming and error prone.

Currently, we are taking part in the second phase of the ParlaMint project, in which we will extend the COVID-19 sub-corpus with new sessions starting from December 2020 onwards. In this context, we will explore the possibility of deriving the data from the Akoma Ntoso format, which might provide a useful result for a wider community due to its becoming good practice in a number of government bodies in several countries all over the world. As regards corpus annotation, in order to avoid tokenisation mismatches, we plan to employ the same pipeline for performing all token-based annotations, with STANZA still being the best candidate. Ideally, we would like to train a specific NER model for Italian in the neural pipeline; however, since a model has become available in the meantime, we will first experiment with it, and assess the quality of the results first.

As regards exploitation, the corpus has already been used in preliminary political studies. For instance, Cavalieri and Del Fante make use of the ParlaMint-IT corpus to compare topics discussed in Senate plenary sessions with the expenditure across budget categories. According to the authors, combining the analysis of parliamentary debates carried out by means of quantitative text analysis techniques with the analysis of final expenditures trade-offs "helps to better grasp dynamics which public budgeting is subject to and constitute a very promising venue for future research both for political science and linguistic scholars" (Del Fante and Cavalieri, 2021).

The availability of the Italian corpus, together with the other ParlaMint corpora, is also greatly beneficial for pedagogical applications. The corpus for instance was selected by a team of students of the 2021 Helsinki hackathon[22], who plotted timelines of COVID-word frequencies using relative occurrences, and added a curve indicating the number of COVID cases, thus illustrating the relation between the parliamentary debates and the epidemiological situation in four countries, including Italy. Furthermore, the corpus is currently being used in Italian universities, for various purposes. For classes in computational linguistics, the interest lies especially in the linguistically annotated sources. From this perspective, it has been used in the framework of the teaching activities of two of the authors in a Computational Linguistics course addressed to Master students within the "Digital Humanities" degree program at the University of Pisa. By manually

[20]The sentence node can also be the parent of <name> nodes, which capture information on NEs. The specific conversion algorithm for NEs is reported in the Appendix to the paper.

[21]In cases of multi-token items the word node can also include other <w> sub-nodes.

[22]*Parliamentary Debates in COVID Times* https://www.clarin.eu/impact-stories/helsinki-digital-humanities-hackathon-2021-parliamentary-debates-covid-times

revising the output of automatic linguistic annotation, students are confronted with the real problems connected with the automatic analysis of specific varieties of language use. Students from the "Master in Gestione e Conservazione e dei Documenti Digitali" at the University of Calabria are querying the ParlaMint corpus via the NoSketch Engine platform[23], thus learning basic notions of corpus annotation, usage of metadata for sub-corpus selection and querying. Also, a tutorial in Italian aimed at non-computationally savvy researchers in political and social sciences with no prior knowledge of corpus linguistics is now available (Del Fante, 2022), and might encourage further studies.

The availability of machine-actionable transcripts of parliamentary debates are indeed an important asset for many disciplines, but, especially for political studies, they are not enough. Future work might thus include not only an extension of the corpus with debates of the other parliamentary chamber and from other time periods, but also with other types of data connected with the parliamentary sittings, such as the annexed documents mentioned in section 3 above: e.g. bills under discussion, voting records, and so on.

Finally, the possibility will be explored to start a project dedicated to adding audio-video files of the sittings, possibly linked and aligned to the transcripts.

8. Acknowledgements

This work was supported by CLARIN-ERIC as part of the ParlaMint project, as well as by CLARIN-IT, CNR-IGSG and CNR-ILC as part of their missions. Special thanks go to Andrea Cimino for his valuable help with the alignment and merging of linguistic and NER annotations.

9. Bibliographical References

Bański, P., Haaf, S., and Mueller, M. (2018). Lightweight grammatical annotation in the TEI: New perspectives. In *Proceedings of the Eleventh International Conference on Language Resources and Evaluation (LREC 2018)*, Miyazaki, Japan, May. European Language Resources Association (ELRA).

Del Fante, D. and Cavalieri, A. (2021). Politics in between crises. A political and textual comparative analysis of budgetary speeches and expenditure. In *Proceedings of the 1st Workshop on Computational Linguistics for Political Text Analysis*.

Del Fante, D. (2022). ParlaMint – IT – Il corpus del Senato Italiano. Una guida pratica per l'interrogazione del corpus ParlaMint-IT con NoSketch Engine, a supporto dell'analisi del discorso politico. https://doi.org/10.5281/zenodo.6526914.

[23]Available from https://www.clarin.si/noske/index.HTML

Dell'Orletta, F., Venturi, G., Cimino, A., and Montemagni, S. (2014). T2K^2: a System for Automatically Extracting and Organizing Knowledge from Texts. In *Proceedings of the Ninth International Conference on Language Resources and Evaluation (LREC'14)*, pages 2062–2070, Reykjavik, Iceland, May. European Language Resources Association (ELRA).

Erjavec, T. and Pančur, A. (2019). Parla-CLARIN: TEI guidelines for corpora of parliamentary proceedings, September.

Erjavec, T., Ogrodniczuk, M., Osenova, P. N., Ljubesic, N., Simov, K. I., Pancur, A., Rudolf, M., Kopp, M., Barkarson, S., Steingrímsson, S., Çagri Çöltekin, de Does, J., Depuydt, K., Agnoloni, T., Venturi, G., Pérez, M. C., Macedo, L. D., Navarretta, C., Luxardo, G., Coole, M., Rayson, P., Morkevicius, V., Krilavicius, T., Dargis, R., Ring, O., van Heusden, R., Marx, M., and Fiser, D. (2022). The parlamint corpora of parliamentary proceedings. *Language Resources and Evaluation*, pages 1 – 34.

Fišer, D. and Lenardič, J. (2018). Clarin resources for parliamentary discourse research. In Darja Fišer, et al., editors, *Proceedings of the Eleventh International Conference on Language Resources and Evaluation (LREC 2018)*, Paris, France, may. European Language Resources Association (ELRA).

Gildea, D. (2001). Corpus variation and parser performance. In *Proceedings of the 2001 Conference on Empirical Methods in Natural Language Processing*.

Nencioni, G. (1976). Parlato-parlato, parlato-scritto, parlato-recitato. *Strumenti critici*, (29).

Nivre, J. (2015). Towards a universal grammar for natural language processing. In *Computational Linguistics and Intelligent Text Processing - Proceedings of the 16th International Conference, CICLing 2015, Part I*, pages 3–16, Cairo, Egypt, April.

Palmirani, M. and Vitali, F. (2011). Akoma-ntoso for legal documents. In Giovanni Sartor, et al., editors, *Legislative XML for the Semantic Web.*, volume 4 of *Law, Governance and Technology Series*. Springer, Dordrecht.

Qi, P., Zhang, Y., Zhang, Y., Bolton, J., and Manning, C. D. (2020). Stanza: A python natural language processing toolkit for many human languages. In *Proceedings of the 58th Annual Meeting of the Association for Computational Linguistics: System Demonstrations*, pages 101–108, Online, July. Association for Computational Linguistics.

10. Language Resource References

Bosco, Cristina and Montemagni, Simonetta and Simi, Maria. (2013). *Converting Italian Treebanks: Towards an Italian Stanford Dependency Treebank*. Association for Computational Linguistics, PID https://aclanthology.org/W13-2308.

Erjavec, Tomaž and Ogrodniczuk, Maciej and Osenova, Petya and Ljubešić, Nikola and Simov, Kiril and Grigorova, Vladislava and Rudolf, Michał and Pančur, Andrej and Kopp, Matyáš and Barkarson, Starkaður and Steingrímsson, Steinþór and van der Pol, Henk and Depoorter, Griet and de Does, Jesse and Jongejan, Bart and Haltrup Hansen, Dorte and Navarretta, Costanza and Calzada Pérez, María and de Macedo, Luciana D. and van Heusden, Ruben and Marx, Maarten and Çöltekin, Çağrı and Coole, Matthew and Agnoloni, Tommaso and Frontini, Francesca and Montemagni, Simonetta and Quochi, Valeria and Venturi, Giulia and Ruisi, Manuela and Marchetti, Carlo and Battistoni, Roberto and Sebők, Miklós and Ring, Orsolya and Darģis, Roberts and Utka, Andrius and Petkevičius, Mindaugas and Briedienė, Monika and Krilavičius, Tomas and Morkevičius, Vaidas and Diwersy, Sascha and Luxardo, Giancarlo and Rayson, Paul. (2021a). *Multilingual comparable corpora of parliamentary debates ParlaMint 2.1.* PID http://hdl.handle.net/11356/1432.

Erjavec, Tomaž and Ogrodniczuk, Maciej and Osenova, Petya and Ljubešić, Nikola and Simov, Kiril and Grigorova, Vladislava and Rudolf, Michał and Pančur, Andrej and Kopp, Matyáš and Barkarson, Starkaður and Steingrímsson, Steinþór and van der Pol, Henk and Depoorter, Griet and de Does, Jesse and Jongejan, Bart and Haltrup Hansen, Dorte and Navarretta, Costanza and Calzada Pérez, María and de Macedo, Luciana D. and van Heusden, Ruben and Marx, Maarten and Çöltekin, Çağrı and Coole, Matthew and Agnoloni, Tommaso and Frontini, Francesca and Montemagni, Simonetta and Quochi, Valeria and Venturi, Giulia and Ruisi, Manuela and Marchetti, Carlo and Battistoni, Roberto and Sebők, Miklós and Ring, Orsolya and Darģis, Roberts and Utka, Andrius and Petkevičius, Mindaugas and Briedienė, Monika and Krilavičius, Tomas and Morkevičius, Vaidas and Bartolini, Roberto and Cimino, Andrea and Diwersy, Sascha and Luxardo, Giancarlo and Rayson, Paul. (2021b). *Linguistically annotated multilingual comparable corpora of parliamentary debates ParlaMint.ana 2.1.* PID http://hdl.handle.net/11356/1431.

A. Appendix: Named Entity Recognition Management

As illustrated in the description of the conversion algorithm from CoNLL-U to TEI ParlaMint, between the Sentence node and the Word nodes there can be an intermediate degree of kinship if one or more entries are Named Entities. In this case the Word nodes that form the Named Entity are grouped as children under a Node `<name>` which in turn will have the Sentence Node as the parent Node. The entry.named field is in IOB format, that is the type of the Named Entities is prefixed by a prefix that assumes values, "B-", "I-" or "O-" which respectively stand for Begin Intermediate and Outside. Algorithmically, the management of Named Entities is achieved by implementing a two-state automaton:

- Stato_0 :
  label{tag == B-} : Action A1 → Stato_1
  Label{ } : Action A2 → Stato_0
- Stato_1 :
  label {tag == B-} : Action A3 → Stato_1
  Label{tag == I-} : Action A4 → Stato_1
  Label{ } : Action A5 → Stato_0

The labels correspond to logical conditions and are executed in the order in which they are written, so empty labels correspond to the complementary condition of the previous. The Actions are described in pseudo programming code:

- Action A1 : {
  NodeName = generateNewNode(<name>);
  setParentOfNode(NodeName,NodeSentence);
  setAttributeNodeName(type);
  CurrentNode = NodeName;}
- Action A2 : { no action; }
- Action A3 : {
  CloseNode(NodeName)
  CurrentNode = NodeSentence
  OtherNodeName = generateNewNode(<name>);
  setParentOfNode(OtherNodeName,NodeSentence);
  setAttributeNodeName(type);
  CurrentNode = OtherNodeName; }
- Action A4 : { no action; }
- Action A5 : {
  CloseNode(NodeName);
  CurrentNode = NodeSentence; }

The part of the code that implements the automaton is within the cycle in which the linguistically annotated entries are scrolled, something like:

```
while(getline(entry)) do:
    ...
    //CurrentNode == SentenceNode
    Tag = IOBof(entry);
    execAutoma(tag);
    analize(entry);
    ...
```

Therefore, the XML Nodes corresponding to the entries can be children of the Node Sentence or of a Node Name set by the automaton.

Proceedings of ParlaCLARIN III @ LREC2022 pages 125–130
Marseille, 20 June 2022

ParlamentParla: A Speech Corpus of Catalan Parliamentary Sessions

Baybars Külebi[1,2], Carme Armentano-Oller[1],
Carlos Rodríguez-Penagos[1], Marta Villegas[1]
[1]Barcelona Supercomputing Center - Centro Nacional de Supercomputación
[2]Col·lectivaT SCCL
{baybars.kulebi, carme.armentano, carlos.rodriguez1, marta.villegas}@bsc.es

Abstract

Recently, various end-to-end architectures of Automatic Speech Recognition (ASR) are being showcased as an important step towards providing language technologies to all languages instead of a select few such as English. However many languages are still suffering due to the "digital gap", lacking thousands of hours of transcribed speech data openly accessible that is necessary to train modern ASR architectures. Although Catalan already has access to various open speech corpora, these corpora lack diversity and are limited in total volume. In order to address this lack of resources for Catalan language, in this work we present ParlamentParla, a corpus of more than 600 hours of speech from Catalan Parliament sessions. This corpus has already been used in training of state-of-the-art ASR systems, and proof-of-concept text-to-speech (TTS) models. In this work we explain in detail the pipeline that allows the information publicly available on the parliamentary website to be converted to a speech corpus compatible with training of ASR and possibly TTS models.

Keywords: speech corpus, automatic speech recognition, data, found data

1. Introduction

Although Natural Language Processing is fast becoming a mainstream, readily-usable technology, for many of its core tasks it relies on a vast amount of data being available for development and training, especially in the age of neural networks-based Artificial Intelligence. Speech processing, be it recognition or synthesis, require many hours of recorded and transcribed data in order to be used reliably for electronic assistants, translation, voice operated interfaces, etc.

For some of the world's languages with many millions of speakers available, this data gathering is not especially challenging. For other less-resourced languages, it can be a matter of survival in an increasingly digital world.

Catalan is a romance European language spoken or understood by more than 9 million people, with deep roots in culture and history, and with a significant online presence, for example, in Wikipedia [1], popular media outlets and in print literature. Even so, it is not recognized as an official language in the EU, nor is it incorporated in many of the major apps and services from Big Tech (Amazon, Google, Apple, etc.) that people increasingly rely on for communication and even daily chores like using maps or scheduling appointments.

For some years now, a diverse and vibrant collaboration between regional government agencies, volunteer tech collectives and research institutions has promoted and supported projects that have produced state-of-the-art tools and resources, such as: translators, datasets, (Külebi and Öktem, 2018), dictionaries, correctors,[2] corpora,[3] pipelines,[4] massive Transformer-based language models and language benchmarks.[5]

These somewhat scattered efforts and the direct involvement of the Catalan government have led to the AINA initiative,[6] enabling the generation of high-quality corpora and datasets which, along with extensive language models, are being made available through various open platforms[7][8] in order to promote Natural Language Understanding (NLU) capabilities for any institution, organization, company or individual. The objective is for people to be able to engage in the digital world in Catalan to the same degree as speakers of a global language such as English, thus preventing the digital extinction of the language.

In this work, we explain the preparation of a Catalan speech corpus based on the Parliamentary recordings and metadata. The corpus is published with a CC-BY license and is fully downloadable from https://zenodo.org/record/5541827(Külebi, 2021).

2. Data Compilation

In order to contribute to the openly available speech resources for Catalan, we have compiled the parliamentary speeches and processed them with their corresponding transcriptions, as well as segmented them into a format that is compatible with ASR training pipelines.

[1]The Catalan version is the 20th largest language edition

[2]i.e. see the resources provided by the NGO Softcatalà

[3]Catalan has consistently been in the top 5 languages of the Mozilla Common Voice initiative

[4]CLIC, TALP and other university research labs.

[5]Barcelona Supercomputing Center, Text Mining Unit

[6]`https://www.projecteaina.cat`

[7]`https://huggingface.co/projecte-aina`

[8]`https://github.com/projecte-aina`

The use of parliamentary recordings for generating speech corpora is well established, with the earliest example for a limited resource language has been the creation of the Althingi, Icelandic parliamentary speech corpus (Helgadóttir et al., 2017). Parliamentary content has certain advantages, such as readily available transcripts, relatively natural speech and a controlled recording environment. Additionally, due to the transparency laws, it is customary to find parliamentary content with open and/or free licenses, hence facilitating the release of the final processed dataset with open licenses.

The complete process, which takes various types of parliamentary content and converts them into a speech corpus, takes advantage of different types of tools and algorithms. In the following subsections, we first explain the details of the publicly available content, and follow with the specifics of the preprocessing steps applied first to textual data and metadata and later to the audio content.

2.1. Catalan Parliamentary Data

The Catalan Parliament (Parlament de Catalunya) consists of 135 elected representatives from an ideologically diverse group of political affiliations. In the last decade, the Catalan Parliament has witnessed lively and intense debates about topics such as social equality, national identity and statutes, language preservation, etc. In this work, we have profited from this diverse content to create a speech corpus.

In order to build our corpus we have first extracted the available content, directly from the Parliamentary website, taking advantage of an earlier easy to access version of it.[9] The audio segments were extracted from recordings of the Catalan Parliament plenary sessions, and the dates chosen were between 2007/07/11 and 2018/07/17, when the scraping was made.

Within the old version of the website, the video files were presented per plenary session and per speaker intervention. For each plenary session, the sequence of interventions per speakers were accessible in the DOM, in addition to a link to the complete transcripts in pdf format.

In short, the overall preparation of the corpus involves matching metadata from two different sources, namely the website and the transcripts in pdf format. Furthermore, the combined data is processed in order to create the ASR training ready corpus. The visual summary of the whole data processing can be found in Fig. 1. Apart from the matching of the metadata from both sources, the most time-consuming aspect of the data preprocessing has been the development of the pdf parser for the parliamentary transcripts. In addition, the existence of multiple official languages has been an extra inconvenience specific to our case.

[9] the old version of the site can be seen in web archive

2.2. Preparation of Session Metadata

The data processing pipeline starts with the scraping of the webpage of the Catalan Parliament, where a recording of a speaker during an intervention per session are available separately. Since the audiovisual content is speaker specific, the first important step was to associate each video file with the corresponding session, intervention and actual speaker and finally the corresponding text. Although the speaker list was provided in the DOM of the session video page, this information had to be aligned with the parsed pdf of the official transcript of the session, converted into structured data, showing the speaker and the corresponding text.

As a first step we have downloaded the list of interventions, the name of the corresponding speakers and the pdf of the full transcription per session, and the corresponding video files for the speaker. Furthermore we have repeated the whole process for each plenary session. As explained before, the intervention recordings are conveniently organized as per speaker per intervention, hence for the given time window we downloaded in total 12918 recordings, with lengths ranging between 10 seconds and up to 30 minutes. The pdfs or "diaris" in Catalan, include the interventions for each topic discussed during one specific day of a plenary session. Due to the content of the sessions, we have concentrated only on the regular sessions and not the extraordinary ones which might include constitutive sessions, with only the voting processes that are contentwise uninteresting for a speech corpus.

In addition to the structured metadata of the audiovisual content page, the pdf files also needed to be converted to structured data, comprising the sequential speakers with their corresponding scripts. For this task we used a two-step process, in which we first extracted the xml information from the pdf, where each line of text have their own coordinates and typographical information. And on a second step we implemented the template logic into a parsing script where the undesired parts of the text, like headers, footers and lists of contents were eliminated, and exploiting the typographical information, text versus speaker name were recognized. Since the structure of the official scripts changed only once during the chosen period, our parser needed to consider only two alternatives.

At the end of this process, we ended up with a structured data file which included the sequence of speakers with their associated speeches within a session.


```
{
  "_id" : "0fa8ea289797a5c40a9106",
  "value" : {
  "urls" : [
  [["Sra. Eulàlia Reguant i Cura
     (Membre)"],
    "4a20b06b2748a0060b3b.mp3"]
  ],
  "text" : [
  ["La presidenta",
```

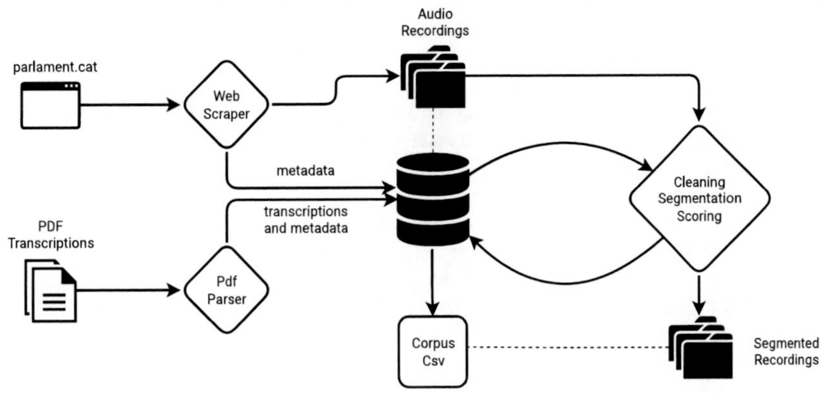

Figure 1: The flowchart of all the processes to generate the speech corpus. All the information persisted in a database, and as a final step a csv file is exported with the relative paths to the audio segments and their corresponding transcriptions.


```
    "Gràcies, president. Té la paraula
     la senyora Reguant."],
   ["Eulàlia Reguant i Cura",
    "Gràcies, president. Arrelada a
     Parets, amb el setanta-cinc per
     cent de la seu financera a
     irlanda:(...)"]
   ],
   "ple_code" : "2017_04_26_212616"
   }
}
```


Finally, to generate the input for the audio-transcript alignment process, we needed to merge this metadata coming from two separate sources, i.e. a sequence of speaker interventions with the corresponding video urls, and another sequence of speaker interventions with the corresponding text. However, the names of the speakers within these two different sources were not consistent: for example *H. Sr. Oriol Junqueras i Vies (Conseller)* vs *El vicepresident del Govern i conseller d'Economia i Hisenda (Oriol Junqueras i Vies)* from the pdf. Or in extreme cases, the names of the ministers did not appear corresponding to their appointment within the transcriptions, for example *H. Sr. Lluís Miquel Recoder i Miralles (Conseller)* vs *El conseller de Territori i Sostenibilitat*.

Furthermore, the audiovisual metadata did not include the minor interventions, neither from the President of the Parliament nor from the interrupting parliamentary members, whereas the data extracted from pdfs did include them. Hence, we used yet another step to align the speakers sources, using first a fuzzy match for the names within an intervention, and assigning them an index, and later sequence matching these indices using the Smith-Waterman Algorithm (Smith et al., 1981).

At the end of this process we ended up with a single database of metadata which include the session, its speaker intervention in the correct sequence with their corresponding text and video urls. The scripts implementing all these processes can be found at the repository of the project. [10]

2.3. Preparation of Audio Corpus

The metadata file we have prepared provided us with the audio file against its corresponding text, but the recording for each intervention had various lengths, up to 20 minutes, which needed to be segmented to 5-15 second clips in order to be applicable for ASR training pipelines. Thus to segment these long audio files into desired sizes, we executed a forced alignment process. We initiated the process downloading all the content in video format and converting them into single channel wav files with a sampling rate of 16kHz. Furthermore, we processed the merged structured metadata file to eliminate all the non-Catalan speeches through the use of a basic language detector,[11] which gives a percentage of Catalan words for an intervention, based on a clean corpus. Finally, for the remaining set we applied a method very similar to the original LibriSpeech article (Panayotov et al., 2015).

We did a first pass of speech recognition using the Catalan CMU Sphinx models [12] trained with TV3, the public Catalan television corpus (Külebi and Öktem, 2018), with the language generated from the self-text of the intervention. This method gave us the word based timestamps for the text; however the resulting word se-

[10] `https://github.com/gullabi/parlament-scrape`

[11] The Catalan parliamentary discussions include Spanish as well as Aranese Occitan interventions, all three being the official languages of the autonomic region.

[12] `https://cmusphinx.github.io/`

quence did not correspond fully to the input text, partly due to the old ASR architecture and partly due to the non-literal transcription of the official records (omission of repetitions and disfluencies). However, we used the results of the ASR decoding, aligned them to the original text using the Smith-Waterman algorithm and used this information to define the text/audio "islands" (Panayotov et al., 2015) in order to segment the audio. For the segmentation, we have taken into account both the silences (minimum 300 ms) and the punctuation. We have used an algorithm similar to beam search, but with assigned probabilities, to find the most optimal segment. This way the algorithm prefer silences which coincide with punctuations (specifically comma, dot, question mark, colon, semicolon and exclamation mark).

The algorithm accepts minimum and maximum durations, but since it is probabilistic, in situations where it is not possible to segment the long audio (due to lack of silences for example) it allows for segmenting pieces that are longer or shorter than the given limits. This is preferable in order to ensure the quality of the resulting segments, and not introduce truncated speech in the corpus. The lengths of the resulting segments can be seen in Fig. 2. In the end, we have manually eliminated the segments longer and shorter than the desired limits, and ended up with corpora of bits between 5 and 15 seconds. The processing pipeline is available on github. [13]

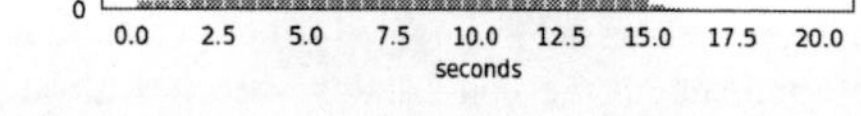

Figure 2: The histogram of segment lengths, the durations are in seconds. Although the duration interval is between 5 and 15 seconds, our method yields some segments with durations outside this interval in order not to generate segments with truncated utterances.

On a second pass, we have further processed the resulting segments in order to assess their quality. Namely, we applied once more the ASR models to the segmented audio and depending on the similarity of the results of the decoding versus the original text, we defined the quality thresholds for the corpus. The quality results were calculated according to Levenshtein distances with 100, complete equivalence of the two strings, and 0, no character overlap. Although we have ensured that our false negatives (i.e. segments with low score) are kept to a minimum through the use of finite-state-transducer based grammars built with the original text of the segment, similarly to Librispeech process (Panayotov et al., 2015), our scoring method was still prone to the quality of the ASR models. Specifically the fact that the ASR models that we used are biased against the non-central Catalan dialect, it is possible that these accents are also penalized by the scoring. However at this moment we don't have the dialectal metadata of the speakers to check this possibility.

In short, in order to eliminate the outliers, possible errors in transcription and/or segmentation pricess we have eliminated all segments below the score of 65 for the global corpus, and ended up with a total of 611 hours of total speech recordings.

2.4. Postprocessing ParlamentParla

For the final published speech corpus, we further processed the data in order to make it compatible with ASR pipelines. First, the text is all in lower-case, which is standard for the speech corpora. Furthermore, for the v2.0 we have included the speaker information, specifically anonymized ids and the corresponding gender. For detecting the genders, we have simply used the information provided in the metadata, using the gendered honorific titles in front of the name of the speaker. Specifically; Sra. (senyora) signifying female, and Sr. (senyor) signifying male.

Finally, using the quality values per segment, we have separated the corpus into clean and other. We have chosen all the segments above the quality score of 91 as clean and left the rest as other. This way we ended up with 211 hours of clean and 400 hours of other quality segments. Furthermore each subset was divided into three parts, training, dev and test, where dev and test datasets have 4 hours each and the rest goes to the training corpus. We have made sure that the speakers that are included in the test and dev subsets are not included in the training subset.

The final gender distribution of the corpus ended up being male dominant with female voice percentages of 28,7% for "other" and 39,3% "clean" subset. In total, the female voices comprise 32,4% percent of the total duration of ParlamentParla. The details of the total durations per subset can be seen in Table 1.

For the v2.0 of the corpus we have used a format similar to the Common Voice dataset since it became a *de facto* standard for most of the modern ASR training architectures during the recent years. Hence we released the dataset in a single file csv (comma separated values), with the speaker ids, the audio filename and the corresponding text, as well as the speaker gender and the duration of the utterance.

The corpus is currently available through the Zenodo

[13] https://github.com/gullabi/long-audio-aligner

Subcorpus	Gender	Duration (h)
other_test	F	2.516
other_dev	F	2.701
other_train	F	109.68
other_test	M	2.631
other_dev	M	2.513
other_train	M	280.196
other total		400.239
clean_test	F	2.707
clean_dev	F	2.576
clean_train	F	77.905
clean_test	M	2.516
clean_dev	M	2.614
clean_train	M	123.162
clean total		211.48
Total		611.719

Table 1: The total duration of all the subsets, with gender distribution.

platform (Külebi, 2021) and Huggingface datasets,[14] with the latter allowing for a convenient interface for inspection of the published data.

3. Current and Future Work

The dataset was already used to train state-of-the-art ASR models, fine-tuning the pretrained multilingual models of wav2vec2.0 with 300m[15], 1b[16] parameters. For the training, ParlamentParla was used in addition to TV3Parla and the Common Voice Catalan v8.0 dataset. The achieved WER (word-error-rate) for these models on the Common Voice test set is 6,8% and 6,1%. Although these models do not solely rely on ParlamentParla, these wav2vec2.0 results are a good showcase of the importance of the corpus in achieving high quality ASR systems for resource-limited languages. We are currently making experiments training wav2vec2.0 models with Common Voice corpus vs Common Voice plus ParlamentParla corpus, and our results will be published in the Huggingface, within the AINA project[17] models.

Due to the innovative segmentation method introduced in the process, and the clear delineation of individual speakers, it is possible to use the corpus for training of text-to-speech (TTS) systems. In order to test this hypothesis, we have used 15 hours of speech from former Catalan President Artur Mas to train the NVIDIA implementation [18] of Tacotron2 (Shen et al., 2018). For privacy considerations, we did not publish the trained model, but synthesized speech snippets can be found on the webpage of the Catalan TTS project Catotron v1.0 [19]. The details of the architecture and part of the experiment are also explained in the original Catotron paper (Külebi et al., 2020).

The most important future work underway is the development of a data pipeline which the ParlamentParla speech corpus can be easily updated and published regularly. Currently, the biggest obstacle is the new structure of the website in which the assets are loaded dynamically; moreover, the connection between the session videos and the official transcripts is broken. However, there is development underway by the Departament d'Informàtica i Telecomunicacions (Department of Informatics and Telecommunications) to provide the session and intervention information via a RESTful API (application programming interface) as part of the improvement of the transparency standards of the Catalan Parliament. Thanks to this effort, the necessary information will be available by a simple API call without having to scrape the website.

Additionally, there is work underway to apply the methodology developed for ParlamentParla to process other parliamentary recordings, most importantly the Valencian Parliament (Corts Valencianes) and possibly also the Parliament of the Balearic Islands (Parlament de les Illes Balears), both Catalan-speaking territories.

3.1. Acknowledgments

The initial preparation of this corpus was partly supported by the Department of Culture of the Catalan autonomous government, and further development with the preparation of v2.0 was supported by the Barcelona Supercomputing Center, within the framework of the project AINA funded by the Generalitat de Catalunya, Departament de la Vicepresidència i de Polítiques Digitals i Territori, through the projects ECIA PDAD14/20/00001, AINA PDAD46/21/000001

4. Bibliographical References

Helgadóttir, I. R., Kjaran, R., Nikulásdóttir, A. B., and Guðnason, J. (2017). Building an asr corpus using althingi's parliamentary speeches. In *INTERSPEECH*, pages 2163–2167.

Külebi, B. and Öktem, A. (2018). Building an Open Source Automatic Speech Recognition System for Catalan. In *Proc. IberSPEECH 2018*, pages 25–29.

Külebi, B., Öktem, A., Peiró-Lilja, A., Pascual, S., and Farrús, M. (2020). CATOTRON — A Neural Text-to-Speech System in Catalan. In *Proc. Interspeech 2020*, pages 490–491.

Külebi, B. (2021). ParlamentParla - Speech corpus of Catalan Parliamentary sessions, doi:10.5281/zenodo.5541827, October.

Panayotov, V., Chen, G., Povey, D., and Khudanpur, S. (2015). Librispeech: an asr corpus based on public domain audio books. In *2015 IEEE international*

[14]`https://huggingface.co/datasets/projecte-aina/parlament_parla`

[15]`https://huggingface.co/PereLluis13/wav2vec2-xls-r-300m-ca-lm`

[16]`https://huggingface.co/PereLluis13/wav2vec2-xls-r-1b-ca-lm`

[17]`https://huggingface.co/projecte-aina`

[18]`https://github.com/NVIDIA/tacotron2`

[19]`https://collectivat.cat/catotron`

conference on acoustics, speech and signal processing (ICASSP), pages 5206–5210. IEEE.

Shen, J., Pang, R., Weiss, R. J., Schuster, M., Jaitly, N., Yang, Z., Chen, Z., Zhang, Y., Wang, Y., Skerrv-Ryan, R., et al. (2018). Natural tts synthesis by conditioning wavenet on mel spectrogram predictions. In *2018 IEEE international conference on acoustics, speech and signal processing (ICASSP)*, pages 4779–4783. IEEE.

Smith, T. F., Waterman, M. S., et al. (1981). Identification of common molecular subsequences. *Journal of molecular biology*, 147(1):195–197.

Proceedings of ParlaCLARIN III @ LREC2022 pages 131–134
Marseille, 20 June 2022

ParlaMint-RO: Chamber of the Eternal Future

Petru Rebeja[1], Mădălina Chitez[2] Roxana Rogobete[2], Andreea Dincă[2], Loredana Bercuci[2]
[1]Alexandru Ioan Cuza University of Iași, 11 Carol I Bvd., Iași, 700506
petru.rebeja@info.uaic.ro
[2] West University of Timisoara, 4 Vasile Pârvan St., Timișoara, 300223
madalina.chitez, roxana.rogobete, andreea.dinca, loredana.bercuci@e-uvt.ro

Abstract

The paper describes the ParlaMint-RO corpus of parliamentary debates in Romania. It analyses several trends in parliamentary debates (plenary sessions of the Lower House) held between 2000 and 2020. We offer a short description of the data collection, the workflow of data processing (text extraction, conversion, encoding, linguistic annotation), and an overview of the corpus. The paper then moves on to a multi-layered linguistic analysis, which offers an interdisciplinary perspective. We use computational methods and corpus linguistics approaches to scrutinize the future tense forms used by Romanian speakers in order to create a data-supported profile of the parliamentary group strategies and planning.

Keywords: ParlaMint-RO, linguistic analysis, future tense, data-supported parliamentary profile

1. Introduction

The discourse of the Romanian Parliament has been analysed by several studies, which have investigated such topics as the use of institutional forms of address (Ilie, 2010), epistemic markers (Ştefănescu, 2015), or situational argumentative strategies (Ionescu-Ruxăndoiu, 2015). These studies, however, do not conduct quantitative analyses, nor do they consult large corpora. Consequently, they do not offer a diachronic and statistical perspective. In this paper, we use a representative Romanian parliamentary discourse corpus, ParlaMint-RO for the first time. Compiled in the framework of the project ParlaMint - Towards Comparable Parliamentary Corpora, the corpus was financially supported by CLARIN ERIC[1], whose aim is to create free-access corpora of parliamentary discourse from as many as possible National Parliaments in Europe. ParlaMint corpora are created and encoded according to pre-established criteria and they are also uniformly encoded so that national datasets can be exchanged, reused and compared in different research scenarios (Erjavec et al., 2022).

The present study intends to introduce the ParlaMint Romanian sub-corpus (ParlaMint-RO) and to exemplify how the data can be used for interdisciplinary studies. After a short description of the data collection process, of the workflow of data processing, and an overview of the corpus, the paper will offer a linguistic analysis. We use computational methods to validate a study on the distribution of future tense forms across parliamentary groups. By analysing future tense forms, we aim to create a data-supported profile of some parliamentary groups' strategies and planning without extending the analysis towards the effectiveness of these strategies, i.e. whether future tense form use is associated with winning or losing parties (Kameswari and Mamidi, 2018). We extend, in this way, an exploratory study conducted by Grama (2022), which explored the discursive context of future tense forms in a corpus of interviews and press releases by Romanian local politicians. The study demonstrated that "promises for the better are made with every election season" (Grama, 2022, p. 31).

Level	Value
Number of transcribed sessions	1,832
Number of processed speeches	552,103
Number of words	109,304,196
Period	2000 – 2020

Table 1: Basic corpus statistics of ParlaMint-RO.

2. Data Collection: Parliamentary Records

The current corpus consists of transcripts of the plenary sessions of the Lower House, the Chamber of Deputies, as published on the official website[2]. Although both Romanian parliamentary chambers have published their transcripts (since 1996 for the Chamber of Deputies and since 2002 for the Senate), the structure of the source documents differs and is not very consistent. Therefore, as shown in Table 2, we limited the data selection to the Lower House. The time span covered ranges from 2000 to 2020 (five full legislative periods). The ParlaMint-RO corpus consists of 1833 files, one for each plenary session (a total of 1832 sessions, and the corpus root file), and comprises over 109 million words.

[1]Visit https://www.clarin.eu/content/parlamint-towards-comparable-parliamentary-corpora for more information about the ParlaMint project.

[2]http://www.cdep.ro/pls/steno/steno2015.home

2.1. Processing Parliamentary Transcripts

The transcripts are published in HTML format and were received in bulk from the Information Technology Service of the Chamber of Deputies, after asking permission to use data for research and enquiring about additional / improved data sets. The data was extracted from the HTML files and converted to XML files using the `lxml` library[3] in Python. Alongside the default processing built into the lxml library (for encoding correction, HTML cleanup), we applied on-the-fly normalization of diacritics.

2.2. Corpus-Specific Metadata

The only metadata added to the corpus consists of the names, gender, and, for some deputies, their profile picture (if available). This data was scraped from the web site of the Lower House. The website also contains affiliation data. However, scraping that data resulted in a lot of erroneous records due to lack of a common structure in presentation. Thus, we did not include that data in the corpus since it needed to be manually corrected or supplemented by project members.

2.3. Encoding Transcripts into XML Format

The transcription began with an analysis of the ParlaMint schema, and in order for the team members to get accustomed to the schema, several sample sessions were manually coded by team members in Notepad+, according to the TEI format and documentation. The manual tagging made it possible to establish a set of tagging patterns and to extract specific recommendations for an automated process.

After identifying the patterns for locating and tagging sections of each transcription, we developed several Python scripts that automate the encoding of HTML transcriptions into XML format as much as possible:

- A crawler script downloads the names, gender and profile picture of the deputies,
- A parser script parses the session transcripts one by one and converts them into the XML format,
- Another script builds the corpus root file,
- After the corpus root file is built, another script is executed that applies the linguistic annotations to the existing corpus files, and creates the `.ana.xml` and `.conllu` files.

Despite our best efforts, we were not able to completely automate the encoding process. As such, after building the corpus root file, it still fails schema validation and needs manual intervention to correct the errors. Only after correcting the root file we could execute the script to perform linguistic annotation. Making the process fully automated is an ongoing task within the team.

The resulting XML files are structured according to the ParlaMint schema, which is based on the standard TEI structure[4], and is adapted to reflect the specific traits of Parliament sessions.

The source code for encoding raw transcripts from HTML format into the XML format required by the ParlaMint schema is available on Github[5], and will be updated to match the requirements of future versions and data.

2.4. Linguistic Annotation

The script that applies linguistic annotation iterates over the corpus files and queries the UDPipe Web API service[6] to perform tokenization, sentence segmentation, lemmatization, Part-of-Speech and morphological tagging, and dependency parsing. Unfortunately, the UDPipe service does not have a NER module for Romanian language so no NER was performed. We also tried to use the `spacy` library[7] which has a NER module available for Romanian but the library that converts the output from spacy to CoNNL-U format[8] has minor processing issues when used with the Romanian models. However, the results are not affected in the end.

3. Data Analysis

Since the future tense in Romanian is an analytical form, existing computational methods (such as UDPipe) extract the particular components of each form (auxiliary verb "to want" + root - infinitive form of the conjugated verb), therefore failing to automatically recognize the verbs we needed for the study. The difficulty of using UDPipe is represented by the fact that numerous verb tenses in Romanian are formed with auxiliary verbs, therefore the instrument cannot distinguish between different tenses built on the same auxiliary + root form, such as "will talk" ("voi vorbi" - formal future, indicative), "to talk" ("a vorbi" - infinitive), "talked" ("a vorbit" - compound perfect, indicative). The downfall of the low-resourced language as Romanian is that the data analysis requires more manual stages. As such, we decided to combine data from several sources for performing our analysis.

In the first step of data gathering, we downloaded the database dump from dexonline.ro[9], which contains Romanian word definitions that are not restricted by Intellectual Property rights. From the aforementioned database we extracted a list of 47,318 entries that were tagged as verbs.

For each of the extracted terms from the previous step, we try to obtain its inflections from conjugare.ro[10]. Retrieving data from conjugare.ro also validates whether the specified term is a verb or not; as such we narrowed

[3] https://lxml.de

[4] https://tei-c.org/

[5] https://github.com/romanian-parlamint/parsers

[6] http://lindat.mff.cuni.cz/services/udpipe/

[7] https://spacy.io/

[8] https://spacy.io/universe/project/spacy-conll

[9] Electronic version of Romanian Explanatory Dictionary, accessible at https://dexonline.ro

[10] htts://conjugare.ro

down the initial list of terms to 9,288 with more than 55,729 verb forms.

From the verb forms we selected the ones that represent the formal future tense (auxiliary + root, while omitting informal constructions such as particle "o" + conjunction "să" + conjugated verb in present: "o să vorbesc"; auxiliary verb "to have"/"a avea" + conjunction "să" + conjugated verb in present: "am să vorbesc"), this final list is then used to perform a cross-search on all the utterances from the corpora for the presence of each form. As such, we iterated through the whole corpus and built two sets of tuples from which we extracted the results: $(speaker, date, count_of_all_forms, count_of_all_words)$, and $(speaker, date, verb_form, count)$. Finally, we used `pandas`[11], and `matplotlib` libraries to aggregate the data and visualize the results.

The Python scripts, alongside the collection of verb forms are available on the Github page of our project[12].

4. Results

Romanian political discourse in general has been subject to various linguistic debates, mostly regarding the pragmatic or rhetoric dimension, such as stancetaking (Vasilescu, 2010), the practice of addressing (Saftoiu, 2013) or even verbal aggressiveness (Roibu and Constantinescu, 2010). In contrast, our data analysis focuses on a more specific topic - the distribution of future tense forms. It seems that a common rhetorical strategy in the Romanian Parliament is to refer to future projects or broader aims rather than ongoing projects. This permanent projection is not a sign of activism or concern for future policies. In different contexts, studies (Bertrand, 2021) have shown it is a sign of non-engagement, of the lack of solid commitment and of a tendency to delay actions. Unlike other languages, the cases when the Romanian present tense marks prospective actions are to be found mostly in literary texts - thus in stylistically rich contexts.

4.1. Verb Analysis: Future Tenses

Our analysis revealed the identity of the 10 politicians who use future tenses most frequently (4.1).

The 10 speakers, some of whom have shifted allegiances, were at the time of their speeches affiliated with the following parties: PSD, PNL, PRM (4.1).

Six of the speakers are affiliated with the Social Democratic Party (PSD), the largest in the country, which held the majority and control in most of the legislatures. This explains their high number of interventions (and the total number of future tense verbs: 33,728). The party's discourse consists of verbs of action projected into the future. Another four speakers are members of the National Liberal Party (PNL), with a total of 11,169 future verbs. One speaker belongs to the far-right nationalist party, Great Romania Party (PRM), which was not present in all national mandates.

Examples of use show a lack of tangible projects for the development of the country: "We will never again guarantee the governmental assumption of responsibility"; "Let's all think about the many and we'll see that we really are a different kind of politicians.". Moreover, when analysing the most frequent nouns and verbs present in the corpus, we noticed a preference for terms usually present in law voting procedure and meeting agenda ("law", "committee"), discourse mark-

Speaker	**Count**	**Pct**
Valer Dorneanu	10,859	0.73
Tudor Ciuhodaru	7,842	1.55
Emil Boc	4,480	1.48
Valeriu Ștefan Zgonea	4,190	0.51
Florin Iordache	3,837	0.62
Adrian Moisoiu	3,775	0.98
Doru Ioan Tărăcilă	3,602	0.73
Gheorghe-Eugen Nicolăescu	3,421	1.40
Nicolae Văcăroiu	3,398	0.85
Bogdan Olteanu	3,268	0.76

Table 2: Most frequent users of future tenses. The column *Count* displays the total number of future forms used by a speaker, and the column *Pct* shows the percentage of future forms from the total number of words spoken by the same person.

Speaker	**Affiliation and time-span**
V. Dorneanu	PDSR/PSD-Social Democratic Party (2000–2008)
T. Ciuhodaru	PSD/Independent/ PPDD-People's Party–Dan Diaconescu (2008–2016)
E. Boc	PD-Democratic Party – now PNL-National Liberal Party (2000–2004)
V. Ș. Zgonea	PSD-Social Democratic Party (2000–2016)
Fl. Iordache	PDSR/PSD-Social Democratic Party (2000–2020)
A. Moisoiu	PRM-Greater Romania Party (2000–2008)
D. I. Tărăcilă	PSD-Social Democratic Party (2000–2008)
Gh.-E. Nicolăescu	PNL-National Liberal Party (2000–2017)
N. Văcăroiu	PSD-Social Democratic Party (2000–2008)
B. Olteanu	PNL-National Liberal Party (2004–2009)

Table 3: Affiliation of the 10 politicians who most frequently use future tenses.

[11] https://pandas.pydata.org/

[12] https://github.com/romanian-parlamint/future-tense-usage

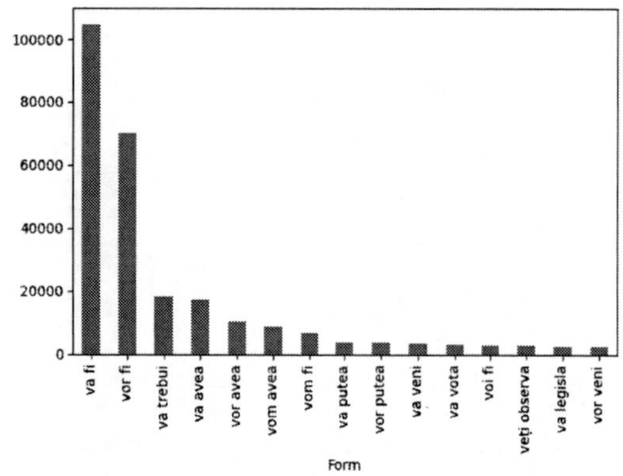

Figure 1: Top 15 inflections in future tense used in Lower House transcriptions.

ers ("thank" as a closing remark, direct addresses such as "mister president"), but likewise general ones that focus on the state of the country: "Romania", "project", "state", "years" etc. The top 15 inflections in future tense (1) reveals only three forms in first person ("will have", "will be" - singular and plural) and eleven in third person (either singular or plural: "will be", "will have to", "will be able to", "will come", "will vote", "will legislate"), which suggests an impersonal tone related to shifting responsibility onto others. Another sign of projection apparent in the deputies' speeches is the frequent use of "ar trebui să", a conditional tense that can be translated with "should".

5. Conclusions and Future Work

The present corpus still needs adjustments in order to obtain accurate data and optimize the workflow. Additionally, the linguistic analysis should be expanded and detailed in future studies in order to make more verb patterns available. We also had several difficulties in processing such large amounts of data with corpus linguistics tools that do not involve programming skills. When the ParlaMint-RO corpus is completed, numerous research directions can be pursued, such as investigating direct addressing, appellations used during debates (divided by parties and gender), or parliamentary topics and political ideology, thus opening valuable pathways for comparative research in political, linguistic or intercultural studies.

6. Acknowledgements

The study would have not been completed without the data provided by online resources such as dexonline.ro and conjugare.ro. The ParlaMint-RO corpus was compiled in the framework of the ParlaMint project supported by CLARIN ERIC.

7. Bibliographical References

Bertrand, D. (2021). Future or past future tense? what political timeframe? *E—C*, (32):34–41, Nov. https://mimesisjournals.com/ojs/index.php/ec/article/view/1500.

Erjavec, T., Ogrodniczuk, M., Osenova, P., Ljubešić, N., Simov, K., Pančur, A., Rudolf, M., Kopp, M., Barkarson, S., Steingrímsson, S., et al. (2022). The parlamint corpora of parliamentary proceedings. *Language resources and evaluation*, pages 1–34. https://doi.org/10.1007/s10579-021-09574-0.

Grama, E.-M. (2022). The language of romanian administration: an interview-based corpus case study. In Madalina Chitez, et al., editors, *Corpus Related Digital Humanities: Interdisciplinary Micro Perspectives*, pages 27–32, Timișoara. Editura Universității de Vest.

Ilie, C. (2010). Managing dissent and interpersonal relations in the romanian parliamentary discourse. *European parliaments under scrutiny*, pages 193–223. https://doi.org/10.1075/dapsac.38.11ili.

Ionescu-Ruxăndoiu, L. (2015). Discursive perspective and argumentation in the romanian parliamentary discourse. a case study. *L'Analisi Linguistica e Letteraria 2008-1*, 16:435–441. https://www.analisilinguisticaeletteraria.eu/index.php/ojs/article/view/423/359.

Kameswari, L. and Mamidi, R. (2018). Political discourse analysis: A case study of 2014 andhra pradesh state assembly election of interpersonal speech choices. In *Proceedings of the 32nd Pacific Asia Conference on Language, Information and Computation*. https://aclanthology.org/Y18-1028.pdf.

Roibu, M. and Constantinescu, M. N. (2010). Verbal aggressiveness in the romanian parliamentary debate. past and present. *Revue roumaine de linguistique*, 54(4):353–364. https://www.lingv.ro/RRL%204%202010%20art04Roibu.pdf.

Saftoiu, R. (2013). The discursive practice of addressing in the romanian parliament. *The Pragmatics of Political Discourse: Explorations across Cultures. Amsterdam: John Benjamins Publishing*, pages 47–68. https://doi.org/10.1075/pbns.228.04saf.

Ştefănescu, A. (2015). Analysing the rhetoric use of the epistemic marker eu cred că (i think) in romanian parliamentary discourse. *Persuasive Games in Political and Professional Dialogue*, 26:101. https://doi.org/10.1075/ds.26.06ste.

Vasilescu, A. (2010). Metastance in the romanian parliamentary discourse: Case studies. *The proceeding of Institutul de Lingvistica al Academiei. LV*, 4:365–380. https://www.lingv.ro/RRL%204%202010%20art05Vasilescu.pdf.

Author Index

Association for Computational Linguistics
209 N. Eighth Street
Stroudsburg, Pennsylvania 18360

ISBN 978-1-7138-6132-4

CURRAN ASSOCIATES INC.
proceedings.com